Selling Welfare Reform

Selling Welfare Reform

*Work-First and the
New Common Sense
of Employment*

Frank Ridzi

NEW YORK UNIVERSITY PRESS
New York and London

NEW YORK UNIVERSITY PRESS
New York and London
www.nyupress.org

Library of Congress Cataloging-in-Publication Data

Ridzi, Frank
Selling welfare reform : work-first and the new
common sense of employment / Frank Ridzi.
p. cm.
Includes bibliographical references and index.
ISBN-13: 978-0-8147-7593-6 (cl : alk. paper)
ISBN-10: 0-8147-7593-4 (cl : alk. paper)
ISBN-13: 978-0-8147-7594-3 (pb : alk. paper)
ISBN-10: 0-8147-7594-2 (pb : alk. paper)
1. Public welfare—United States. 2. Welfare recipients—
Employment—Government policy—United Staes. 3. Poor—
Government policy—United States. I. Title.
HV95.R53   2009
362.5'5680973—dc22   2008045877

New York University Press books are printed on acid-free paper,
and their binding materials are chosen for strength and durability.
We strive to use environmentally responsible suppliers and materials
to the greatest extent possible in publishing our books.

Manufactured in the United States of America
c 10 9 8 7 6 5 4 3 2 1
p 10 9 8 7 6 5 4 3 2 1

*Dedicated to the noble human services workers
and administrators in this book and
the families they seek to empower.*

Contents

Acknowledgments

The late Senator Daniel Patrick Moynihan (D-NY) was keen on assigning extra homework. In our last conversation I expressed concern about a need to carefully and critically consider the pros and cons of neoliberal public policy. As a former student of his, I anticipated his grinning response: "Write it up for me!" In some ways this manuscript is part of that write-up, though not completed in time for the senator to critique. There were also many others who encouraged and inspired this project and to whom I owe a great debt. First and foremost I must thank my academic mentor and continuing collaborator, Marjorie L. DeVault. Conversations with her, and at times her tag-team approach with Dorothy E. Smith, helped to convince me to rescue this project from the hopelessly broad and make it concrete, grounded, and doable. This project has had many lives and along the way has benefited from the good will and constructive critique of excellent scholars. I thank them in somewhat chronological order.

At Syracuse University's Maxwell School, Jackie Johnson, Monisha Das-Gupta, Bob Bogdan, Sari Knopp Biklen and Gary Spencer all had a hand in helping me to shape the early scope of this project. Scott Allard, Susan Borker, Andrew London, Madonna Harrington-Meyer, Nancy Mudrick, and Diane Murphy all put in countless hours scrutinizing and masterfully offering advice from their public administration, sociology, social work, and feminist perspectives.

I am indebted too to my colleagues from graduate school: Payal Banerjee, Corey Colyer, Cheryl Najarian, Catherine Richards Solomon, Lauren Eastwood, Jeremy Brunson, Charleen Tuchovsky, and Brenda Solomon.

Beyond this, I have been fortunate to also have the support, encouragement, and example of the community of IE (Institutional Ethnography) researchers: Suzanne Vaughn, Paul Luken, Ellen Pence, Joan Acker, Marie Campbell, Tim Diamond, Kamini Maraj Grahame, Alison Griffith, Nancy Jackson, Ellen Scott, Bonnie Slade, Susan Turner, and many others.

Thanks to those who read and commented on all or various parts of this manuscript (most are listed above) including Nancy Naples, Cory Blad, Murali Venkatesh, and Mary Giegengack Jureller. Mary's work to make this readable to a nonsociologist was crucial. Also, thanks to Clinton Smith for his excellent bibliographic work, and to Joshua Grant McIntosh for hosting me and my family at Harvard during the final stages of this project.

I would also like to acknowledge support from the Kauffman Foundation and the Center for Urban and Regional Applied Research and the faculty and staff at Le Moyne College. I could not hope for a better group of colleagues. Thanks also go to my editor Ilene Kalish, managing editor Despina Papazoglou Gimbel, and the fine staff at NYU Press.

Finally, and with greatest appreciation, to my partner Jody, who sustained me throughout this project, and to our wonderful children, whose inspiration carried me through and whose nap times allowed the analysis that follows to make it to pen and paper.

1

"Selling Work-First"
Introduction

Common sense is not something rigid and stationary, but is in
continuous transformation, becoming enriched with scientific no-
tions and philosophical opinions that have entered into common
circulation. —Antonio Gramsci, 1985, 421

PERHAPS the sentiments contained in the following pages, are
not yet sufficiently fashionable to procure them general favor; a
long habit of not thinking a thing wrong, gives it a superficial appearance of being right, and raises at first a formidable outcry in
defence of custom. But tumult soon subsides. Time makes more
converts than reason. —Thomas Paine, *Common Sense*, 1791

The philosophy of one century is the common sense of the next.
—Henry Ward Beecher

Have you heard about the Republican and the Democrat
who were locked in the White House for 20 years? They agreed to reform welfare. During the 1976 presidential campaign, Republican Ron-
ald Reagan's stump speech introduced a story about a Cadillac-driving
welfare queen from Chicago: "She has 80 names, 30 addresses, 12 Social
Security cards. . . . She's got Medicaid, getting food stamps, and she is
collecting welfare under each of her names. Her tax-free cash income
alone is over $150,000."[1] Reagan's comments brought welfare criticism
into the national spotlight. Over a decade later, Democratic candidate

1

William Jefferson Clinton made a campaign pledge to "end welfare as we know it." Though efforts were made along the way, the convergence of Republican and Democratic platforms culminated in the 1996 welfare reform that was passed by a Republican Congress and Democratic president. Indeed, over those 20 years it seems that nearly everyone came to agree that welfare produced an unacceptable state of affairs. In an age where political partisanship and social polarization are the norm, we can learn a great deal from occasions when opposing agendas coalesce around shared ideas. In this case there are lessons to be gleaned about one of the most powerful tools in the arsenal of an institution—common sense.

People have both local and extra-local reasons for doing what they do. By local I mean the everyday decisions that we make about our work and leisure lives. They may be based on interests such as personal preference, needs, or values. Local actions, however, are not completely isolated from the actions of others. To the extent that individual actions are coordinated with each other, we can glimpse the extra-local reasons for our actions—such as national identity, economic principles, social values, or, of course, common sense. These extra-local reasons account for the trends in societal behavior that sociologists notice—people's participation in holidays or civil rights movements, for instance. When individuals do not see any clear self-interest in a situation, it is quite likely common sense that will lead to the course of action chosen.[2] Nevertheless, the social power of common sense to marshal support and action, and the role of institutions in forging it, is routinely overlooked.

We assume that common sense originates on its own and is somehow natural. As with "street smarts," it seems to us an innate dimension of intelligence rather than the adroit perception of and acclimation to distinctively contemporary rules of the street. In other words, we overlook that common sense on the streets of Brooklyn several hundred years ago would be anachronistic in the same location today. Yet, even this realization does not acknowledge the degree to which common sense is socially constructed in concrete and observable ways, often via social institutions.

Selling Welfare Reform is about the U.S. welfare institution's efforts since the 1996 reform to convince poor families to buy into a new common sense about what welfare should be. The common sense of work-first, the dominant version of welfare since the reform, has not been an easy sell; it has required a massive overhaul of the way administrators, staff, and clients are treated. Still, there are some in each of these groups who do not fully buy in: some caseworkers insist, "I'm not in this for the welfare reform, I'm in this to feed my children"; some clients claim that work-first is "creating a workforce of slave laborers." These individuals notwithstanding, work-first, as a national institution, has been phenomenally successful in forging a new common sense among the general public. Research portrays unprecedented support for work-first among both caseworkers and clients.[3] Political leaders and the news media herald the 1996 legislation as a monumental achievement that has succeeded in reducing welfare caseloads by over 50 percent.[4]

This book, however, is more concerned with understanding *what* was intended than in judging the extent to which the reform achieved what was intended. It will show where the current "common sense" of work-first originated, why it has come to dominate, and how it is conveyed to the poor families whose lives it affects. It certainly was not the prevailing way of thinking under the pre-1996 system. I will argue that the common sense of the work-first approach is best understood as neoliberal; it is a new (or neo) take on how to structure society, and welfare, according to principles of economic liberalism. Liberalism's perhaps best-known variant is the laissez-faire approach to fostering "free markets" by limiting governmental involvement. This "neoliberal" approach is at odds with the preceding Keynesian philosophy that dominated U.S. welfare since the New Deal. Keynesianism, championed by British economist John Maynard Keynes, advocated governmental protectionism for working people and markets.

Understood in this context, the selling of work-first common sense to those who would presumably buy into it is a creative enterprise. It enlists the innovative energies of social entrepreneurs to re-envision welfare. At the same time, however, work-first has a destructive element as it dismantles the prior work of Keynesian social engineers. In this changing of the guard, the inevitability of power is apparent. Macrostructural ideologies about how best to structure society are at odds; and in this case there is a clear victor. Though the ongoing battle between opposing liberal and protectionist meta-philosophies is a necessary backdrop for understanding common sense at the welfare office, it is not at this level that this book largely focuses. It is an instructive case study of institutional change and an opportunity to examine the structural power dynamics that institutions uphold. Most of all, however, this is a study of the way local and extra-local interests merge in the production of the nation's foremost welfare program for poor families. To the extent that I am successful, I will provide a window into the everyday lives of administrators, caseworkers, and clients in the nationally exemplary work-first program that developed in East County, New York.[5] As I hope to illustrate, understanding their work and experiences requires attention to both local and extra-local ingredients of the common sense that is forged at the welfare office.

A Rising Star: Welfare Reform in East County

Welfare reform in East County was conceived in the back of a Toyota as local movers and shakers returned from a conference on curbing the spread of illegitimate births and welfare dependency. Less than two decades after Reagan's campaign stump speech about Cadillac-driving welfare queens gave voice to a groundswell of anti-welfare sentiment, public administrators in East County set out to devise a way to reform the unpopular system. According to Roger, one of the top administrators in East County, "we could see the writing on the wall. . . . You keep your ear to the ground. You've got a new governor, a new president, Clinton, who made a big deal about how welfare reform was going to happen. You know something is going to happen and you know it's going to emphasize work. You just don't know how it's going to sort of settle in." There was a sense of urgency and a need to hit the ground running so as to be well-prepared by the time the federal government passed binding reform legislation. It was the calm before the storm that would become the Personal Responsibility and Work Opportunity Reconciliation Act (PRWORA) of 1996. This would replace Aid to Families with Dependent Children (AFDC) with Temporary Assistance for Needy Families (TANF) and set a new course for the nation's primary cash assistance (welfare) program for poor families.

Roger, who eventually became director of East County's program, recalls the years just prior to 1996 as a time of excitement and innovation in which synergy among local social entrepreneurs was aglow.

> Starting our program was a highlight. I will always remember that as such a creative time, because we had a lot of energy, a lot of enthusiasm. We worked great together to create something from nothing. What's not to like about that? We weren't necessarily building on something; we weren't having to fix something. We had a new building, we had new employees, we had a new direction! It was fun.

The idea behind East County's program, and behind the national legislation that would follow within a few years, was that of work-first, or moving a large percentage of TANF recipients into work and work-related activities as quickly as possible. As a result, welfare services should not focus on long-term training, human resource development, or income maintenance. Rather, workforce preparation should involve activities that are "authentic and replicate to the greatest extent possible actual labor force conditions."

Work-first was a change from previous approaches that had emphasized an entitlement of poor families to a safety net below which they would not be allowed to fall and long-term developmental programs, some of which had even paid for community college. As might be anticipated, East County's program at first faced daily challenges from those who saw value in the previous approach. Roger recounts:

> Sometimes it was a real challenge. If you were being asked by a quote unquote "liberal" group, what they were saying was basically to the effect of "isn't this awful that you are making all these people work?" . . . People on the other side of the political aisle felt that welfare reform was terrible, that we were hurting people who already had tough lives, and making people work in unpaid work experience [workfare] was a terrible thing. And there were a lot of articles about all right what you are going to have is an increase in the prison population, an increase in food bank problems, all that kind of stuff—none of which ever happened. But the idea was that this was just such a terrible punitive system.

As Roger recalls, he had to diffuse this carefully. After all, this was not an extremist position; "I understood the thinking" and "I really had a lot of respect for people who wanted to help other people, and that's what you were getting there—people who were trying to step up and help people, and sometimes they were right and we were doing things wrong." He admitted, "I understood because I used to feel that same way. . . I grew up in the '60s." "Looking at the [professional] things I had done before, I was certainly of that bent and I would never call myself a conservative now, I don't know what I would call myself."

Though Roger had not switched political parties, the common sense from which he viewed welfare had changed. In the midst of national and state discussions and excitement, he recalled: "You really start seeing it in a different way. You really start seeing yourself more as someone who should be encouraging work as opposed to just making sure people get their benefits and get out of the way. That probably doesn't sound like a big thing but it was a big thing." As he explains, this forced him to rethink his position on requiring labor market participation.

> Work had been sort of the bad thing before. It was like you don't want to make anyone work in a minimum-wage job. And I totally changed my mind about that. When you really think about it, I worked at minimum-wage jobs. That's how I learned all the basic work skills that everybody is still complaining that people don't have, not just people on welfare, kids out of school. All of the basic stuff about being a professional at work, getting to work on time, knowing how to interact with your supervisor, being consistent, even going to work, you know those kinds of things. That's how you learn that and a lot of these folks had never experienced that. So I kind of changed my mind about the value of work, even if it was minimum wage, or even if it was what was then called "unpaid work experience" [workfare].

Though work-first seemed like a pro-business answer to dissatisfaction with the existing welfare system, gaining the support of the business community was not without its own challenges.

> They didn't think that welfare reform was a big economic development issue. And I will never forget the look on their face when I explained to them that [taxes will go up if people stay on the rolls after the federal five-year limit], and I remember one of them looked up and said, "We need to make sure people know about this!" We were trying to get employers to see that this is to their benefit too, to give people a chance. . . . Some were really good, but the hard thing is—and this is still the balance—you want to get an employer who will be willing to take a chance on somebody, but you really have to send them some great people to begin with or they will never come back to you. And that is so hard; they need the soft skills, showing up on time etc. . . . So that was always a very delicate balance to keep.

Faced with a public relations challenge in relating to both potential employers and advocates for the poor, East County's work-first program set out on a marketing campaign. "We knew what we wanted to do, the concept was there, and we knew why we wanted to do it. The challenge was then to sell it to the county." Strategizing with the marketing department at a local community college and relying on the work of a marketing person on staff, East County's program "held receptions for everything."

> We had a lot of local publicity when we opened. We did that intentionally because we wanted to raise awareness; . . . we would emphasize both the educational and welfare reform portion. . . . We had a lot of innovative programming and one of our staff members had a background in marketing and I would be ready to just do it, but she would say, "No, you have to get some information out about this." That's why we had receptions for everything. I will never look at punch and cookies again. So I guess that's how [we were discovered]. Because it brought awareness. And it was also the topic of the time. People were talking about welfare reform. We would get the press coming to us and say, "I need a story about such and such, what do you have?" So it really worked both ways. And we really did feel like we had some interesting things we were doing.

In addition to public attention, the program was performing as planned. The director recalls, "We had great numbers, we really did, our numbers were great."

Stemming from the publicity and outcomes, others took note. A neighboring county executive unexpectedly flattered East County in her state of the county speech, by declaring, "Why can't we be more like East County?" As the director recalls, "Then we started getting all these phone calls." A national organization invited East County to present on the specifics of what they were doing, "and that kind of got us out there and we got a lot more calls of people interested in what we were doing. There were people from all over the country." This led to a much broader than expected level of national outreach. Roger beams:

> We did a lot of presentations at the national level. We had some ideas of what other places were doing from attending national conferences, but mostly people came to us. . . . We had a lot of people come and visit us. We did presentations, wrote an article in a journal, so we were aware of what other people were doing, but it was more because when they came to us we would ask them, "Well, how do you do this?" And if we heard a good idea, we would steal it.

All of this attention led to visits from the governor and from the president's secretary of transportation. East County also received accolades as a "bold proposal" from then Health and Human Services Secretary, Donna Shalala. Even an international delegation from Namibia visited before they set out to replicate parts of East County's program. Somewhat humbly the director commented, "I think once you are out there, it just happens."

In the midst of East County's rise to prominence, national welfare reform was enacted. The PRWORA was signed into law by President Clinton on August 22, 1996, with bipartisan support. It was activated on July 1, 1997, and replaced the AFDC program and the Job Opportunities and Basic Skills Training (JOBS) program with TANF. Combining the scopes of its predecessors, TANF's overall mission was to "provide assistance and work opportunities to needy families by granting states the federal funds and wide flexibility to develop and implement their own welfare programs."[6] Thus, East County was well-situated. Abolishing family aid's status as a guaranteed entitlement to all with low enough means, welfare reform also transformed the national welfare system by limiting lifetime receipt of benefits to five years, requiring participation in work-related activities as a condition of assistance, and giving states discretion over eligibility and program content through a new system of block grant funding.

The East County experience is instructive on multiple levels. First, it was a nationally recognized prototype on which other locales based their reform design. Second, the East County case highlights the paramount role of common sense in the institutionalization of a neoliberal perspective. Common sense has increased in importance in large part because the top-down hierarchy of the AFDC system, which had limited local discretion, was replaced. The decentralized structure of TANF, also known as the style of new federalism, allows states and localities to create their own welfare programs as long as they are within the PRWORA legislation's guidelines. This has tremendous implications for the role and nature of common sense in welfare offices. In effect, local innovators rely on it to borrow "what makes sense" from other communities with whom they interact. Given a national mandate to innovate locally, and a plethora of "good ideas" that administrators can "steal" from other programs, direct influence of local caseworkers and administrators on each other has become the rule rather than the exception. Advances in travel and digital publication have enhanced these dynamics. The result is a climate that Jamie Peck has described as "fast policy transfer," in which local-level welfare offices like East County are "no longer merely the territorial outposts of a centrally managed system, they now have a role in making policy as well as implementing it."[7] Some have even pointed to innovative local communities such as East County as the likely sites of future transnational trends and "policy fix[es]."[8] In this sense, East County's visit from a Namibian delegation is not so surprising. In the estimation of some, governments all over the world are considering whether to follow America's lead. As just one example of this, the Blair government moved to emulate U.S. welfare policy in its efforts to retool British welfare for a global economy. It even went so far as to lecture its more resistant European counterparts in a fashion Peck succinctly describes as, "this is the future; get used to it."[9]

TANF, however, is more of a work in progress than a finished policy. Even though TANF was enacted following years of local experimentation with AFDC waiver demonstration programs, much about the actual implementation of TANF has changed in the years between PRWORA's passage in 1996 and its reauthorization in 2006. As with the East County experience, states and localities continue to tweak their programs, apply for grants to support auxiliary services, and strive to find better ways to meet federal benchmarking goals given local fiscal priorities. Work-first common sense, thus, is itself continuing to evolve.

As we forge ahead in the early twenty-first century, East County's administrators are joined by social scientists, policymakers, and policy implementers as they continue to wrestle with the dilemma of how to restructure welfare in the midst of a global labor market. Relatively little has stayed the same in the more than 70 years since the U.S. welfare state was born in the wake of the Great Depression. It is true that the economy has been relatively stable between the time of the Depression and now in that we have not hit the same economic straits since, but the playing field that has emerged in the wake of the New Deal is hardly comparable to the labor market its policies were intended to stabilize. Downsizing, outsourcing, off-shoring, the rise of contingent labor—these problems hardly seem solvable within a solely domestic paradigm. Poverty, employment, livelihood, and social safety nets are all connected to international flows of commerce and population.

In the creation and re-creation of welfare states, several questions arise. What basic human rights should be guaranteed? Whose interests and needs should the welfare state ultimately serve? Who should bear the brunt of economic risk in the new international economy?

What role should the federal, state, and local governments play in matters of family structure, gender, race, income inequities, and class animosities? These questions are at the heart of welfare office common sense.

Work-First Common Sense

Selling Welfare Reform addresses the questions that continue to loom about the future of welfare by charting the complex and contradictory ways in which the dominant approach to welfare since 1996—work-first—responds to these questions. Under the mantra, "get a job, any job, then get a better job," the "work-first" approach to welfare presumes a stepping stone career ladder in the low wage economy. It de-emphasizes education, training, and even career advancement under the pretext that motivating people to take any job they can get will jumpstart the long and arduous process of climbing the career ladder from the very bottom up. This, however, is a politically contentious assumption and there is little evidence to suggest that the work-first approach does anything more than leave poor parents permanently stranded in the low wage labor market.[10] Regardless of which side of the debate is correct, it is clear that welfare as presently deployed opts not to create an infrastructure to support a "high road approach" to economic prosperity that would press career and wage advancement for poor workers as immediate goals. Rather, across nearly all states, welfare implementers have adopted what some have labeled a "low road/work-first approach," committed to propelling clients into low wage jobs. Work-first proponents are undaunted by the potential vulnerability of their clients to exploitation by a global labor market seeking the cheapest and most flexible labor possible.

As with all policy decisions, work-first has political winners and losers. The existing literature on welfare reform to date has been nothing short of precedent setting in its volume and detail. The literature is also broad in scope. It includes a wealth of insightful program evaluations, caseload analyses, surveys of clients and workers, organizational case studies, and national statistical reports. Yet, most of the literature takes the "common sense" of work-first for granted. As a result, the implications work-first holds for the wider political economy of poverty in the global labor market have been largely unprobed. This book journeys to the core of these dynamics—examining welfare caseworkers at the many welfare offices and outposts that comprise one county's welfare system, as well as the applicants and clients of this program—to explore the complex, subtle, and obvious ways in which the post-1996 work-first approach charts a new course for welfare states in the era of globalization.

Work-first common sense is as much about destruction as it is about the creation of new and innovative program implementation. In order to move policy and society toward the neoliberal ideals of work-first, the barriers to this model must be undermined and removed. Preparing poor mothers to think about and sell their labor power as a true commodity requires elimination of the family protections that allow them to stay out of the labor market to raise their children. Shifting personal responsibility for economic survival to individuals requires an attack on union protections and entitlements to aid. Encouraging employers to utilize clients as low wage workers entails dismantling the previous bureaucracy that protected workers from market exploitation. The new structure must be nimble enough to respond to employers' demands at the expense of uniform practice. Coaxing clients to buy into low wage jobs even against their own prerogative necessitates a contortion of client-directed social work ethos. Vital to the ability to carry out all of these necessary destructions is a dismantling of centralized federalism and the creation of space for market-driven policy innovation on the local level. The flourishing of local entrepreneurial spirit occurs at the expense of central planning and guarantees of equity. In themselves, these transitions are neither good nor bad, but they are political.

I am concerned with uncovering the dynamics of political economy underlying the common sense that prevails in work-first programs across the nation. These dynamics have a tremendous effect on the daily lives of needy families who have little if any political clout. In addition, the absence of a critical perspective on work-first's common sense constitutes a significant absence in the literature to date. It has precluded comprehensive debate about the precedents the PRWORA sets for future welfare policy. Analytically, debates have been stalled at an impasse of diametrically opposed abstractions about whether poverty is due to structural or individual failings; in the current tenor of the time, individual arguments tend to win out. In this context, there is little room for concrete analysis of the ways in which neoliberal policy affects the material interests of all workers. Scholars and policymakers still do not have a clear picture of what caseworkers and administrators do to form the foundation of our contemporary social safety net and to enforce a neoliberal approach to social well-being.[11] For this reason, it is critical to examine the transition and reconfiguration of the welfare state through the eyes of the workers and clients who live it, *and* with attention to their material interests.

Finally, a wealth of scholarship focuses on institutions and the role they play in society. Recently, there has been growing interest, particularly in the area of institutional ethnography, in the subtle and complex ways in which local and extra-local interests interact within modern institutions. I see the social construction of common sense as crucial to this work.[12] Here I draw on the work of other institutional ethnographers to make the case for the analytical and theoretical importance of common sense in our understanding of how social power dynamics and politics organize our everyday lives.

Politicizing Work-First Common Sense

In the midst of heated debates about welfare reform in the late 1990s, the *Washington Post* published a political cartoon that speaks to the heart of the macropolitics behind the welfare office. It features a downcast and bedraggled woman leading three children by the hand with a fourth on her back, through the streets of an urban jungle of looming office buildings, presumably searching for a job. A conversation can be heard from several stories up in a skyscraper labeled "Corporate Welfare" that towers overhead: "*Don't worry. . . . The idea is to get rid of welfare as they know it, not as we know it.*"[13] Corporate welfare in the forms of government subsidies and tax breaks to large and often transnational employers have garnered public concern as of late because their expenses in the billions dwarf the amount spent on welfare aid for the poor.[14] This choice of diction invokes President Bill Clinton's campaign promise to "end welfare as we know it" and makes it clear that it is welfare for poor families that TANF ended, not welfare for corporations. Quite to the contrary, the welfare reform seems to have expanded the aegis of corporate welfare.

The article accompanying the *Post*'s cartoon, entitled "Making Public Assistance a Private Enterprise," suggests a new angle to corporate welfare—what I will call corporate-centered welfare. The idea is to make welfare for the poor also beneficial to corporate interests—a new frontier for profit that TANF adds to existing corporate welfare policies. Though the article deals with one aspect of this, allowing the privatization of welfare services so that commercial entities can turn a profit from welfare reform, it is not the only one. Throughout this book I will discuss corporate-centered welfare by examining the ways in which the work-first approach to welfare serves to empower investment-savvy employers who are entrepreneurial enough to take advantage. This is an inherently political aspect of work-first that shifts the balance of social power away from poor families and toward employers.

Certainly at other points in U.S. history "work-first" would have been considered harsh, punitive, and draconian because it rejects food, shelter, and economic security as basic rights.[15] Yet today, in the midst of global economic restructuring, one need only look at the vast majority of research literature and media publicity to see that the assumptions of work-first—that the free market is politically neutral and that only the poor who commit themselves to participation in the labor market are deserving of aid—are taken for granted as obvious and self-evident.[16] I question whether these assumptions are themselves part of the ideological vanguard of an effort to dismantle welfare as a safety net and transform it into something else—a corporate-centered approach to welfare. This would not be the first time:

> From Lochner to twenty-first century neoliberalism, opponents of a welfare state have aimed not simply to defend impartial market forces against government distortion, but rather to enlist the state in constructing a particular substantive version of the market in which the partisan interests of an elite appear as natural and necessary to the public interest.[17]

The thesis of this book is that the 1996 welfare reform is an attempt to adapt the U.S. welfare system to the demands of the global economy by employing a neoliberal rather than labor protectionist strategy.

The ascendancy of neoliberal thinking, as one of the most dominant contemporary U.S. frames of interpretation, has pre-empted sustained skepticism of its underlying assumptions. It has also served to crowd out other perspectives to the point where, in the words of Gregory Albo, "central policy disputes in Washington [now] occur totally on the terrain of neoliberalism."[18] Embedded within welfare offices on the local level as well, the neoliberal approach carries a valence of being "natural" and "common sense."[19] The result is a phenomenon also observed by institutional ethnographer Ellen Pence in her research on domestic violence response systems:

> Workers' tasks are shaped by certain prevailing features of the system, features so common to workers that they begin to see them as natural,

as the way things are done—and in some odd way—as the only way they could be done, rather than as planned procedures and rules developed by individuals ensuring certain ideological ways of interpreting and acting on a case.[20]

But how did the neoliberal approach to globalization come to be adopted as the dominant strategy for adapting the U.S. welfare state to a global economy and how did it find its way to East County and other local communities?

Policy solutions do not originate in a vacuum. Sociologists such as Paul Burstein and scholars of public administration such as Anthony Downs argue that organizations and cultural constructs are critical to understanding policy domains and the inner workings of policy creation.[21] Public policy analyst John Kingdon has presented a similar argument through his identification of what he calls "policy windows" that must open in order for a policy change to occur.[22] According to Kingdon, a policy window is "an opportunity for advocates of proposals to push their pet solutions or to push attention to their special problems."[23] Such windows open due to national mood swings or administrative turnover. When they do, Kingdon asserts that it is policy entrepreneurs who take advantage of the opportunity.[24] But how is it that policy windows open?

Members of society, like policymakers and implementers, approach society from a variety of standpoints. Common sense represents a convergence of these perspectives in certain places. I focus throughout this book on how a characteristically neoliberal common sense is socially constructed through a variety of means in the welfare office. To understand how this is possible, however, requires familiarity with certain societal trends. These trends both created the policy window for the 1996 welfare reform and fostered a common sense that begins not with lived experience of poverty but with suburbanization, racial politics, and globalization. More important, making sense of the daily experiences of local caseworkers and clients has required me to understand these larger trends.

The concentration of poverty in cities has led to suburban speculation about the deficiencies of poor urban families. Gender is an implicit part of this speculation, since women and children make up the vast majority of welfare families. Politics of race date back to before the New Deal, but popular understanding of the significance of race has changed. Race plays a considerable role in the common sense of dealing with welfare since black families comprise a disproportionate amount of the TANF caseload. Finally, dominant perspectives on how to adapt to the global economy are influential because the work-first approach is one of integrating poor families into the labor market. Labor market integration is seen as a way to both adjust to a global labor market and facilitate its growth.

Suburban Common Sense

The critiques of welfare's clientele that led to the 1996 reform are built on representations of the poor framed by ghetto ethnographies and individualizing discourse. This is evident in legislative debate and policy, which have served to "reinforce the idea that the family, not public or political institutions or the workplace, [is] the primary institutional location for intervention into poor life."[25] This perspective is not necessarily shared by work-first clients. Rather, the idea is grounded in and born of a homogeneous suburban common sense that was created by government actions such as the post–World War II Interstate Highway Act of 1956 and the Serviceman's Readjustment Act of 1944 (including the GI bill and federal mortgage interest deduction). These bills not only provided roadways for suburban sprawl but also supplied 8 million free college educations and 16 million new suburban homesteads as they radically transformed the U.S. landscape.[26] Supported by pro-suburbanization policies, suburbs grew "forty times as fast as cities" in the 1950s, and the national suburban population more than doubled between 1950 and 1970. With 83 percent of total national population growth occurring in suburbs in this time period, by 1970 more U.S. citizens lived in suburbs than in cities or rural areas, "a first for any society in recorded history."[27] Labor too was a part of this suburbanization of America as employers joined the exodus to these newly opening spaces. Suburbs became the main location of employers for the nation's cities by the 1970s and became home to two-thirds of the nation's manufacturing industry by the early 1980s.[28]

The widespread suburbanization of the post–World War II period enabled "white flight" from cities just as more southern blacks were migrating to cities in search of jobs. The racial exclusions that accompanied suburbanization also created a nationally homogeneous suburban white population—what Michael Lind termed "the white overclass."[29] Describing this same phenomenon in Gramscian terms, Matthew Ruben asserts that a national hegemony was created, by virtue not only of its "high degree of sociopolitical homogeneity," but also because its own outlook and life experiences took over center stage and "had come to appear universal" or national. This completed "a three-way equation among location, whiteness, and American-ness" that re-constructed urban dwellers, especially non-whites, as "the other" and as aberrant to the extent that they failed to follow suburban white norms.[30] This suburban hegemonic establishment ushered in the rise of neoliberalism.[31] It joined conceptualizations of the two-parent, heterosexual, Standard North American Family (SNAF) with what Paul Luken and Suzanne Vaughan describe as the Standard American Home (SAH) to universalize the perspective and sensibilities of white, middle-class, suburban, nuclear families.[32] In the suburbanized-neoliberal-context, "The nationalized suburban position is *the necessary point of observation and enunciation for urban diagnosis*, providing a vantage point from which the city may be apprehended precisely as a site of national otherness."[33]

The construction of a suburban, hegemonic, white, American, middle class (SHWAM) not only preceded the 1996 welfare reform; it also made the reform politically feasible. Previous attempts at wide-ranging welfare reform had been hindered, stalled, and even blocked by chronic and persisting "helping conundrums."[34] Policy expert David Ellwood examined how four basic values seem to underlie much of the philosophical and political rhetoric about poverty. The values of autonomy of the individual, the virtue of work, the primacy of the family, and a desire to provide economic security to all members of the community can never be mutually satisfied in a single poverty policy.[35] With the rise of the SHWAM, autonomy and work were elevated over security, particularly economic security for aberrant urban others. Once urban welfare clients came to be seen as "others," the SHWAM was able to mentally overcome the conundrums that had stalled previous reforms and be at peace with its decision to adapt a "tough love" approach toward the perceived "dysfunctionality" of poor urban families.

In the context of suburban hegemony, welfare reform appears as an endeavor of neocolonialism, an attempt not to end poverty but to "make them more like us." Ironically, though, the SHWAM hegemony is also implicated in the creation of this otherness. As jobs followed the white majority out to the suburbs, they left a vacuum in inner cities. The ascendancy of classical liberal individualism and liberal feminism to mainstream sensibilities has been credited with overall national rises in female labor force participation and female-headed households. However, for urban African American women the narrative also includes the structural unemployment and resulting dearth of "marriageable" African-American men, precipitated by many of the same social forces that concurrently brought about the rise of the suburbs.[36] The suburban majority did not experience the daily realities of increasing joblessness among urban men and subsequent female-centered adjustment of families, as did urban families of color.[37] As such, there is little to prevent SHWAM families from viewing poverty, joblessness, and single-parent households as the fault of those on whom such familial restructuring fell. This has allowed a critical mass of public opinion to support a shift in welfare policy from anti-poverty to anti-behavior.

As social commentators have noted, "today's political rhetoric is vastly more concerned with ending welfare dependency than with ameliorating poverty."[38] The debate of the late 1980s and early 1990s which was led by such neoconservative thinkers as Charles Murray and Lawrence Mead, revived Oscar Lewis's "culture of poverty" concept of the 1960s. A new thesis emerged of a stereotypically black urban "underclass" that was "isolated" and "dislocated" from the rest of society, rife with moral weakness, and in need of "tough love" attempts to shock them out of a "culture of dependency."[39] These arguments were based on suburban subjectivities and found fertile ground in the minds of suburbanites who had not experienced the flight of jobs out of cities just as they arrived, as did many nonwhite urbanites. Thus, a collusion of suburban hegemonic subjectivity and popular discourse of dependency paved the way for the common sense of tough love. This was also a new chapter in the ongoing politics of race and economic transformation.

The Politics of Race

Though publicly downplayed, race was also a substantial subtext of the 1996 reform. Welfare was a key political wedge that spanned the 1960s through the 1980s largely because of its racial and gender undertones. Built on the foundations of a growing literature that scrutinized an "underclass" of black Americans—helped along by stereotypes such as that of the Cadillac-driving black welfare queen—race had become so entangled in the issue of poverty that any mention of welfare conjured images of blackness in the public eye. Nicholas Lemann's observations in 1986 epitomized this cognitive connection when he observed, "President Reagan has commissioned a major study of welfare reform, which is a polite way of asking what we should do about the black underclass."[40]

In the 1960s, an increasing number of blacks gained access to the welfare roles due to socially liberal efforts to ensure that the considerable population of poor blacks was not systematically excluded from governmental safety nets. As a result, socially liberal Democrats who had supported Lyndon B. Johnson's Great Society programs and racial equality in welfare became associated with poorer African-American and Latino voters. Given the growing concentration of nonwhites on welfare, the initial intent of the program to protect white mothers from having to leave their children to work in menial labor lost its political support. In addition, women of all colors were increasingly entering the labor market, which gave rise to a new way of thinking about the appropriateness of work that was critical to the undermining of support for AFDC. As some vocalized, "Wage earners get no supplement when they have another child, so why should welfare recipients?"[41] In the tradition of what Mike Davis terms "the have revolution" of the 1970s, in which white middle-class suburbanites reacted to recession, high oil prices, inflation, and increased economic insecurity in part by obsessing about the "pathologies of the poor," the work-first approach, and TANF in general, has been "based on the assumption that the cure for poverty is participation in the paid labor force for all able-bodied adults, including single mothers of infants and young and/or disabled children."[42] Collectively these political changes made AFDC "politically indefensible at worst, [and] unattractive at best, even among many committed to women's equality (or racial justice)."[43]

A backlash began in the 1970s with Nixon's "silent majority" of white voters who, though they would never vocalize it for fear of being seen as racist, resented having their tax monies going to support the disproportionately nonwhite urban poor. Corresponding with Reagan's caricature of Cadillac-driving black welfare queens, Republicans increasingly used welfare as a wedge issue in the 1980s in an effort to separate white voters from the Democratic Party. By the time of the 1992 presidential campaign, Democrats were in a bind such that they felt forced to do something to disassociate themselves and their welfare policies from race politics. As Ann Shola Orloff explains:

> Democrats were put in the unenviable position of defending a deeply flawed welfare program in order to defend poor people and a safety net, and lost support among traditional white working-class constituencies, among others, because of it.[44]

With rising popularity making a reform seem inevitable, both Republicans and Democrats pressed welfare as a key issue in their efforts to attract voters. In the process, the politically centrist Democratic Leadership Council, led by Bill Clinton, sought to "inoculate" its party from Republican attacks by both pledging to "end welfare as we know it" and embarking on a gender- and color-blind approach to poverty.[45]

The color-blind approach that dominated public discourse hence was a product of political wrangling as much as anything else. Conservatives who claimed that "anything was better than the old system" of welfare "were really interested in . . . politically exploiting the issue and painting the Democrats as defenders of 'amoral' black women in ghettos."[46] In response, social liberals rationalized a color-blind welfare reform as necessary, since it provided "a way of banishing race, and racialized poverty from the political lexicon."[47] For both parties, welfare reform was as much about poverty as it was about navigating race politics to secure the vote of middle-class white (SHWAM) voters. Democrats had lost their support to Republicans following Great Society programs aimed at helping inner-city nonwhite poor.[48] Corresponding with broader postmodern trends in thinking, the reform rhetoric assumed that "all human beings are the same under the skin." This rhetoric claimed that "seeing racial differences is to *be* racist [just as] pointing out gender differences is to *be* sexist."[49]

Contemporary domestic politics contributed immensely to the character of the 1996 welfare reform, but so did a legacy of imperial colonialism. Under the imperial paradigm, the extent of generosity offered by welfare states has historically varied by dynamics of race and class.[50] In short, racial homogeneity at home has historically allowed for the fostering of national solidarity through generous welfare policies in nations such as Britain.[51] In such cases, providing a strong, centralized, and deeply penetrating welfare state was politically feasible because it included only white residents of the homeland, excluding nonwhite members of the kingdom living abroad. Thus, it left colonialism's racial hegemony unchallenged.[52] This dynamic not only helps to explain Scandinavian nations that have not been hindered by racial cleavages in their construction of generous universal welfare states, but it also points out one possible cause of the comparatively un-generous policies of the United States.[53]

Unlike the British and French empires, both of which comprised considerable nonwhite majorities that lived abroad from the homeland, the particularities of the United States' involvement in slave trade and southern agrarian economy led to a minority nonwhite population (approximately 10-12 percent) that lived domestically within the homeland at the time of welfare-state creation in the 1930s.[54] In global comparison, Robert

Lieberman notes, "Where the boundaries of imperial and racial citizenship were more permeable, the possibilities for social policy were restricted by the possibility of racial inclusion."[55] In other words, the United States did not adopt a strong and generous centralized welfare system because it would have risked disrupting the nation's established racial hierarchy.

> In such countries, the problem of distinguishing between those who were and were not entitled to consideration as members of the solidaristic national community was a more complicated political and administrative enterprise, since one could not simply presume that social and national boundaries coincided. Rather, welfare states in these countries were more likely to take complex institutional forms, involving decentralized decision making and administration rather than constructing direct links between citizens and the state.[56]

This framework for understanding the dynamics between race and the welfare state provides an explanation for the emergence of racially exclusive New Deal policies in the United States that systematically excluded certain predominantly black employment sectors (excluding over three-fifths of the black labor force from social insurance in the process) and took shape amidst a complexity of north-south racial politics.[57] New Deal policies were thus "built on racial rather than class hierarchy" through a "cross-class coalition" that united disparate white constituencies of white northern urban workers, white southern workers, and the white southern planter-class elite.[58]

As Lieberman documents, in both the United States and Britain, race became "one of the central axes around which the politics of welfare revolved" since the construction of cross-class coalitions was predicated upon racial animosities. Britons were united across class levels against "a racially defined threat from outside," while in the United States, whites of various classes banded together against an internal racial threat to create the welfare state of the 1930s.[59] The result in the United States was a welfare state that did not design inclusive and universal national approaches, opting instead for policies that were exclusionary and decentralized in nature.

Contrary to contemporary associations of blackness with welfare, a large part of U.S. welfare history has thus involved overlooking the plight of poor blacks such that poverty was portrayed as a white problem. As such, the majority of efforts to alleviate poverty were directed at whites (see table 1.1). It was not until the 1960s that black migration to northern

TABLE 1.1
Race and the Welfare State

Era	Program	Mechanisms that Excluded Blacks From Welfare Aid
Colonial Period to 1935	Mother's Pensions— state and locally created policies	• local implementers strictly interpreted eligibility to exclude black and/or unmarried women to protect their programs from public criticism • programs often not established in areas with high black populations
1935	New Deal Programs— Federal Aid to Dependent Children	• agricultural and domestic workers who were disproportionately Black were left out of new deal provisions due to legislative compromise between northern and southern legislators • states retained rights to determine eligibility and used standard of "suitable home" to exclude Black and unmarried women • seasonal employment policies cut people, largely Black, off welfare rolls during harvest season • higher standard budgets used for Whites then Blacks assumed that Blacks "could get by" with less
1947	ADC Rules Tightened— discrimination reduced due to more uniformed eligibility rules	• state administrators reframed image of clients from deserving White mothers to lazy Black mothers of questionable morality • sexual behavior and childbearing of stereotypically Black recipients linked in public discourse to increasing costs to taxpayers • "suitable home" was determined often on the basis of whether a child was illegitimate, Blacks had a higher rate of illegitimacy
1960s	Great Society and Civil Rights—push for equal rights in social policies	• county officials cut Blacks off welfare rolls or suspended benefits when they participated in voter registration • "suitable home" regulations made more stringent in southern states • states slow to comply with 1964 Civil Rights Act which prohibited discrimination in federally funded programs • "man in the house rules" defined any man with whom a mother had sexual relations as a "substitute father" thus making children ineligible for aid - struck down by Supreme Court King V. Smith 1968 • welfare rights leaders' homes were subject to gunfire in the south • great society programs created in 1960's not implemented in states until 1970s
1996	TANF— created by the Personal Responsibility and Work Opportunity Reconciliation Act	• neoliberal Personal Responsibility approach denies or minimizes contemporary significance of overt and institutional racism in welfare case management and the labor market • greater discretion returned to states and local caseworkers to determine how the legislation applies to individuals, this allows for racial stereotypes and biases to be incorporated into implementation • more punitive policies enacted in areas with higher Black concentration • racial disparities in caseload declines, case management services, and employment outcomes

Sources: Gooden 2003, Soss, Schram, Vartanian, & O'Brien 2001, Abramovitz 1988, Quadagno 1998, Valocchi 1994.

cities, urban riots, and the civil rights movement forced black poverty into the public spotlight. However, simultaneous with the shift from focus on white to black poverty, news attention given to the poor became less sympathetic and African Americans became associated with the "undeserving poor."[60] This shift in media attention has increased in importance as the post-1996 return to local discretion elevates the role of public attitudes. Negative stereotypes are more consequential not only among frontline workers, their administrators, and state officials, but also among the wider public to whom they cater and who are less likely to be sympathetic to or support aid for poor families, especially those of color.[61]

This association between race and laziness or unworthiness of aid is more than merely a suspicion or paranoia. Survey research reveals that believing that welfare recipients are black is correlated with a higher likelihood to blame "lack of effort on their part" and lack of desire to work rather than "circumstances beyond their control."[62] Such evidence suggests that the ability of black clients to manage their own image in the welfare office may be compromised by media portrayals that have predominantly associated the underclass of lazy welfare recipients with blackness. In one examination of news magazine stories between 1950 and 1992, for instance, researcher Martin Gilens found that people pictured in stories on the "underclass" were nearly universally "black," as opposed to other more sympathetic stories on poverty, welfare, and hunger which, though having appreciably higher proportions of nonwhites, were more racially diverse.[63] This depiction of a large, nearly all black underclass prevailed despite estimates that only 5 percent of all Americans are thought to belong to an "underclass" and only 59 percent of these are African Americans.[64] The result is a process of media representation in which the "undeserving poor" have been represented as mostly black, and racial stereotypes are perpetuated that lessen public support for anti-poverty programs in general, and assistance for blacks in poverty in particular.[65]

Given these broad historical developments, America's historical racism has changed but not dissipated. "Although America is much less segregated and much less outwardly racist than it was a half-century ago, race remains one of the deepest and most intractable dividing lines of contemporary American politics."[66] While the poverty rate overall has fallen in recent years to 10 percent for all families in 2003, it has remained disproportionately high among blacks as compared to whites (28.7 percent versus 8.9 percent among families with children under 18, and 42.8 percent versus 28.1 percent among *female headed* families with children under 18).[67] These statistics keep race in the public eye even if official welfare policy is color-blind. Race is a major factor as well in the common sense that has developed to address the problem of welfare in a global economy.

Politics of Globalization

Work-first common sense embraces a neoliberal vision of globalization in which the government focuses less on protecting its people than on encouraging them to "sink or swim" in the global labor market. This represents a monumental shift away from the common sense of earlier eras in which national welfare and solidarity were higher priorities than global commerce. This shift, however, was not an overnight process. The rise of neoliberalism as a strategy for globalization and the favoring of corporate-centered welfare are rooted in massive structural, political, and economic changes. These have brought about a new way of seeing government as less viable in its Keynesian role, that is, as a steward and protector of national economy and culture. Because of neoliberal globalization, and its attendant international competition and rising public debt, old models of state guardianship have come to be seen as antiquated. A consensus has grown around the necessity that governments become leaner and meaner to adapt to global market forces. These forces do not guarantee job stability and do not tolerate the inefficiencies of social protections for families and workers.[68]

Globalization is implicated by the very nature of East County as depicted in its local newspapers and common locution. At its geographic center is a rust-belt city, built on the manufacturing eruption of the industrial revolution and modernity. As with the other major northeastern urban centers with declining populations, out-migrations have created a vacuum, drawing the youth to other areas of opportunity in the south and overseas. Those left behind are disproportionately the retiring baby boomers who have managed to keep their jobs or patch together employment until retirement, all the while pining for their distantly relocated children and grandchildren. The literature has much to say about the trajectory of well-paying industrial jobs—out of cities to suburbs, from the rust belt to the sun belt, and from expensive U.S. labor markets to overseas havens from taxes and organized labor.

Yet, the critical piece of this scholarship for the purpose of the present analysis is the ideology that has arisen to instruct people on how exactly to deal with this tumultuous labor market. People can no longer expect to spend a career with the same company, and no career training—not even computers—is a surefire means to a lifelong livelihood. In this context, work-first seems like a cost-effective stance for government to take, since job-training investments run a high likelihood of proving futile. Further, government is seen as having little choice in the matter, since its former toolbox of economy boosters and job creators has proven ineffectual in the new economy. Governments can no longer guarantee to stabilize communities by luring business investments from elsewhere with promises of tax breaks. This is clear from the stream of failed attempts by U.S. senators, representatives, and state assembly members to lure businesses to East County only to be undercut by cheaper labor elsewhere, or by other senators making better bids.

Community anchor businesses prove far too elusive and their capital is far too mobile. They are eager to rush on to the next blighted community offering to sacrifice just a little bit more for even a few less jobs than were offered to the community before them. In this climate, downsized, outsourced, and outmoded professional workers are taught in job-search workshops to embrace the challenge, accept the risk inherent in the global economy, and actively manage their careers so that they are always making themselves marketable to the next potential employer. Unfortunately, this will continue until their current job inevitably expires.[69] In the case of welfare in the post-reform era, a distant cousin to this discourse emerges in the neoliberal work-first rhetoric that similarly individualizes the burden of global dynamics.

But how did globalization come to mean the complex and volatile mixture that is today both praised for the exchanges of culture and goods it produces and blamed for unemployment, pollution, and destabilization of daily life?[70] As James Midgley points out, globalization is blamed for these social ills "when they are not in fact the result of some objective 'thing' exerting its own, malevolent volition but the result of a complex set of human activities with intended and unintended consequences."[71] If indeed the problem is not international capitalism, but rather "international predatory capitalism" as some have suggested, then understanding the genesis and evolution of this approach is critical to gauging and addressing its influence at the welfare office.[72]

In the era leading to the end of World War II, working classes had flocked to the state for protection and business rallied around the market to represent their interests.[73] The rise in neoliberal popularity, however, has enabled a welfare reform that merges capital interests with that of the state in the name of more efficient service. Simultaneously, the reform has provoked a condition in which those whom it affects most directly—clients, caseworkers, administrators, and taxpayers—are "unsure as to what their interests actually are, let alone how to realize them."[74] This condition, which Mark Blyth labels "Knightian uncertainty" following from the work of Frank Knight, is a by-product of both the complexity of contemporary society and the persuasive power of neoliberal ideas. Figuring out where our personal interests lie requires examining the origins of the neoliberal common-sense approach to globalization.

The words of Karl Polanyi regarding the 1800s are instructive for understanding the emergence of today's neoliberalism: "While in imagination the nineteenth century was engaged in constructing the liberal utopia, in reality it was handing over things to a definite number of concrete institutions the mechanisms of which ruled the day."[75] This history can be seen to repeat itself, though with contemporary nuance. The present contours of the neoliberal approach to global economy similarly result from a series of twentieth-century decisions, events, and "handing[s] over" of reins that were initially intended to create a utopia. These began with the July 1944 United Nations Monetary and Financial Conference held in Bretton Woods, New Hampshire. While this conference laid a foundation for facilitated global trade by establishing a system of rules, institutions, and procedures to regulate the international monetary system, its interests were more along the lines of ensuring stability of nations, economies, and working citizens in the wake of the Great Depression and World War II.

In the process, however, the imbalance of power accorded to the United States as an up-and-coming postwar economic and military superpower set the stage for "a hegemonic monetary regime centered on the dollar."[76] It also set a precedent for international leadership and normalized the existence of a global regime that would "act as a sort of governance mechanism between sovereign states."[77] A shift away from nation-centered economic growth and planning seemed a logical next step. Planning based on capital accumulation through international investment rather than national well-being became popular.[78] This was part of a broader transnationalization of financial capital and weakening of national control over monetary policy similar to the "haute finance" identified by Polanyi in the early twentieth century.[79]

There were numerous milestones for this late-twentieth-century shift. In 1971, the Nixon administration decided to abandon the gold standard to facilitate the international flow of currency. Keynesian approaches to centralized economic planning within nations were replaced with neoliberal economic policies that were favored by the west, particularly in the 1980s. Prominent in this paradigm was the notion popularized by business writers (such as Kenichi Ohmae 1991, 1996) as the declining relevance of the nation-state in an era in which global markets are the last word.[80] Things would work out for the best and most prosperous if everyone—regardless of race, gender, and caregiving responsibilities—pursued their own economic interests internationally and governments focused on helping them do so.

In this age of highly mobile global capital, and an expendable international labor force, within-nation solidarity and welfare supports were no longer needed to maintain profitability for policy-influencing elites. The tenor of the time in some ways embodies a version of the cosmopolitan perspective on globalization, in which national loyalties and prejudices are rejected in favor of recognizing commonality among the world's peoples. In this version, however, global elites often have more in common, both in terms of material interests and lifestyle, with the elites in other countries than with the poor and working classes in their own nations.[81]

Seeking to augment their continued accumulation of capital, elites have enlisted the aid of the state through massive lobbying efforts. Accordingly, "rejecting the libertarianism and hard-line laissez-faire ideology of the right, neoliberalism embraces efficiency and 'good government' by shifting public resources away from the promotion of social equality and toward the promotion of targeted economic growth."[82] In the course of this transition Bretton Woods institutions, such as the International Monetary Fund (IMF) and the World Bank (and in 1995 the World Trade Organization), are increasingly used to promote the interests of powerful western commercial financial institutions across the globe. In addition, U.S. corporations have begun to restructure their employment strategies in accordance with neoliberal approaches to capital accumulation.[83]

Since "the Great U-Turn" that Bennett Harrison and Barry Bluestone identified in 1988, elites seeking continued capital accumulation have adopted a "low road" approach to adapting to the global market. This entails a hyper-focus on cutting labor costs through "the breakup of internal labor markets and seniority systems, the increased use of 'contingent labor' through subcontracting and through the employment of temps, casuals, part-timers, and contract workers, the enforcement of pay freezes and two-tier pay systems, and increased hostility to organized labor."[84] In this new paradigm, "good business climate" equals "no social wage."[85]

Racialized minorities and overseas workers and corporations are no longer threatening competitors used to galvanize national solidarity. Offshoring often involves "increasingly yielding fundamental technology, manufacturing management experience, and design and engineering skills to what, in another era [of nation-centered common sense], would have been considered the competition."[86] In the emergent restructuring, racial distinctions that had characterized early imperial colonialism have faded in importance and the lines of class are being re-emphasized. The new adversary of the U.S. capital elite includes those who would stand in the way of the economic agenda of restoring "growth" and renewing "corporate dynamism" through a strategy designed to, in the words of Nixon's assistant secretary of labor, "zap labor" in order to undermine labor union action.[87]

Collectively, neoliberal views on globalization, racial politics, and suburban experiences form the backdrop for welfare reform's policy window and the everyday experience of common sense at the welfare office.

The Approach and Organization of the Book

Whether it is suburban opinions, racial politics, or globalizing logics, people are certainly influenced by the discourses they encounter. However, we also retain a considerable degree of personal autonomy in our lives. The prevailing common sense does not force us to behave in certain ways. Nevertheless, it is the standard by which we judge ourselves and our work and evaluate what we do. Though we may reject it, we remain accountable to common sense, and our resistance is in relation to its status quo.[88] In this way, common sense influences the ways in which we organize our lives. Given the complexity of today's world and modern forms of communication by which we are exposed to discourse, it is seldom, if ever, possible to comprehensively understand the factors that influence our daily lives by looking only at local factors. Social reality is continually reproduced by what we say, do, and write, but the "we" involved is now much broader than in the past.

The approach I take to exploring the construction and politics of common sense is inspired by the work of Dorothy E. Smith. She incorporates this understanding of the interaction between local and extra-local within institutional ethnography. Like Smith, I am hopeful that this book provides an accessible means to understanding how what seems like naturally occurring logic in our daily lives, and in this case in the welfare office, is more a product of how we decide to organize society. By "we" I mean the aggregate of local people like you or me who both live our lives locally and become sources of "extra-local" influence on others in other locations when we write, do, or say something that influences them (whether we ever meet them or not). By the same token, I am conscious of how others influence us from their extra-local standpoints.

Power is not necessarily a part of the relationship between our local life and its extra-local influences, though it often is. For instance, this is the case in work-first when federal officials mandate that state and local officials behave in certain ways, or when policymakers regulate the labor-market participation of local families. Smith's aim is to improve our understanding of how our daily lives are involved in power dynamics by working to make clear how social organization links people's everyday world with generalized social relations. Though some ways in which we organize society are blatant—such as military ranks, zoning laws, and organizational hierarchies—others are much more subtle. Institutional Ethnography is designed to attend to the subtle ways that society is organized through the flow of consciousness and ideas from person to person and across local and extra-local locations. These ideas and common-sense assumptions become the rules that we navigate in our daily lives, whether we choose to follow them or not. In aggregate, these rules are held in place by ruling relations—that is, by the interpersonal bonds that encourage us to play along. This may involve the relationships between a boss and employee or a wife and husband. It may also be seen in the fear of gossip that keeps new parents always in line with societal expectations of child rearing.

Smith asserts that it is possible to empirically investigate the connections between local people and the extra-local influences on their lives by paying close attention to the mediums by which people share ideas and adopt them. In practice, this often involves: interviewing people about what they are thinking when they do things; examining the texts, forms, letters, and books that people engage as they do things; and following up on the connections people make by then going to the extra-local sources they reveal to see what in turn has influenced them. In this case I begin with caseworkers and clients. I trace their work through texts and interviews to the work of caseworkers in other locations within the welfare bureaucracy, to administrators, and ultimately to thoughts and communications, or discourse, of people who are beyond East County. The result resembles a map that extends from people's lives outward to the social

TABLE 1.2
Summary of Chapter Findings

Chapter theme	Work-first common sense is constructed by:
2. Innovation and Common Sense	national discourse and entrepreneurial efforts that champion a corporate-centered approach
3. Work-First Performance Measures	budgetary responsibilities and program goals
4. New Technology and New Stakeholders	hard-wired protocols and paperwork
5. Work-First Case Management	coordination of case work strategy and discretion
6. Work-First and Families	reframing family life expectations
7. Work-First and Resistance	countering resistance of caseworkers and clients

organization of work-first common sense. Though I begin from people's daily lives and extend outward, I present my findings in reverse for the sake of clarity. The following chapters closely examine the details of the work-first institution of today by beginning with the extra-local creation of work-first common sense and then tracing it as it is sold to administrators, caseworkers, and eventually, to poor families. See table 1.2 for a summary of chapter findings.

I systematically demonstrate how the neoliberal restructuring of thinking about welfare in extra-local places is connected with the local day-to-day welfare office practices in East County's TANF program. I begin by examining the work of local entrepreneurs who created work-first in East County. I demonstrate how the common sense that guided their local work was guided by national politics, including a well-organized lobbying effort. I then examine how this common sense was institutionalized through performance measures and technology. From there, I explore how work-first has transformed the common sense of case management and changed caseworker understandings of how best to deal with the needs of poor families. Finally, I address the process of buying into the ideology of work-first and the reasons for resistance among administrators, caseworkers, and clients.

Chapter 2 sets forth the concept of corporate-centered welfare as a lens through which the neoliberal restructuring of U.S. welfare can be understood. I explore how the values of corporate-centered welfare have entered into the thinking of local welfare leaders who have pioneered work-first.

In addition, I seek to frame this "common sense" in the context of the wider politics of neoliberal restructuring.

Chapter 3 broadens the field of analysis by turning to the federal, state, and county infrastructure behind welfare reform's work-first approach. It explores how the logic of the welfare reform's performance measures corresponds with the neoliberal paradigm of the new federalism. I explore how the reform has increased both worker accountability and worker vulnerability by creating contingent government workers, by imposing performance measures, and by retreating from client rights.

Chapter 4 allows for a closer scrutiny of how welfare technology has been restructured according to work-first priorities and how, given organizational restructuring, surveillance has become a case management strategy. This case management style fosters work-first "common sense," as caseworkers sort and inspect clients. This surveillance serves to undermine client labor market bargaining power and divert clients from aid, because it establishes employers as gatekeepers to aid and also as central customers of work-first's employee screening and conditioning functions. I argue that the restructuring of work-first technology further acts to prioritize the interests of employers and the state over those of clients. Thus, it simultaneously redefines the customers of welfare and acts to ensure a steady supply of labor for the increasingly unstable work of the new economy.

Chapter 5 provides an in-depth analysis of how the daily function of human services casework has changed to accommodate neoliberal sensibilities. Work-first abandons a structural understanding of poverty for an individualistic approach. Chapter 5 offers an examination of the cognitive work involved in maintaining this neoliberal and individualistic approach to case management. National discourse and administrative efforts to coordinate discretion among caseworkers frame work-first as a form of moral work. They describe casework in terms of "tough love" and offer caseworkers a chance to take a stand against welfare abuses of fraud and dependency. Ideological buy-in to work-first serves to reinforce a neoliberal agenda in the minds of both clients and staff. Ideological buy-in on both of these accounts is perhaps most evident in instances where work-first clients become caseworkers themselves after participating in the program. The neoliberal framework views any type of work, regardless of how degrading and undercompensated, as good, thus fostering self-exploitation in the hopes of ultimately achieving prosperity. By encouraging poor adults to internalize a moral compass that steers them away from all dependency as wrong, work-first also teaches clients who internalize its philosophy to blame themselves rather than the institution should they fail in the labor market, as most do.

Chapter 6 examines how the stages of work-first processing employed in East County demand that both motivated and unencumbered mothers enter the labor force. The work-first approach to welfare reform is used in such highly regarded programs as Wisconsin's W-2 and California's GAIN programs, and it involves a series of pre-aid work preparation requirements that must be completed successfully to gain entry to the welfare rolls. However, not all clients successfully enter the rolls. Many are diverted and still others must repeat the intake processing indefinitely. Diversion and struggles to gain admittance to welfare are aspects of work-first's gauntlet approach to weeding out families and only selectively providing benefits. In the process, applicants learn that a disembodied and unencumbered worker becomes a pre-requisite for aid and that the economic roles of poor families are now valued over their caregiving and child-rearing potential.

Relationships between clients and staff become strained in the course of selling work-first at the welfare office. Caseworkers seek to change behavior of clients via punishments and rewards. They also engage in various forms of evasion, such as with respect to the relevance of gender and race within the labor market. The intent is to pacify clients whose first reaction is to resist work-first, sometimes violently. In Chapter 7, I approach these forms of everyday resistance as personal and political protests against what is problematic about work-first from the standpoint of everyday life. I use the disjuncture between work-first as anticipated and as experienced as a starting point from which to offer recommendations for future policy reform. To this end, I offer suggestions for future research, legal action, legislation, and grassroots strategy.

Chapter 8 holistically assesses the post-reform regime in an effort to ascertain which aspects of work-first common sense are most problematic and which are worth building upon. Though the problems that neoliberalism presents are considerable, retreating to pre-reform welfare is not an option. It would neither gain traction in the contemporary popularity of neoliberal political thinking nor empower poor families and their workers. There is, however, much to improve upon if welfare is to transition from pro-work to pro-worker in an honest, good faith attempt to live up to the rhetoric of the new welfare contract. We have much to learn from our own history and the experiences of other nations.

2

"You're All Doing the Wrong Thing"

Innovation and Common Sense

Work-first presents communities with a shocking new objective: the goal is to serve fewer people rather than more. The first half of this chapter provides a bird's eye view of the work-first program in East County, highlighting how diverting poor families makes sense given the goals of welfare reform. The second half focuses on how top administrators in East County came to see the previous goal of trying to serve as many poor families as possible as "doing the wrong thing." This exploration shows how local innovation of welfare was due to the entrepreneurial spirit of local leaders. It, however, was also heavily reliant on a work-first common sense that was politically manufactured and sold for local consumption. Whereas this chapter is dedicated to the larger politics by which work-first is sold and bought into, future chapters fill in the local details.

Welfare's New Goal

Nearly everything caseworkers in East County do as they process applicants for aid is oriented toward the goal of encouraging immediate employment and reliance on work instead of welfare aid. Associated with near immediate caseload reductions and relatively low per-client expenditures, the work-first approach has been adopted not only in New York State, but also by such high-profile welfare-to-work programs as California's Greater Avenues for Independence (GAIN) and the Wisconsin Works (W-2) program.[1] It is also featured in nationally distributed "best practices" manuals that closely reflect the approach as employed in East County.[2] But how does *Work-First* look close up and who made it what it is today? This chapter focuses on the administrators who designed the program in East County. Through their eyes I explore both how the program works and the origin of the common-sense logic of work-first that is central to its design.

In general terms, work-first is a strategy of "workfarism." This term, initially coined to represent an exchange of work for benefits, has in recent years become transformed "in a much broader sense to include, as a condition of income support, the requirement that recipients participate in a wide variety of activities designed to increase their employment prospects."[3] Nationally, over 60 percent of states (32) impose pending application requirements that base eligibility determination on participation in such employment-related activities as signing personal responsibility contracts, attending orientation, completing assessment and drug screening, conducting job searches, beginning work activities, and cooperating with child support.[4] Evident in the words of Tim, an eight-year veteran of the work-first system, these practices have also become associated with the intentional diversion of applicants from entering the welfare rolls. "You know . . . the application is to keep you out, not to get people in, it's to weed people out. . . . I mean that's why we have an application here, to weed people out." However, as this chapter explores, these practices extend beyond limiting access to aid; they entail a radical transformation of the U.S. approach to safety net provision.

Structural Overview of Work-First in East County

Figure 2.1, developed from my fieldwork, provides a general diagram of the reformed flow of welfare in this local site as well as the caseworkers involved in each processing stage. While the actual processing flow differs for those not considered eligible for TANF, this chart, like this research, is limited to an exploration of the TANF route for several reasons.[5] As in the nation, TANF is the aid structure in East County and the state of New York that provides means-tested (or need-based) public assistance to families that include children. In addition to being the most commonly sought means of assistance, this is also the aid structure at which federal performance measures and welfare reform in general are most clearly aimed. Other services such as Safety Net (SN), Emergency Assistance (EA), and Food Stamps (FS), while often administered in conjunction with and/or at the same location as TANF, are separate state and/or federal programs. As such, they have distinctive concerns, guidelines, and regulations. FS is primarily concerned with providing food vouchers, EA with immediate short-term assistance, and SN, a general assistance program, with providing cash assistance to individuals who do not have children.

In figure 2.1, each box of the main diagram (signified by a letter) represents a stage of the welfare process for a TANF applicant. The perforated boxes at the right indicate the distinctive caseworker teams present to take part in processing at each of the three main locations of intake processing (the welfare office, work-first office, and fair hearing offices).

As figure 2.1 shows, those who become involved with the reformed welfare system begin by filling out an application for TANF in the county welfare office (A). In order for their application to be processed, applicants must complete a series of steps (including being screened for FS, EA, and Drug and Alcohol addiction) before being allowed to attend a welfare orientation (B), which begins to explain the themes and complexities of the reformed welfare system. Following this orientation, the application is sent to eligibility workers who follow pre-established means-tested criteria in determining whether a person is eligible for a grant or not (C). This process takes 30 days on average. In the time that it takes the application to be processed, work-first begins processing the applicant through their program. As indicated in the diagram, applicants who complete the welfare orientation are then referred to attend a work-first orientation (D) held at the work-first office, usually the next day. Work-first orientation is focused primarily on explaining what is expected of applicants in order to be considered compliant.

From work-first orientation, TANF applicants are passed on to a stage of processing involving supervised job searching (E). Clients are required to apply for ten jobs a week. They remain in this stage of "job search" until a decision is announced on their application (F). This signifies the end of their intake processing. If their application is denied (if they are for instance ineligible, fail to comply with requirements, or they did not fill out the forms completely or correctly), the family is diverted and can begin the process over again—if they are still in need of assistance and have not become disillusioned or discouraged (G). TANF's interaction with applicant families whose cases are denied formally ends with this denial.

If, on the other hand, an application is approved, the TANF public assistance (PA) case is opened, a TANF recipient family begins to receive their grant, and they are referred to the next stage, called Job Preparation Class (H). An administrator explains, "Up till now, everything has been voluntary and [an applicant is] not receiving benefits. However, from now

FIGURE 2.1
Overview of TANF Processing

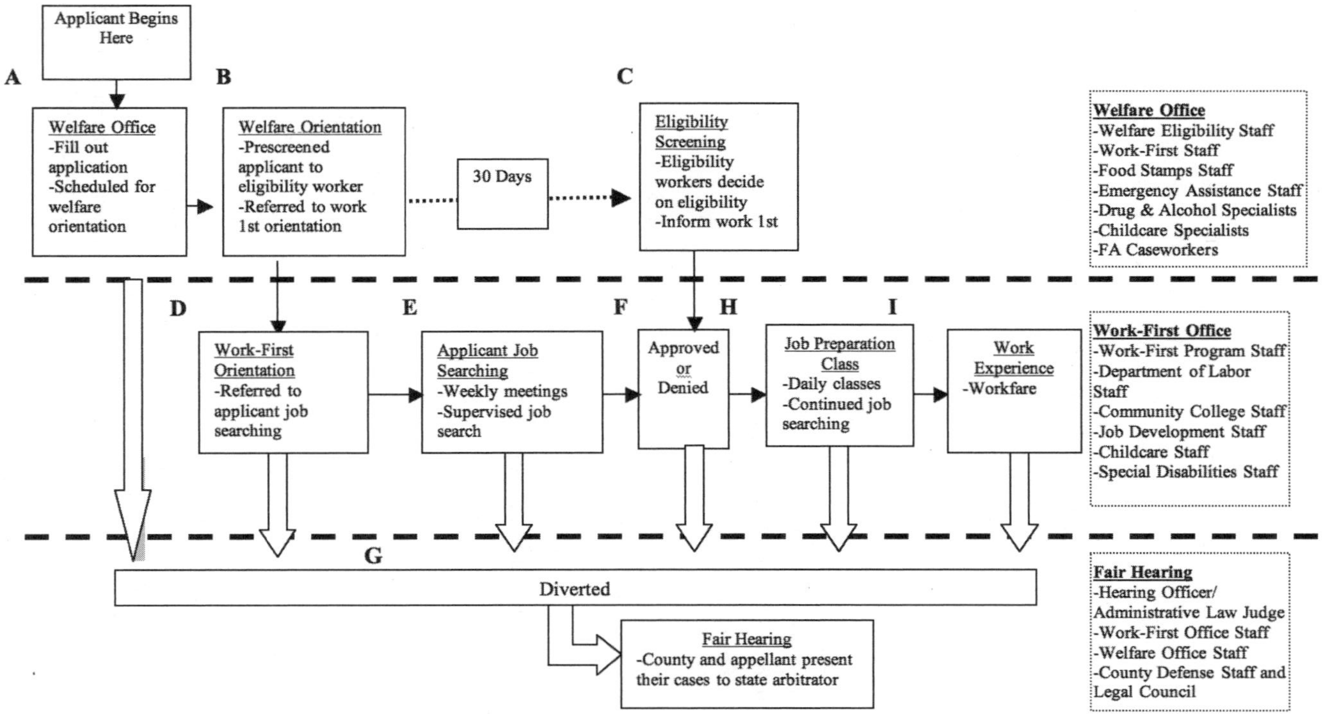

Welfare Office
-Welfare Eligibility Staff
-Work-First Staff
-Food Stamps Staff
-Emergency Assistance Staff
-Drug & Alcohol Specialists
-Childcare Specialists
-FA Caseworkers

Work-First Office
-Work-First Program Staff
-Department of Labor Staff
-Community College Staff
-Job Development Staff
-Childcare Staff
-Special Disabilities Staff

Fair Hearing
-Hearing Officer/ Administrative Law Judge
-Work-First Office Staff
-Welfare Office Staff
-County Defense Staff and Legal Council

A Applicant Begins Here

B Welfare Office
-Fill out application
-Scheduled for welfare orientation

Welfare Orientation
-Prescreened applicant to eligibility worker
-Referred to work 1st orientation

30 Days

C Eligibility Screening
-Eligibility workers decide on eligibility
-Inform work 1st

D Work-First Orientation
-Referred to applicant job searching

E Applicant Job Searching
-Weekly meetings
-Supervised job search

F Approved or Denied

H Job Preparation Class
-Daily classes
-Continued job searching

I Work Experience
-Workfare

G Diverted

Fair Hearing
-County and appellant present their cases to state arbitrator

on you are on welfare and if you don't do what or go where you are assigned, you can be sanctioned."

Upon completion of a two-week class focusing on soft employment skills (in addition to continuing to job search), the recipient is then referred to a Work Experience (WE) site (I). This is equivalent to workfare; applicants must work 35 hours a week in an internship-type setting, all the while seeking outside employment, in order to continue receiving their full grant. If a recipient does not secure full-time employment, she continues to cycle through WE assignments that change on a six-month basis.

Recipients are encouraged to leave work-first at any stage by obtaining full-time paid employment. Making this clear, an administrator asserts:

> As with all of the stages in this welfare-to-work program, the goal is for the participant to not make it to the next level. The goal is for them to find a suitable job and get off welfare before moving to the next stage of the program.

The arrows that lead from each of the processing phases to diversion below represent the preferred institutional outcome of having applicants drop out of the welfare system. Once a family is diverted, they may begin the process all over again, or, if they feel they have been treated improperly, they may file an appeal to have a fair hearing regarding their case. Fair hearings were instituted following the 1970 U.S. Supreme Court case *Goldberg v. Kelly* as a check on local administrative discretion.[6] This ruling guaranteed due process to welfare clients who believe that benefits have been wrongfully denied, reduced, or discontinued.[7] This includes an impartial legal decision maker, and a chance to address the actions of welfare agency caseworkers through the confrontation of adverse witnesses.

To those familiar with the old "way of doing business," the reconfiguration depicted in figure 2.1 constitutes a dramatic change from the pre-reform structure that focused primarily on determining financial (means-tested) eligibility of applicants for assistance. As a welfare caseworker trainer described the change, "The reform added a larger front door [to welfare]." It is no longer as simple as applying for aid and being accepted or denied. Caseworkers in East County's revamped welfare system are called to a high level of interagency cooperation and now must attend to an over-arching concern for the work-related behavior of their clientele in addition to ascertaining means-tested eligibility. In this way they are active participants in what emerges as a work-first gauntlet that is intent on weeding out or diverting as many clients as possible.

Welfare Intake as Gauntlet

Though not advertised as such, the work-first approach serves the function of a gauntlet that diverts those who do not learn to comply, or who resist compliance. Much like the fabled gauntlet method of punishment or torture in which people armed with sticks or other weapons arrange themselves in two lines facing each other and beat the person forced to run between them, the work-first welfare intake structure is meant partly to punish or shame those who pass through it, partly to teach a lesson and issue a challenge for "improved" behavior, and partly to weed out those who are not strong enough to withstand its demands.

Reform implementation literature has highlighted the importance of changes at the intake level as being crucial to the accomplishment of the reform's goals of behavioral change among the poor, but exactly how this occurs has been the object of much speculation.[8] In addition to emphasizing work and self-sufficiency, many states and local sites of implementation across the nation have heavily incorporated processes aimed at weeding out and diverting clients as a favored alternative to benefits.[9] As a result, nationally, not only have caseloads declined by over half, but the proportion of financially eligible families who actually make it through new intake processing and enroll has dropped drastically, from nearly 80 percent in 1996 to 48 percent in 2002.[10]

As social work scholar Sanford Schram argues in *After Welfare*, in this new regime "personal responsibility organizes discrimination" such that those who fail to demonstrate responsibility as institutionally defined are culled from the system.[11] This organized discrimination is evident in Tim's comments that "the application is to keep you out, not to get people in." Emily, another veteran welfare employee, offers a similar outlook:

Some women just came in earlier complaining about all they have to go through in this system. They wanted it to be easier, not have to do so much. "You're missing the point!" I tell them. "Social Services doesn't want your case to open."

This message has become clear to clients as well. Andrea, a former welfare recipient who now leads a support group for those interacting with the public assistance system, offers her assessment of the situation:

> We're seeing more problems in the area that I call . . . "Jumping through the hoops." People say, "But I've done everything, now what's the problem?" [They're] frustrated, just not wanting to go through with it. You have people who are eligible for benefits who don't want to apply because they don't want to go through the system.

In addition to discouraging applicants from receiving TANF assistance, intake practices serve another function in screening. They become the first line of contact and interaction between applicants and the demands of the state. The state begins to carry out its work of organizing applicants according to ideological and conceptual standards. This includes attempting to change lifestyle through teaching preferred behavior and shaming those who do not perform adequately.

Despite the promise of aid at the end of intake processing, insistence upon conformity to compliance standards means that poor families seldom successfully negotiate the work-first intake gauntlet on the first attempt. Rather, work-first comes to resemble a training ground to which clients re-submit themselves on a repeated basis until they either get it right or become diverted. The data in figure 2.2 illustrate this recycling of families through intake processing, as it becomes visible in the high incidence of delayed case openings of TANF applicants (in many cases for over a year). The chart begins in March 2000, and illustrates the number of case openings for this particular month's applicants (only) over the course of the subsequent 13 months.

In the initial application month (March 2000), welfare intake caseworkers approved 16 percent (201) of the total March applicants (1,101) for TANF and correspondingly opened their public assistance cases.[12] As seen in April 2000, caseworkers activated cases for another 8 percent of the initial March 2000 applicants in the following month. Since an application can remain on file only for 30 days, the distribution of case openings suggests that the rest of the March 2000 applicants failed to make it through the application process on the first try and hence were not granted open cases until later months if at all. Figure 2.3 shows that 71 percent of the initial March 2000 applicants eventually opened TANF cases over the subsequent 13 months.

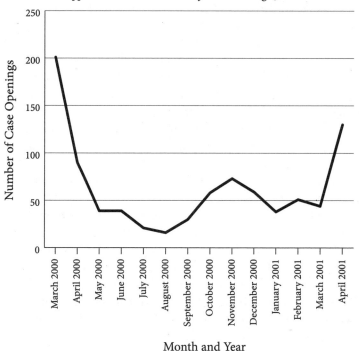

FIGURE 2.2

*Family Assistance (TANF) Case Openings For All March 2000
Applicants Over the Course of the Following 13 Months*

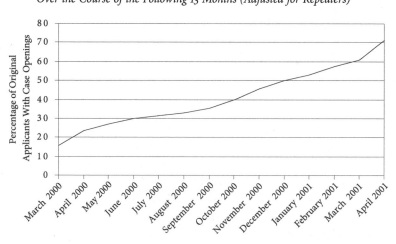

FIGURE 2.3

*Cumulative Percent of March 2000 TANF Applications With Opened Cases
Over the Course of the Following 13 Months (Adjusted for Repeaters)*

Such a cumulative distribution reveals that the application process, that is, navigating the welfare intake apparatus, is more complex than simply qualifying financially for means-tested benefits. Unless 55 percent (71 percent minus the initial 16 percent approved in the first round) of the initial applicants were originally ineligible, a possibility that my fieldwork suggests is highly unlikely, a large proportion of economically qualified applicants (approximately 77 percent of those who eventually opened a case) were simply unsuccessful, at least initially, at navigating the demands of work-first. To navigate the demands of the new welfare system successfully requires negotiating both need and deservingness with intake workers (and producing the correct papers). In effect, it requires successfully running a gauntlet of welfare intake.

The stages of work-first intake processing are structured to encourage work instead of welfare in several ways. First, they introduce a "hassle factor" by adding an array of new compliance requirements on top of, rather than in place of, the former means-tested requirements that existed under AFDC. Thus, TANF is both means-tested and work-readiness tested. As a caseworker explains, these additional "hoops" that families must now jump through are a considerable means of discouraging aid in favor of paid employment; "You figure with all of the stuff they now have to go through to get aid, they might as well just get a job." Second, the stages of intake processing collectively serve to orient clients to the reform's new goals of emphasizing employment as the new replacement for aid. Third, via presenting paid employment as the socially desirable, and even morally correct thing to do, intake processing contributes to the socialization of applicants to see work as good and dependency as bad.

Throughout the stages of work-first processing, caseworkers strive to instill an ideology of work and self-sufficiency in all applicants. It is a distinctively neoliberal approach.

> In the neoliberal view, the undeserving poor . . . [consists] of those who are still "dependent" on state largess and are not "productive" in the private sector. Those among the poor and unemployed who invest in the ideology and practices of the market re-enter the lowest echelons of the labor market. Those who, for whatever reason, do not become acculturated to the market are written out of the public sphere and subject to malign neglect—or worse.[13]

This ideological approach produces standards for deservingness grounded in work readiness or "productiveness" in the labor market, and it justifies malign neglect through diversion from the system. As a result, work-first contrasts markedly with the preceding AFDC program:

> Where welfare stands for principles of needs-based entitlement and universality, workfare stands for market-based compulsion and selectivity. Where welfare implies passive income support, workfare implies active labor market inclusion. Where welfare constructs its subjects as claimants, workfare reconstitutes them as jobseekers: the status of being *on* welfare is replaced by the transitory experience of being processed back into work *through* workfare.[14]

But how exactly did welfare change to work-first in East County? And how did local innovators come to see serving less people as a logical goal? The next section addresses this question from the perspective of the top administrators responsible for this shift in thinking on the local level. In the process it also provides insight into what accounts for the notable variation in welfare offices across the nation and why, despite this variation, there are striking similarities across the nation. The answer to both of these questions lies in the rise of a new entrepreneurial approach to U.S. welfare that was made possible by the 1996 reform. This entrepreneurial approach has allowed for local innovation and creativity. On the other hand, it shares a context of work-first common sense that creates isomorphism.

Entrepreneurial by Design

Entrepreneurship as it emerges in the context of TANF is the product of generations of development of entrepreneurial thinking. While commonly associated with the for-profit sector, entrepreneurship is increasingly viewed as a means for encouraging innovation in the nonprofit world by employing the same principles.[15] Analyses dating back to noted economist Joseph Schumpeter have emphasized that entrepreneurship entails doing something fundamentally new and different from the automatic behavior of preceding scenarios.[16] Sociologist Max Weber contrasted the enterprising and dynamic nature of entrepreneurs with the staying power of rationalized and routine bureaucrats (seeing them almost as counterbalances to each other).[17] Ironically, some have argued that this emphasis on being innovative has itself become normalized (and almost universally, uncritically acclaimed) as "a modern western institution."[18] In this sense, entrepreneurship in the field of welfare is an extension of this tendency to apply business principles to the nonprofit and government world.[19]

Entrepreneurship has not always been in fashion, however. As Weber notes, the general attitude toward entrepreneurs was one of hostility and alienation in the years predating the rise of the Protestant ethic. In the esteem of dominant religious ideology across the globe, entrepreneurial activities—associated with greedy market behavior—were "at best tolerated, never embraced."[20] The Protestant ethic helped to normalize and validate the pursuit of moneymaking and the use of innovation to achieve market success. While the U.S. welfare state has always tended toward the liberal economic regime (and has thus been pro-market and pro-business), it was not until recent years that entrepreneurial qualities have come to be seen as a key feature of federal welfare policy.

Rather than conform to the top-down model of program design and implementation that had come to dominate federal welfare policy since the New Deal, the reform movement (that culminated in the 1996 PRWORA legislation and the 1997 welfare reform legislation in New York) fostered entrepreneurial policymaking on the local level as the best way to disassemble large federal programs. The push toward local control, or an approach of "new federalism," was so vocal and sustained in the years leading up to the reform that many localities tried to be proactive by setting up their welfare-to-work programs prior to 1996. In East County, welfare was transformed to a work-first program in 1994, two years before AFDC became TANF. Proactive reform allowed local actors to do what they wanted rather than follow federal orders. As the newly appointed director of temporary assistance at the time recounts, her impetus to reform locally was at least to some degree endogenous.

> I was extremely unhappy doing this [AFDC] and I couldn't figure out why. And eventually it dawned on me that the reason I was unhappy with this responsibility was that I did not believe in what we were doing. It felt like the proverbial rearranging the deckchairs on the *Titanic*. We were trying to make the ship go straight but I didn't believe in the direction. It was institutionalizing poverty. We were all about determining eligibility, crossing t's, dotting i's. We were spending so little time and resources

helping people get jobs. And if the way you allocate resources is a reflection of your priorities, that was clearly the point, we probably had 200 staff at the time and 8 were assigned to employment activities. The vast majority of staff were assigned to initial [eligibility] determination and case maintenance. That was characteristic of the state and the entire national welfare system.

Though initially dismayed, the director felt that she was not alone. Others were also dissatisfied with the status quo. With the approach of the 1996 reform, the time was right for local innovation and she took the opportunity gladly.

It really just came from kind of a general unease about the direction of the system, solidified by a comment, a provocative throw-away comment made by a federal official, and then a couple of us figured it out.

Expanding on this story, the director explains, "Innovative ideas can happen in any way, shape, or form, they can happen through a formal planning process, they can happen when need drives it, or opportunity, or a chance comment" as in this case:

So it really started for us. . . . In this instance what happened was in 1994 the State of New York had decided that the state system was misguided and it wanted to do something but the state was saying "We can't do it ourselves. We're hide bound tied to regulations, and innovation has to occur at the local level."

So a conference was held and I remember quite clearly, the keynote speaker was David Ellwood, who was undersecretary of Health and Human Services in the Clinton administration, and he said to this group of welfare officials, employment officials across the state. He said, "You're all working really, really hard, there's only one problem, you're all doing the wrong thing. You're focusing on eligibility, crossing t's, dotting i's, you're not paying attention to employment." And I remember thinking at the time this was a cheap shot because we are following state and federal rules, but he's absolutely right, he's absolutely right.

And coming back in the car, I brought a couple of people, we started talking about this and doing "what if" scenarios and when we arrived from that city back to our own, we had done enough "what if" scenarios that we pretty much had a game plan on how we wanted to proceed with

increasing our focus on employment. We came back, worked out the details, and then brought it to the county executive's attention, who was
very, very supportive. The executive endorsed it. And we developed a plan
that now employs about 100 staff focused exclusively on employment.

This conference was only one of the many discursive encounters with reform ideas on the national and state levels. Reflecting on the effect of this
abundant discourse on thinking, a local administrator shared:

> You go to this conference, there was a national and state discourse, and
> there was all kinds of literature. . . . You really start seeing yourself in a
> different way. You really start seeing yourself as someone who should be
> encouraging work as opposed to just making sure people get their ben-
> efits. It probably doesn't sound like a big thing but it was a big thing.

Work-first was not the only innovative idea that circulated among East
County's administrators; it was one of many possibilities that emerged
from routine meetings to assess current programs and how they were fitting current needs.

> A lot of ideas are good on paper but then all of the necessary follow-
> up, all the interfaces that are necessary to clarify and work out, they just
> aren't done. So the idea is dropped.

What set this one apart was its perceived potential, and the popular support it received from the media and the federal and state levels.

> We thought it was the right thing to do, the right social policy and we
> figured out how to do it structurally, so that this is something that could
> be paid for. We figured out how to find resources and use existing regu-
> lations to use those resources effectively. . . . It was one of those "aha"
> moments.

Though there were a few detractors, some caseworkers and community
members who objected, overall the plan was met with support. The county
executive and others were "very supportive" of the general idea.

> We kind of started with a broad brush, just the, you know this is the
> overall context, the overall principle of work being the centerpiece—that

we should really work to engage everyone, that the expectation would be that every able-bodied individual should participate in some kind of work preparation program, or if there is some kind of disabling medical issue, to address that. Then we went back and started sitting down with the administrative team, staff, and talking about specifics of what this might look like. And that is where we really brought in staff really significantly to talk about what this means in terms of daily operations. A broad idea, recommendation, is just a starting point. A ton of hard work has to be done to figure out, "What does this mean to the worker on the line and how do they address this?"

As might be anticipated, massively restructuring the local welfare bureaucracy involved significant hurdles.

It's easy to say we are going to make work the center of the system but . . . then the practical issue of how do you redirect this huge enterprise that for decades had been going in this direction? And so everything had to change, not only structure had to change, operations had to change. What the worker on the line, what the clerk who is supporting the worker on the line is doing has to change. You need to develop information systems that support what you are doing. So it was just, it was like President Kennedy saying we are going to the moon, what does that mean? You know you don't just do it. It's just a zillion things need to change.

Changing a "zillion things," as the director explains, included paying attention to the minutiae of the new program before any of it was implemented.

If you talk about job search, what does that mean? Does that mean any job? Does that mean jobs that are hiring? Does it make any sense to say go out and apply for jobs when a person goes to the parking garage, the bagel shop, places that hire two people, or have a staff of two and don't hire? So is that a legitimate job search? So you have to figure out all the nitty gritty stuff.

As the director explained, however, East County was not alone in this process. Other counties had also taken up the call to innovate to varying degrees.

I think we were a little bit ahead of the curve, but we talked with our counterparts all the time. . . . There have been a lot of visitors to our operation from across the state, other states have contacted us . . . [interested in] how it all works. . . . It was very unique, just the way we were set up. . . . Part of innovation, there is no point trying to come up with everything yourself, you steal as much as you can, absolutely. I mean this is not proprietary information, we are not in the private sector, these are not industrial secrets, so I am happy to share whatever learnings we have and I am happier to take whatever learnings others have.

Confident that other locales were copying and adapting what was done in East County, the director also made no bones about their intention to emulate others as well. This cross-fertilization of ideas via "fast policy transfer" no doubt is partly responsible for the sense of isomorphism noticeable across counties and states.

This influence was not solely peer-to-peer, however. It was coordinated by encouragement from higher levels of government.

The state brought us together to talk exclusively about welfare to work. This was like the last year or years of the Cuomo administration, and the new commissioner was Michael Dowling and the national and state discussion on welfare really was beginning to change. More and more the focus was on "this thing is really broken and so how do we fix it" and so the point of this discussion was Commissioner Dowling bringing all the counties in the state and really pushing us to innovate. Basically it was opening the door and saying, "This is the direction we need to head in but we the state can't do it ourselves." . . . I think they felt very bounded by the legislative and regulatory context. They didn't feel that the political climate was right, where, you know their influence was really in legislation, regulation and funding. They didn't feel that the political climate was right, across the state, to seriously change state legislation and regulations, but they felt there were opportunities within the existing regulations that counties could pursue, so they were very much encouraging counties to use those opportunities.

Within this context, there was enough discursive interaction that by the time the 1996 federal legislation and 1997 state reform were enacted, East County was so well positioned that it needed to make only minor changes. "We did what made sense," the director explained, "our focus was engagement," and as a result, "when the legislation changed, it increased the population we were going to work with, it didn't change the expectations." From the perspective of local welfare innovators in East County, the 1996 reform merely tweaked what they began doing in 1994 of their own volition.

Through these dynamics, the welfare reform that culminated in the 1996 creation of TANF was driven both by local concerns and innovations, and by extra-local messages and discourses that were circulating at the state and federal levels. East County's program involved entrepreneurial reform of the preexisting welfare institution and all its inertial tendencies to stick with the status quo. It was an effort to "redirect this huge enterprise that for decades had been going in this direction." Yet it was also extra-local. The local innovators were influenced, encouraged, and perhaps even catalyzed by "the national and state discussion on welfare," and by individuals like David Ellwood, undersecretary of HHS in the Clinton administration, who passed on and legitimated the message that the preexisting welfare involved "doing the wrong thing."

What emerges is a view of institutional change similar to the description offered by researcher Petter Holm in his analysis of the Norwegian fishing industry.[21] In the case of Norwegian fisheries, there is a practical first level based in local everyday concerns and a political second level in which the local level is "nested." This view of institutions "draws a distinction between actions guided by the established order, on the one hand, and actions geared toward creating new or changing old institutions, on the other."[22] According to Holm, it is less important whether innovations originate at the first-order level or on the second-order level (as with one that has been unsuccessfully promoted through public discourse for some time before becoming possible due to larger structural shifts in power). Rather, of greater consequence is the degree to which first- and second-order levels interface:

> Hence, whether a "problem" at the first-order level of action will trigger institutional change depends on the ease with which it can be translated to the second-order level, if it can be attached to a "solution" there, and whether this "decision" can be translated back to the first-order level.[23]

As Holm goes on to argue:

> Replacing one institution with another means that income, power, and status will be redistributed. To succeed, an institutional entrepreneur

must mobilize external and internal constituents behind his or her project. One instrument for doing that will be the construction of accounts that make sense of the proposed institutional project and discredit the alternatives. . . . New ideas can make actors see the situation and their own place in it from a new angle. In this way, ideas constitute interests.[24]

From this perspective, local innovator efforts to "just [do] what made sense" are implicated in the broader construction of common sense in this context. The extent to which extra-local discourse contributed to this sense makes it unsurprising that the local county was well-situated and in need of little further reform by the time the 1996 legislation was passed. It is also unsurprising that East County's director believed that "I'm sure there were other counties that were in a similar position."

Such isomorphic synchronicity points to the importance of examining the nested layers of entrepreneurial activity. Though it is difficult to deny the role of local innovators in creating the work-first program in East County, it is also misleading to allocate full credit locally. Some sociologists see institutions as social constructions that come into existence and change in considerable part due to the work of idea creators and disseminators. This has given rise to the notion of "institutional entrepreneurs" who serve as "authors—generators of influential texts that are aimed at influencing the nature and structure of discourses and, in turn, affecting the institutions that are supported by those discourses."[25] Thus, entrepreneurship is not only a local endeavor but one that has counterparts on the broader extra-local, second level.

Adjusting the Neoliberal Meta-Discourse to Welfare

Though most visible in the 1996 reform, the discursive foundation for the work-first approach seen in East County and elsewhere was built decades earlier. It is what Dorothy Smith might call a local adaptation or "specification" of a broader neoliberal ideological discourse. As a "meta-discourse," or master narrative about society, neoliberal ideology "regulates others that are specialized for specific contexts such as institutions," and in this case, the institution of welfare.[26]

The ideological discourse that has come to govern public discussion on the economy since the early 1980s in North America is the discourse known as neoliberalism. Neoliberalism, as an ideological discourse, is based on economic theories that stress the paramount significance of a free market for general prosperity; government is viewed as costly and inefficient; concepts of citizenship stress individual responsibility for economic well-being and so on.[27]

This meta-discourse, however, did not simply arise; it was intentionally created. As Bourdieu explains, the neoliberal utopia is a "political project." Though it claims to be natural, or "reality," it is in fact achieved through political measures and policies directed at reducing labor costs and public expenditures and making work "more flexible."[28] In her earlier work, Smith describes an "ideological campaign waged by a political apparatus aimed at securing control of the concepts, ideologies, and theories that coordinate multiple sites of power/knowledge generated by contemporary ruling relations."[29] Through this concerted effort to capture sites of knowledge production, political actors, in this case "right-wing conservatives," actively undertook the "manufacturing" and promotion of a neoliberal ideology to suit their own interests in an era of global restructuring. This undertaking was more than economic, however. It included planned and deliberate cultural reconstruction. It intended to depose the socially liberal culture that had dominated politics and civic life since the New Deal and replace it with conservative sensibilities.[30]

The mechanism behind this largely effective ideological coup was to infuse neoliberal ideology into mainstream thought through the creation of a massive "idea industry" or what Robert Stein, former senior advisor to the chairman of the Democratic National Committee, termed the Republican "message machine."[31] Stein described this machine as "perhaps the most potent, independent institutionalized apparatus ever assembled in a democracy to promote one belief system." He explained that it consisted of "fifty funding agencies of different dimensions and varying degrees of ideological fervor, nominally philanthropic but zealous in their common hatred of the liberal enemy, disbursing the collective sum of roughly $3 billion over a period of thirty years."[32] Figure 2.4 details the distribution of $210 million by 12 such foundations between 1992 and 1994, just as debates about welfare reform heated up.

As Ellen Messer-Davidow documents, this money was strategically dispersed to think tanks, training programs, grassroots organizations, and legal centers of kindred culturally conservative and free-market spirits.[33] In this division of labor think tanks sought to "influence the nation's formal policy process by publishing policy studies, holding seminars for political

FIGURE 2.4

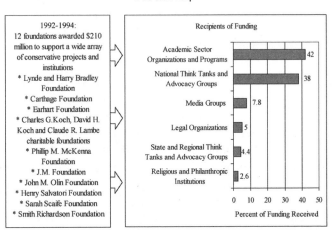

Source: The Strategic Philanthropy of Conservative Foundations. Moving a Public Policy Agenda. From a report by the National Committee on Responsive Philanthropy, www.mediatransparency.org/conservativephilanthropypageprinterfriendly.php? conservativePhilanthropyPageID=1

and business leaders, and banking the resumes of potential conservative appointees to government and judicial positions."[34] Training programs sought "to increase the number and effectiveness of conservative activists" through schools that offered "training programs in youth leadership, grassroots organizing, organizational leadership, direct mail fundraising and mobilizing, preparation for the Foreign Service examination, Capitol Hill staffing, legislative management, broadcast journalism, and student publications."[35] Funded grassroots activities included holding conferences and publishing journals under scholarly auspices, as well as sponsoring political actions aimed at mobilizing membership to "lobby government officials."[36] Finally, legal centers served as a means of bringing into the court system issues of concern and challenges to the status quo. These centers were also used as a means to leverage desired change via legal intimidation.

Together, the multiple voices emanating from these seemingly separate yet essentially coordinated sources crowded out socially liberal opinion and made it seem radical in comparison to the emerging chorus of slightly varied culturally conservative and economically neoliberal perspectives.[37] The result, Messer-Davidow describes, was "not merely a reticulated movement, but . . . a massive apparatus consisting of several institutional systems variously articulated to produce cultural change."[38]

Within the society-wide "meta-discourse" created by this interest-driven campaign, "more specialized and subordinate discourses have been developed that mediate ideological discourse at the general level and the specifics of institutional discourses."[39] Though it is beyond the purview of this chapter to explore the vast mechanics behind this process, we examine a partial view of how this meta-discourse has entered, or become infused, into welfare policy and frontline work-first sensibilities in figures 2.5A and 2.5B, created by consolidating the work of Ellen Reese with that of Ellen Messer-Davidow and Lewis Lapham.[40]

These figures depict the flow of funding from business interests and corporate-funded philanthropic organizations to culturally conservative and economically neoliberal and neoconservative think tanks. The figures then connect these tanks to prominent researchers in the area of welfare who they have funded. Finally, figures 2.5A and 2.5B link these corporate and conservative-funded think tank researchers to some of their most well-known ideas concerning welfare reform. Notably, not only is there much overlap in ideas (especially when the broader writings of these scholars, upon which these summaries are based, are considered), but many of these ideas were encoded in the 1996 legislation. These include: Besharov's five-year limit, Mead's and Rector's obligation to work, Cove's performance-based contracting, and Horowitz's replacing of entitlements with block grants. Others, such as Mead's charge against illegitimacy and dependency, and Gilder's assertion that welfare only hurts the poor, were encapsulated in the spirit of the legislation and transmitted to local implementers. This is not a coincidence. Many of the researchers noted in figures 2.5A and B testified before Congress in pre-reform hearings, and they produced numerous publications and appeared on talk shows and in widely distributed news media. Consequently, as depicted in figure 2.6, these 11 corporate and conservative-funded think tank scholars were cited numerous times in the congressional records, particularly in the 104th Congress, during which welfare reform debates were taking place.

The listing of scholars profiled here is by no means comprehensive, nor is this chapter intended to represent the many nuances of their arguments. Rather, as with other institutional ethnographies, my intent is to demonstrate how relations of knowledge production and dissemination function in institution-specific settings such as that of the contemporary welfare structure that created work-first.

It is important to note that, though in this instance conservatives and Republican-leaning benefactors are highlighted because of their prominent

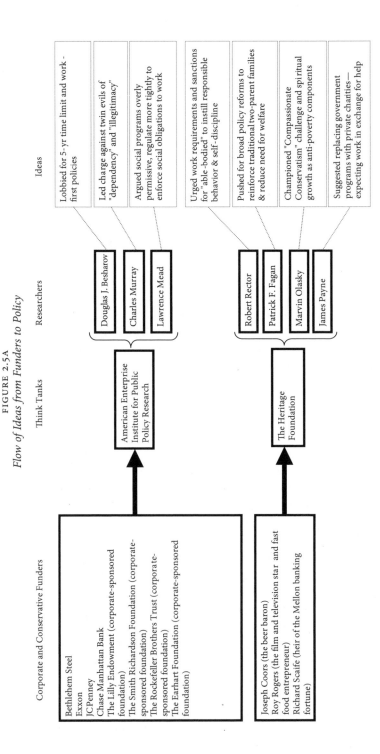

FIGURE 2.5A
Flow of Ideas from Funders to Policy

Corporate and Conservative Funders

Bethlehem Steel
Exxon
JCPenney
Chase Manhattan Bank
The Lilly Endowment (corporate-sponsored foundation)
The Smith Richardson Foundation (corporate-sponsored foundation)
The Rockefeller Brothers Trust (corporate-sponsored foundation)
The Earhart Foundation (corporate-sponsored foundation)

Joseph Coors (the beer baron)
Roy Rogers (the film and television star and fast food entrepreneur)
Richard Scaife (heir of the Mellon banking fortune)

Think Tanks

American Enterprise Institute for Public Policy Research

The Heritage Foundation

Researchers

Douglas J. Besharov

Charles Murray

Lawrence Mead

Robert Rector

Patrick F. Fagan

Marvin Olasky

James Payne

Ideas

Lobbied for 5-yr time limit and work-first policies

Led charge against twin evils of "dependency" and "illegitimacy"

Argued social programs overly permissive, regulate more tightly to enforce social obligations to work

Urged work requirements and sanctions for "able-bodied" to instill responsible behavior & self-discipline

Pushed for broad policy reforms to reinforce traditional two-parent families & reduce need for welfare

Championed "Compassionate Conservatism" challenge and spiritual growth as anti-poverty components

Suggested replacing government programs with private charities—expecting work in exchange for help

Source: References used in the chart include: Reese 2005; American Enterprise Institute 2002; Besharov 2002; Murray 2002; Heritage Foundation 2002; Rector 2002; Fagan 2002; Manhattan Institute 2002; Hudson Institute 2002.

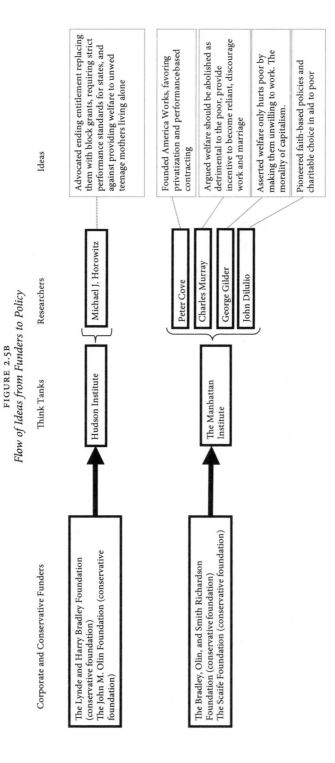

FIGURE 2.5B
Flow of Ideas from Funders to Policy

Corporate and Conservative Funders

The Lynde and Harry Bradley Foundation (conservative foundation)
The John M. Olin Foundation (conservative foundation)

The Bradley, Olin, and Smith Richardson Foundation (conservative foundation)
The Scaife Foundation (conservative foundation)

Think Tanks

Hudson Institute

The Manhattan Institute

Researchers

Michael J. Horowitz

Peter Cove

Charles Murray

George Gilder

John Dilulio

Ideas

Advocated ending entitlement replacing them with block grants, requiring strict performance standards for states, and against providing welfare to unwed teenage mothers living alone

Founded America Works, favoring privatization and performance-based contracting

Argued welfare should be abolished as detrimental to the poor, provide incentive to become reliant, discourage work and marriage

Asserted welfare only hurts poor by making them unwilling to work. The morality of capitalism.

Pioneered faith-based policies and charitable choice in aid to poor

Source: References used in the chart include: Reese 2005; American Enterprise Institute 2002; Besharov 2002; Murray 2002; Heritage Foundation 2002; Rector 2002; Fagan 2002; Manhattan Institute 2002; Hudson Institute 2002.

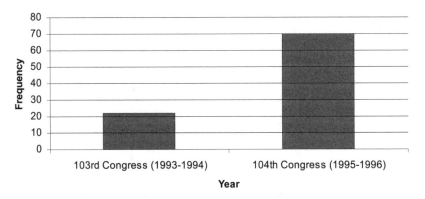

FIGURE 2.6
*Frequency With Which Think Tank Funded Researchers' Names Appear in the Text of
the Congressional Record for both U.S. House of Representatives and U.S. Senate*

role in creating the discourse that has come to structure the 1996 welfare reform, the power relations of discourse and knowledge production are neither inherently liberal nor conservative.[41] Mechanisms for disseminating viewpoints exist for both ends of the political spectrum, though in this case socially liberal-leaning organizations were severely outgunned due to the massive financial support of corporate and conservative interests. In 1995, the year prior to welfare reform, the top five conservative institutes received $77 million from foundations, compared to the $16.6 million received by the top eight progressive institutes.[42] The following year, as the welfare reform was debated and passed, "conservative think tanks were cited seven times more than progressive think tanks by the mainstream media."[43]

Furthermore, though figures 2.5A and B depict relations of power and ruling by linking the interests of wealthy capitalists to reform discourse used to regulate the lives of poor families, "it is misleading to reduce them to relations of domination or hegemony, or to view them as monolithic or manipulated."[44] Rather, consistent with Karl Polanyi's conceptualization of the "double movement," the influence of the conservative and neoliberal lobby can be seen as an episode in the tug of war between liberal market pressures and protectionist demands.

Polanyi's double movement approach conceptualizes modern history in terms of pushes toward liberal market capitalism that create unfavorable conditions for local populations. These populations in return demand protection from unbridled market forces. Thus, protectionist policies and economic liberalism (or in this case neoliberalism) are diametrically opposed forces that keep each other in check. In the words of Polanyi:

> For a century the dynamics of modern society was governed by a double movement: the market expanded continuously but this movement was met by a countermovement checking the expansion in definite directions. Vital though such a countermovement was for the protection of society, in the last analysis it was incompatible with the self-regulation of the market, and thus with the market system itself.[45]

Important to Polanyi's approach, however, is debunking the idea that free-market forces are in any way natural or inevitable. Instead, as he documents in the period of "the great transformation," both the liberal economic and protectionist movements are essentially cultural and political processes of forging nationally dominant ideology.

In the Polanyian sense of the shifting tenor of the times then, the tracing of discursive relationships (as seen above) demonstrates the outline of what D. Smith refers to as historically situated "ruling relations," a term that "identifies an historical development of forms of social consciousness that can no longer be adequately conceived as arising in the life conditions of actual individuals" such as welfare families and their caseworkers.[46] "It directs investigation to a complex of objectified relations, coordinating the activities of many, many people whose consciousness as subjects is formed within those relations."[47] Awareness of this connection between objective material realities and shared consciousness, though here specific to the terrain of the 1996 reform, can be found as early as the writing of Marx and Engels.

> The ideas of the ruling class are in every epoch the ruling ideas. i.e., the class which is the ruling material force of society is at the same time its ruling intellectual force. The class which has the means of material production at its disposal, consequently also controls the means of mental production, so that the ideas of those who lack the means of mental production are on the whole subject to it. The ruling ideas are nothing more than the ideal expression of the dominant material relations grasped as ideas; hence of the relations which make the one class the ruling one, therefore, the ideas of its dominance.[48]

This interpretation is by no means limited to Marxian analysis. Adam Smith voiced a similar assessment of the way government can be made to institutionalize the interests of the wealthy in his famous treatise, *The Wealth of Nations*:

> Civil government, so far as it is instituted for the security of property, is in reality instituted for the defence of the rich against the poor, or of all those who have some property against those who have none at all.[49]

While Adam Smith's and Marx's and Engels' treatment of ideology, knowledge, and civil government suggests a monolithic state that acts as an arm of class interest, from a Polanyian perspective, this is only half of the "double movement."

In Polanyi's eyes, class tensions are entangled in the balance between liberal and protectionist forces. Differing class interests predispose classes to advocate opposing forces in the double movement and to fortify themselves in opposing market and governmental strongholds:

> The working class was an influential factor in the state [due to universal suffrage]; the trading classes, on the other hand, whose sway over the legislature was no longer unchallenged, became conscious of the political power involved in their leadership in industry. . . . When tensions between the social classes developed, society itself was endangered by the fact that the contending parties were making government and business, state and industry, respectively, their strongholds.[50]

In this sense, government is less a stable advocate of either the elite classes or the working classes, but rather a contested site which could be claimed by either side depending on the tenor of the time.

Also crucial to Polanyi is the role of the state in maintaining balance by not appearing to be overtly partisan. As James O'Connor reminds us, cultural legitimacy is a key aspect of this balance:

> A capitalist state that openly uses its coercive forces to help one class accumulate capital at the expense of other classes loses its legitimacy and hence undermines the basis of its loyalty and support.[51]

In this light, the present chapter involves tracing the construction of the dominance and legitimacy of economically liberal forces of the double movement as a cultural phenomenon. This is done not so much to appraise the accuracy of Adam Smith's, Marx's and Engels', and Polanyi's claims. Rather, the intent is to use a similar approach to examine the extent to which the roots of the power exercised by frontline welfare caseworkers extend into and are circumscribed by the wider sociopolitical and economic shift in power. Discourse, however, is only one aspect of the cultural shift that opened a policy window for work-first. Yet, it is a critical catalyst in what emerges as a shifting of the welfare pendulum toward neoliberalism.

A Welfare Pendulum

In 1696, noted English thinker John Locke proposed a labor-rate system that would handle poverty by allocating the village poor to work for local community members.[52] Three hundred years later, U.S. President William Jefferson Clinton signed into law a welfare-to-work system that would pair poor mothers with local employers. Such juxtaposition may suggest that little has changed in the field of welfare over the past three centuries. However, this would be an error similar to measuring the distance between the crests of waves without taking into consideration the troughs between them. In fact, welfare policies between Locke and Clinton are not bound to schemes that integrate the poor into the labor market. Instead, a vast number of policies, such as the 1795 English Speenhamland Law and the 1935 New Deal in the United States, have resisted efforts to solve the problem of poverty by forcing the poor to survive in the labor market (i.e., commodifying them).[53] Instead, these policies have guaranteed all citizens the right to a basic standard of living and certain family protections. In effect, they served to de-commodify survival by separating subsistence from labor market aptitude. Indeed, the history of welfare that has brought us to the 1996 U.S. welfare reform can be characterized as that of a pendulum swinging between championing liberal free markets and protecting citizens from them.

In the context of growing international economic competition in the late 1970s and early 1980s, U.S. economic strategy was faced with a choice. It could either invest in U.S. workers to bolster national ability to compete against other nations, or it could instead seek to capitalize on wage savings for businesses through fostering increased global labor market competition. As Harrison and Bluestone chronicle, the choice selected was a "low road" approach intended to maintain capital accumulation for investors by cheapening labor.[54] Part of this strategy was to shore up corporate profitability by, in the words of Nixon's assistant secretary of labor, "zap[ing] labor" to undermine collective action and mold workers into a more flexible and compliant mentality.[55] Restructuring welfare figured prominently into this equation. Morgen and Maskovsky wrote in 2003:

> In the context of declining profitability, the business class has forced the abandonment of welfare-state policies, conceived since the Great Depression as an effective way of achieving long-term economic growth, avoiding capitalist boom-and-bust business cycles, and managing class antagonism. Instead, the welfare state is downsized to loosen labor markets, and the social wage is attacked in an effort to redistribute wealth in an upward direction. The abrogation of the Fordist social compact and the pursuit of cheap labor across the globe join welfare state downsizing, supply-side corporate welfare, and welfare-to-work as aspects of the post-Fordist strategy of flexible capital accumulation.[56]

Placed in the context of welfare states internationally, work-first can be seen as shifting U.S. welfare toward increased commodification of workers (i.e., the degree to which they are bought and sold in the free market). De-commodification refers to "the degree to which individuals, or families, can uphold a socially acceptable standard of living independently of market participation."[57] In general, welfare states can be understood as existing along a continuum that stretches from least commodified to most. The least commodified (or most de-commodified) (such as Sweden, Norway, Denmark, and the Netherlands) serve to strengthen the hand of labor and particularly poorer working classes by seeking to redistribute wealth and removing certain goods and services from the realm of commodities.[58] These social democratic welfare states are first and foremost democratic. They are also based loosely on the Beveridge principle of universal rights of citizenship, favoring programs that benefit all equally and ensure a certain level of subsistence apart from the market.[59] On the opposite extreme (most commodified) liberal-style welfare states (such as the United States, Canada, the United Kingdom, and Australia) tend to strengthen the hand of commerce by fostering liberal laissez-faire economic policies. They also engage government in efforts to maximize "capitalist acts between consenting adults."[60] Liberal welfare states focus on reinforcing reliance on the market for survival and providing welfare only on the basis of means-tested need (residualist). Thus, they tend to weaken the bargaining power of workers who hire themselves out for sustenance, and concomitantly they tend to strengthen the leverage of those who do the hiring.

In the context of welfare-state restructuring, work-first can be seen as "strengthening the engine of capitalist accumulation" by increasing the need for individuals to engage in the labor market for survival.[61] In the words of a caseworker, the work-first approach involves removing the aspects of the AFDC system that were intended to de-commodify poor mothers so that they could attend to family caregiving. Instead, work is less a free choice and more a necessity.

> When you need to survive, you work for it. But the [AFDC] system provides for survival so the only way people will move from it is if the punishment gets greater or the reward gets greater, and everybody's preference for rewards is different.

Caseworkers needed to develop a new goal as they sought to implement this commodification of welfare clients. Rather than "helping people get their benefits and then getting out of their way," they became involved in moving them off of the system and into the labor market:

> [We are moving them] from point A, unemployed and on welfare, to point B, employed and on welfare, to point C, employed and on reduced welfare assistance, to point D, employed and off welfare, or self-sufficient.

Taken as a whole, work-first engenders a new approach to welfare based on the principles of increased commodification and de-emphasis of structural matters that had previously been the focus of anti-poverty programs. The goals are no longer to protect poor families from the labor market and remedy racial inequities. Rather, "welfare reform aimed to extend the compulsion of the market to welfare recipients."[62] Along with this shift in state emphasis is a shift toward an individualized way of looking at poverty that emphasizes the need for behavioral change among the poor.

Work-First Caseworkers, Moral Ideology, and Power

Though caseworkers in East County by and large strive toward unbiased practice, they cannot avoid the fact that they are far from neutral actors. While the common belief is that bureaucracy and administrative functions serve to depoliticize power relations by ushering them out of the realm of politics and into the regime of executive authority, Barbara Cruikshank argues that in effect they do the opposite: the "'regulation', 'professionalization' or 'depoliticization' of social life is better understood as an extension of the political and an extension of power's reach."[63] This has political implications for the relationship between government and the poor in the post-1996 reform era.

Work-first represents an administrative governmental policy, but in the context of the preceding discussion, it can also be read as a bureaucratization of a broader neoliberal agenda that has acquired the middle ground of both Democrats and Republicans.

> Market triumphalism has coalesced as the ideological cornerstone of recent shifts in mainstream liberalism in the 1980s and 1990s. Indeed, the political ideology of the New Democrats and the Democratic Leadership Council (a group Bill Clinton helped form and once chaired) can be characterized as *neoliberal*. . . . Accordingly, George W. Bush's "compassionate conservatism" is best understood as a hard-right variant of the neoliberal project.[64]

Within this context, the contemporary "welfare state retrenchment" of the 1996 reform and its 2006 reauthorization can be seen as an extension of the reach of political ideology's power into the lives of families who are regulated by this policy.

A critical perspective makes the processes of administrator, caseworker, and client buy-in to work-first also visible as what Yeheskel Hasenfeld identifies as the power-imbued moral work of welfare. "The decision of whether a single poor mother qualifies for public assistance is not merely a technical question of assessing her needs in relation to the resources available to her. It is also a moral assessment of her 'deservingness' including a judgment about her commitment to the work ethic and to family values."[65] As Robert Goodin argues, in the neoliberal approach, dependency becomes a "moralized" term and comes to hold a negative valence that is not present in other ideological contexts that value the de-commodification of families.[66] Furthermore, the very act of "rationing resources to clients involves a moral categorization of deservingness."[67]

Under neoliberal work-first, morality and economic ideology conflate to present work-first buy-in as the moral or right way to think. Joel Handler provides a framework for thinking about such moral work within a three-dimensional model of power that he adapts from Steven Lukes to the bureaucratic welfare setting. In this model, the first dimension involves the commonly understood definition of power in that person A has "power over [person] B to the extent that he [or she] can get [person] B to do something that B would not otherwise do."[68] The second dimension, drawn from Bachrach and Baratz, "involves not only who gets what, when and how, but also who gets left out and how."[69] The third dimension draws on Gramsci and Edelman and involves the even broader level of "how power may affect even the *conception* of grievance."[70] In this dimension, "the absence of grievance may be due to a manipulated consensus" such that dominant groups are so powerful that they are oblivious to challenge.[71] In the words of Lukes, "the most effective and insidious use of power is to prevent conflict from arising in the first place."[72] This involves exercising power over people by shaping their "wants" and desires even if there is a conflict between their interests and the interests of those exercising power over them.

Jamie Peck posits that though the work-first methodology is publicly presented in the language of "empowerment," "independence," and "self-sufficiency," its day-to-day functioning is at its heart an effort to gradually socialize a specific neoliberal "work ethic" through "coercion, discipline, and conformity."[73] This ethic is that of living as a commodity in which "good" clients learn to sell themselves on the global market. Though today cloaked in terms of personal responsibility and freedom, commodification has not always been seen this way. As Gøsta Esping-Andersen notes, when policy designed to establish market hegemony among competing economic alternatives emerged in the 1800s, its outcome was seen as unnatural, dangerous, and even prison-like for the general laborer.[74]

> With no recourse to property, and no state to which human needs can be directed, the market becomes to the worker a prison within which it is imperative to behave as a commodity in order to survive.[75]

It is in this sense that "welfare-state restructuring can also be conceived as one of a number of sites where the boundary between coercion and consent is being redrawn in the remaking of the neoliberal state."[76] The local work of redrawing the boundaries of the welfare state can be seen in the present chapter in the progression from seeing a need for change, to buying into work-first's goal of commodification. From a distance, this work emerges as not simply an issue of worker morality but also of power.[77]

Despite being framed in response to the social costs of poor, female-headed families, and despite calling for increases in marriage and "responsible fatherhood and motherhood," the greater emphasis of the 1996 legislation is on work.

> Indeed, at first glance the campaign to reform welfare seemed to be en-
> tirely about questions of the personal morality of the women who sub-
> sist on the dole. Certainly it was not about labor markets. The problem
> was, the argument went, that a too generous welfare system was lead-
> ing women to spurn wage work for lives of idleness and "dependency"
> (Fraser and Gordon 1994). Also, too generous payments, too laxly admin-
> istered, were undermining sexual and family morality among the poor.
> Women, even teenagers, were having sex and bearing out-of-wedlock ba-
> bies whose fathers easily walked away, all because they knew they could
> turn to welfare. . . . None of this talk was about labor markets. Rather,
> everyone focused relentlessly on the ostensibly perverse effects of welfare
> on the creatures who received it. Yet it had a good deal to do with labor
> markets, for it created a national drama which heaped insult on women
> who were poor if they were presumed not to work.[78]

Within this "drama," distinctions dating back to colonial times between the deserving poor and undeserving poor, which at one time were based in family relations of mothering, were reshaped in accordance with the ideology of "market triumphalism."[79] "The deserving poor are now those who embrace the spirit of entrepreneurship, voluntarism, consumerism, and self-help, while the undeserving are those who remain 'dependent' on the state."[80] This transition is accomplished through discursive work which presents a dominant paradigm for understanding and interpreting the lives of clients. In the case of clients who buy into the reform ide-als, but which also holds true for administrators and caseworkers, such ideology "does not straightforwardly determine their actions but instead gives them a lens to interpret their experiences."[81] It furthermore provides them with "discursively legitimate grounds" on which to base their deci-sion-making and actions.[82] These discursive grounds, namely, neoliberal discourses of personal responsibility, are created by and constituent of a wider political economy. Through its impact on frontline casework, this political common sense brings extra-local interests and sensibilities to bear on the day-to-day experiences of local lives in East County. In this way, "local development . . . is patterned on a national (and global) shift toward neoliberalism."[83]

Institutional Change, Entrepreneurship, and Neoliberal Common Sense

The rise of work-first in East County presents us with a case study in institutional change through entrepreneurship. In a global economic environment, it seems that entrepreneurship is being called for from all corners—the White House, private foundations, local efforts at urban revitalization. In this respect, government is no different. Calls for devolution of government responsibilities to local levels where innovation can take place are a hallmark of the new federalism. Though there is a rich literature in the scholarship of business, we know surprisingly little about how such entrepreneurial spirit (or what Vanna Gonzalez refers to as "social enterprise spirit") takes hold in the public sector.[84]

Recent research has highlighted the social embeddedness of innovation and entrepreneurship in the private sector, elucidating how culture shapes value and significance as much as economic concerns.[85] Agents, as Jeffrey Alexander has argued, typically work through prevailing culture, not against it.[86] Hargadon and Douglas argue, "To be accepted, entrepreneurs must locate their ideas within the set of existing understandings and actions that constitute the institutional environment yet set their innovations apart from what already exists."[87]

Certainly professional training socializes certain ways of thinking, but this is not the only cultivator and coordinator of innovations. Neoinstitutionalism has applied itself to uncovering how ways of thinking span various walks of life, giving daily personal experience a conspicuously isomorphic quality.

> Tak[ing] as a starting point the striking homogeneity of practices and arrangements found in the labor market, in schools, states and corporations . . . the constant and repetitive quality of much of organized life is explicable not simply by reference to individual, maximizing actors but rather by a view that locates the persistence of practices in both their taken-for-granted quality and their reproduction and in structures that are to some extent self-sustaining.[88]

Building on the work of neoinstitutionalists who conceive of institutions as broader than organizations and seek to explain "striking homogeneity of practices and arrangements," this chapter examines the ideological discourse of neoliberalism as an engine and orienting force of innovation in this global era.[89]

Though some have characterized the relationship between innovation and institutions in terms of a collision of opposing forces of change and stability, others have acknowledged that "social structures" are not only constraining but also enabling forces of agency.[90] Following from this second approach, I have explored neoliberalism as an example of an institution or social system that greases the tracks, so to speak, for certain forms of innovation by investing in establishing what we come to see as problematic about our social organizations at present and how we go about conceiving of solutions, that is, our common sense about welfare.

While the promise of profit and/or change for the better are generally credited as the engines behind adoption of new ways of doing things, such explanations neglect the social embeddedness of the process by which innovations are introduced to and accepted by the public or the conditions by which they occur in the public sector. To understand how individuals and organizations become involved in public-sector innovations, it is useful not only to observe them as they occur but also to consider how existing institutions shape those responses. A vast literature on innovation relies on historical case studies (post-it notes, light bulbs, etc.), but in this chapter we observe innovation in progress in order to identify the means by which innovations gain purchase and the linkages that connect them to broader relations of contemporary social organization and power dynamics. This yields us important insight into the relationship between ideology and innovative institutional change.

Much attention has been given to what sets successful innovators apart from the unsuccessful and how they displace the status quo. In the private sector, explanations for the successful (and unsuccessful) introduction and diffusion of innovation tend to highlight the inherent functional and economic advantages that new technologies offer compared with traditional ways of doing things.[91] In the words of Herbert A. Simon, "Everyone designs who devises course of action aimed at changing existing situations into preferred ones."[92] What Simon also points out, however, is that innovations are intrinsically "artificial" to the extent that they are contingent on the inherently biased goals or purposes of their designer. Thus, a key question that must be asked of innovations is whose preferences they serve. In the private sector, profit provides a clearer standard of success. In the public sector, however, innovations must appeal to some form of shared understanding of what is "preferable." It is here that examining the role of dominant discourse becomes useful, since it is well equipped as a mechanism to establish what is communally preferred.

A rich nomenclature already exists for such analysis. Sociological and psychological literature argues that schemas offer sets of existing understandings and actions through which individuals interpret novel situations and craft responses. They furthermore assert that institutions play a large role in the establishment of such schemas by constituting an understanding of what interpretations and actions are acceptable.[93] Neoinstitutionalists such as Paul DiMaggio who have appropriated this language argue that "everyday cognition relies heavily and uncritically upon culturally available schemata—knowledge structures that represent objects or events and provide default assumptions about their characteristics, relationships, and entailments under conditions of incomplete information."[94] For DiMaggio, scripts represent localized variants of broader schemata.

Applying similar neoinstitutionalist terminology to understanding the contemporary dilemmas we face in our everyday lives, Dorothy E. Smith employs an institutional ethnography approach to studying neoliberalism as a "meta-discourse" that becomes specified to local situations such that a broader neoliberal ideological discourse can be empirically traced as it "regulates others that are specialized for specific contexts such as institutions."[95] In this case we are concerned with neoliberalism as it can be seen regulating innovations within institutions of welfare.

Though previous analysis treats innovators as catalysts looking to see how their action "invokes and exploits institutionally shaped understandings" in order to successfully challenge institutional stability with a new vision of change, this chapter calls into question this conflation of actors, agents, and their "cultural systems."[96] The East County experience suggests that the culture and social systems in which innovators live, in addition to some individual endogeneity, forms the basis for the knowledge from which they innovate.[97] This does not necessarily entail a shift in locus of control such that extra-local forces control what happens locally in a deterministic way, but there is certainly a shift in the directionality of influence. Local actors retain a degree of control or agency over the innovations they conceive of and implement. Fundamentally, what we learn is that we should not assume that the events of conceiving of need for reform and of brainstorming appropriate directions for reform are wholly endogenous. Quite to the contrary, striking similarities across distinctive sites of welfare innovation lead us to suspect otherwise. In trying not to miss the forest for the trees, East County's experience encourages us to revise the claim that innovators endeavor to cloak truly original ideas in the language and likeness of existing institutions so that they gain acceptance. Instead, this chapter suggests that it is the other way around; familiar ideas are involved from the outset of conceiving of innovations. This understanding is more than polemical as it opens us up to a need for critically examining the common sense that cultivates innovations and the political economy on which they are based.

The following chapters chronicle the achievement of innovative local leaders in one county in New York State as they champion and exemplify the public management called for by the neoliberal approach to welfare reform. I hope to make visible the ways in which work-first common sense is continually constructed and re-constructed through managerial performance measures, technology, and new case management strategies that reinforce the values of neoliberalism.

3

"A New Way of Doing Business"

Performance Measures, Rights, and Common Sense

There has been much talk of reforming government, ushering in the age of privatization, government by proxy, and the emphasis on efficiency over equity.[1] In the time between the 1996 PRWORA and its re-authorization in 2006 (on February 8, 2006 in the federal Deficit Reduction Act of 2005), the focus of research has been on outcomes, such as the decline in caseloads and on the important question of former recipients' long-term quality of life post-welfare.[2] Within the realm of social policy and public politics, these outcome measures are the most visible. In this examination of performance measures and welfare rights, however, I take a closer look at how the elements of reform implementation actually function to order the work of welfare workers and their clients. They enact an inter-scalar restructuring of the welfare state. Responsibility, authority, and power shift both up and down in complex ways between the scales of the individual, household, community/county, state, national, and global. This reconfiguration is largely driven by a neoliberal logic of globalization that encourages the delegation of responsibility to adapt to global economic restructuring. This logic can be seen here to extend to local caseworkers and clients.

In this chapter I examine the institutional relations of worker accountability and vulnerability that the 1996 reform has imposed within the welfare office, as well as its significance for the restructuring of the global labor market beyond. Specifically, I focus on how welfare office reorganization, with its emphasis on performance measures and its de-emphasis on client rights, restructures common sense in the welfare office. This restructuring affects both caseworkers and clients, though in different ways. Caseworkers simultaneously face increased accountability through performance-based contracting and find themselves in contingent work configurations that circumvent civil service and public-sector union protections. Clients, on the other hand, experience an institutional reform that in rhetoric offers "a hand up rather than a hand out," but in practice enforces client responsibility to work while neglecting client rights.

This chapter begins with a description of how TANF has been structurally transformed in the local setting of this study, East County, pursuant to the 1996 welfare reform. I explore what this means not only for its ability to achieve the mission of the reform but also for the workers involved. Prominent in this reconfiguration is the infrastructure of the new federalism, which delegates greater administrative responsibility to states and counties, but maintains tight reins over agency mission through stringent enforcement of participation rates and other performance measures.

Together with workplace restructuring and performance measures, a third component, budgetary pressures through the block grant funding structure, establish an institutional imperative that requires caseworkers to enforce work preparation requirements strictly. This shift has discouraged welfare receipt overall. New performance measures are clearly in sync with demands that clients accept personal responsibility to work toward self-sufficiency. They also reinforce the goal of diversion. A de-emphasized fair hearings appeal process since the reform complements these changes. It serves to undermine government pledges to assist clients and highlights their vulnerability in the post–welfare reform labor market.[3]

A *"New Way of Doing Business"*

Though states have addressed the delegated responsibility for administering a reformed welfare system in various ways, in most cases it involves drastic change as compared with the pre-reform years. The 1996 PRWORA required each state to submit its own plan for complying with the federal reform's demands. New York State produced its response in the 1997 Welfare Reform Act and an accompanying implementation guide that closely mirrored the federal legislation yet radically restructured New York's existing system.[4] As expressed in a letter from the state welfare commissioner addressed to the administrator in charge of East County's program, "we are witness to tremendous change in the way we do business."[5]

Following passage of the 1997 act, state officials appointed county commissioners and assigned implementation responsibilities to local apparatuses that these county officials either created from scratch or arranged via contracts with already existing public and private entities. In East County, a newly established agency, spawned from a partnership between a community college and a city social services department (and piloted even before the 1996 legislation), was granted authority to collect TANF block grant funds and to administer the local work-first program. This arrangement involved a negotiation of responsibility and a blending of resources, which, despite acting to satisfy legislative provisions and existing contingent to grant funding, remained outside of the formal public bureaucracy. As one staffer in the newly formed work-first agency clarifies, although work-first caseworkers work in conjunction with government services and use government funds, "We're not actually public servants; we're paid by the college. We don't have to take a civil service test or anything." Work-first thus came into existence to supplement, not replace, the pre-reform welfare office.

Once created, work-first began to coordinate its services with the existing welfare and aid-granting structure. East County, much like other localities nationwide, took the initiative to reconfigure formerly distinct welfare, employment, and other social services to meet the goals of the reform more efficiently. Satellite branches of these departments were relocated on shared premises and have been further transformed by sharing and/or re-assigning responsibilities that were previously retained by each agency separately.

Throwing Money at Us

Welfare reform, in the larger sense, has been described as entailing two types of behavior modification—that of clients and that of the bureaucrats who administer welfare. While many states and localities have attempted to revamp intake processes to "signal" to applicants that welfare is different now, local administrators were made aware that their behavior too had to change. This expectation was communicated by "strong signals" and large pools of money that emanated from state and federal legislative actions.[6] As one administrator recalls:

> Once welfare reform passed on the federal level and the state legislation had passed, there was so much money. And we looked at that and said "this is not going to be forever, we need to take advantage of this" because that stuff ebbs and flows. There is going to be a time when there is no money for anything, but right now there is a lot of interest in trying

new things and doing new things. One year the county said well we have this much money, do something with it. They were literally throwing money at the counties, saying, here we have this much money, do something with it!

While TANF involved new requirements of participation and new expectations of both clients and staff, it also came with new opportunities for innovative programming. A spirit of innovation was transmitted to frontline staffs by drastic transformations in workplace processes.[7] In East County, new sources of money provided work-first with comparatively lavish office space and the fiscal ability to lure experienced caseworkers from previously existing social services departments with a generous pay structure. As one veteran work-first staffer explains:

> Many of us came from other social services departments and [we] were hired on little by little, as work-first grew. I was one of the first ones hired. Back when we started, there were only five of us.

Such comments present a stark contrast to the long-term existence and seniority system described by a welfare office worker:

> Welfare Office Caseworker: So I've been here 18 years and I'm still low on the totem pole as far as seniority, I'm 13th from the bottom. That's because the Food Stamps workers are counted in, they've been here forever.

Despite a lack of seniority, work-first caseworkers are well compensated. As one explains, "They pay us well. We get paid a lot more here than others who do a similar type of work." By the time of this research, work-first's formal caseworker roster numbered over 100. Thus, the creation of the work-first office was an organic process that started small and accumulated caseworkers as the program matured. In this process, it created a distinctive workforce niche that was in some ways reflective of a broader national trend toward de-skilling the social service professions. In particular, it involved both circumventing gateway mechanisms that regulate the social services—namely social work education credentials and civil service exams—and eroding professional protections. More specifically, it sidestepped unions and made employment contingent on funding and performance.

Circumventing Gateway Mechanisms

The staffing arrangements of welfare reform in East County follow a trend of social service de-skilling that began in the 1970s with the "separation of service." At that time, welfare eligibility determination and service provisions, which previously had both been conducted largely by professional-degree-holding social workers, were split into two distinct functions. This allowed less well-trained and significantly lower-paid workers to conduct routine eligibility determination and separated professional social workers from the purse strings.[8] The 1996 reform can be seen as mounting a similar de-skilling attack on the service provisioning side of welfare.[9] By circumventing traditional gateway mechanisms to social service positions, namely professional training and civil service exams, the reform contributes to further restructuring and de-professionalizing welfare-related social service work. A work-first administrator explains:

> A social work background is not a requirement. Our staff comes from various backgrounds and most have a Bachelor's degree or equivalent work history. They are thoroughly trained by work-first and are screened for personability and communication style and ability.

Similarly, one staff member explains:

> You don't have to take a civil service exam to get a job here. If this were a county welfare job, they would have to interview and hire from the top three scorers on the civil service exam. But here they don't have to do that; they could just hire you off the street. I see it as a positive thing. I'm not sure it is, but I think it is.

Work-first embodies a diverse staff as it draws caseworkers "off the street" and from other social services offices. The diversity is increased by a pool of model welfare recipients who were hired on after successfully completing a work experience internship (workfare) in the work-first office. Those in the higher end of the agency, such as job coaches, typically hold a bachelor's degree or one or two years of college with commensurate experience. Their pay ranges from $25,000 to $30,000 a year. Despite the common list of gripes encountered in any workplace (a grumpy co-worker, a broken photocopy machine, chronic database malfunctions), these higher-paid, higher-educated caseworkers tend to appreciate the position they have. "I don't always love my job, but it's great pay for what I do, great benefits. You really can't beat that."

Another explains:

> Sure I talk about all the things I'm going to do when I leave here, start my own business and all, but I'll never leave here. It's a good job. I like what I do, it gets me up in the morning.

These caseworkers enjoy a flexible, typically white-collar work environment. They receive a number of benefits—health and retirement benefits, a salaried 40-hour workweek, several weeks of vacation, and a lenient and generous sick day policy; and there is relatively little managerial oversight of everyday details. As in other white-collar jobs, absences are noticed, but the autonomy they enjoy allows them to negotiate their workplace responsibilities in relation to other aspects of their lives.

Work-first employees in the lower tiers of the agency, such as technical assistants or receptionists, are not as well compensated (earning $18,000 to $20,000 a year), but they participate similarly in the workplace culture. They dress professionally—wearing khakis, a tie and a shirt, or a skirt or business suit. Lower tiered employees tend to have less education—high school or equivalent—and many are former recipients. Their job tasks are also less flexible and routinized, and there is more managerial supervision. While there is a clear class and authority distinction between these two groups of employees (often evident in different speech patterns and differing amounts of on-the-job "free time"), they, like their co-workers, actively participate in maintaining a certain level of distance between caseworkers and clients.

This distance from clients is also visible among welfare office caseworkers who follow a similar dress code and work within a parallel hierarchy of job titles. Unlike the new work-first office, the welfare office, which existed prior to 1996, does not tend to hire former recipients. As career professionals, welfare office caseworkers tend to be more highly educated, many even holding master's degrees. Though the workers appear quite similar on the surface, however, the 1996 reform has created critical structural differences between work-first caseworkers and their welfare office counterparts.

Eroding Social Service Protections

The 1996 reform facilitated the wider trend of tentative work relations in which capital saves money by employing workers on an exceedingly "as-needed" basis by making immediate work mandatory for welfare clients. It is also implemented in part through the use of contingent work contracts for caseworkers. The work-first employees interviewed in this research, unlike the welfare caseworkers at the welfare office, were largely contingent employees, hired for only as long as the block grants continue and the agency continues to meet performance measure benchmarks. In one work-first caseworker's words:

> We're not permanent workers. Our agency is grant-based so the first TANF grant was for five years. So we were guaranteed employment for five years and since then it has just been year-to-year, contingent on funding from the state, county, and federal government, you know the block grants.

This distinction is consequential not only because it involves temporal contingency but also because these new contract workers are positioned differently from "permanent employees" of government welfare organizations.[10] In particular, the employee status and bargaining rights are explicitly protected in the case of permanent employees who predate the welfare reform and who continue to work in the welfare office.

Amidst massive restructuring and consolidation of departments and functions, these collective-bargaining rights of permanent employees were explicitly recognized in the 1997 New York State Welfare Reform Act:

> §128 Transfer of employees. 1. Upon the transfer of functions from the former department of social services and the former division for youth to the department of family assistance and the appropriate successor offices. . . . 2. A transferred employee shall remain in the same collective bargaining unit as was the case prior to his or her transfer.[11]

Furthermore, assurances were provided that the privatization of welfare functions that brought about East County's work-first agency would not impinge upon permanent employees' primary traditional functions regarding eligibility determination and that permanent employees have a right to bid for contracts offered for privatization.

§151, §20-c, (p205) Privatization. . . . the department shall not enter into any contract with a private entity under which the private entity would perform any of the public assistance and care eligibility determination functions, duties or obligations of the department as set forth in this chapter.

These clauses do not apply to contract workers at the work-first agency. Work-first caseworkers are contingent and lack the long-term job security of pre-reform welfare staff. They also lack the ability to join established unions such as the CSEA (Civil Service Employees Association) or the AFSCME (American Federation of State County and Municipal Employees). One work-first employee explains:

The majority of the work-first staff, we are not unionized. Over in the welfare office they are all part of the CSEA [The Civil Service Employees Association which is a local 1000 of the American Federation of State County and Municipal Employees—AFSCME] and they cover a few of our workers here like the information aids and technical assistants. Also, some of the administrators that came from the community college when we were formed are covered under the state community college union. But the rest of us, the job coaches, are not in a union. We don't have one.

As another employee explains, the lack of union representation leads to a muted voice in negotiations over work conditions.

We don't have a union, but, as part of the deal when they created our agency, we job coaches get our benefits based on the faculty over at the community college. We don't have anyone representing us, but we get whatever they negotiate.

Additionally, without the ability to participate in collective bargaining, work-first employees also forgo some of the protections. One work-first employee explained:

As work-first employees we have no protection. They could just call me in the office and tell me see you later. I would be fired and I would have no recourse. That is a big difference for us. Like I know of a union employee who admitted to having a drug problem. They tried to fire her but the union got involved. If that were me, without the union, I would be fired, like see you on down the road.

In addition to lacking the protections of organized labor, work-first case-workers find that their workplace vulnerability is further circumscribed by their need to continually meet mandated performance benchmarks. If the agency as a whole fails to do this, it faces considerable financial sanctions and the possibility that the contract to administer TANF funds will be rescinded and re-issued to another agency, thus rendering them unemployed.

Performance Measure Accountability in the Restructuring of Welfare Work

Welfare services, like many government-provided services in the United States, are undergoing a process of restructuring and rethinking of accountability mechanisms. O'Connell, Betz, and Shepard assert that this trend has been gaining momentum since the 1970s and has corresponded with public demand for greater institutional accountability and the rise in stature of the private sector's efficiency imperative.[12] In response, the federal government's 1996 legislation has increased emphasis on free-market-like efficiency and outcome-tied effectiveness to the task of processing the needy. The result has been a reconfiguration of the old system based on a new premise of performance. By calling attention to certain behaviors above others, this new stress on outcomes instructs caseworkers to emphasize particular parts of their work and de-emphasize others.

Under the old structure, eligibility requirements were pre-determined and local managers had only to apply the rules to each person's situation and concentrate on accuracy. As this TANF worker explains, many of the pre-reform welfare accounting mechanisms continue to exist alongside the new reform imperatives.

> TANF Worker: Yeah the state [still] does audits, . . . [to make sure] check-lists are being done or whatever, re-coups are being initiated properly, . . . whether those types of checklists are being done, if benefits are being issued under the right category. You know, categories meaning, is it federally funded, or state funded, or locally funded. You know, things like . . . that an error percentage is calculated, based on, per county, who's doing what properly.

While local departments of social services have an inherent interest in the amount of money being spent on public assistance, state-mandated eligibility standards have traditionally meant that there was not much they could do beyond monitoring it. Under the new system, this processing of welfare applications according to a set standard continues, but it has been joined by an additional task (undertaken primarily by work-first) of enforcing and keeping track of recipients' participation in work and/or work-related activities.

A conversation with a worker in the welfare department responsible for processing welfare applications illustrates this contrast between the old system and the new work-first component.

> TANF Worker: We've been worried about recidivism for a while over here. "Repeat offenders" we call them. Yeah, we see a lot of the same people coming through again and again. . . . It would save us a lot of money to cut down on repeaters. But we can't really do anything about it here. If they qualify, they get money, . . . but those guys over there [at the work-first offices], they can really do something about it.

This excerpt outlines a major difference between the old system and the new expansion to the system. By contrasting welfare and work-first, this intake worker expresses the sentiments that the institution of welfare is now expected to aim beyond eligibility determination and check cutting. Under the old system, high numbers of welfare-eligible clients and application patterns were merely observed and discussed by workers. They were vaguely reflected within a simple county Department of Social Services budgetary statement of expenses that did not allow for an easy examination of welfare expenditures by either frontline caseworkers or the public. Little detail about county caseloads could be extracted from this form of representation. However, corresponding with the rise in attention given to welfare reform, the county budgets began offering a more in-depth look at county caseloads, dividing them by type of grant and even providing graphical depictions of caseload fluctuations over time.

While the old form of reporting evoked little more than acknowledgment, the new genre of presentation elicits a sense of concern for local case management that complements the goals of welfare reform. The new form of reporting gives a high visibility to local caseload management. It goes beyond reporting aggregate financial grants, indicating as well, according to precise definitions, how many grantees are participating in what programs, and the average cost per individual case. It is part of a larger restructuring that emphasizes outcome measures and makes the

location of weak management results detectable. As a work-first administrator explains:

> Everything is now outcome-based as opposed to how it used to be. In
> the social services we, [she explains to me in an aside] me and the other
> administrators that work here that were in various programs and agen-
> cies before being hired at work-first, we used to just apply for grants and
> then do what we said we would do with them but never be checked. Now
> everything is being outcome-based and our participation rates are very
> important or else the government will take away the money.

The visibility of these measures, tied to funding and accessible to managers at higher levels of the hierarchy, sets a new charge: good management
involves achieving accountability benchmarks.

As the accounting mechanism for work-first agencies is set up in New
York State, county success in fulfilling its mandate is measured in terms
of three things: (1) participation rates, or the number of recipients participating in approved programs as of monthly report tallies; (2) the assessment of employability requirement, a mandate that all applicants must
be assessed to an employability category (this is entered and checked on
the statewide Welfare Management System—WMS); and (3) the 12-month
limit on approved training activities, after which a recipient must be
working (also verified via the WMS). While assessment of employability and limiting of training approval are easily accomplished via internal
casework practices and policies, client participation requires the cooperation of actual recipients and thus presents a greater challenge to local administrators. Success at this task is reflected in the regular reporting of
participation rates.

Once a month, at the end of the month, local administrators calculate participation rates. The work/activity status of each open TANF case
(Family/Household) is evaluated by the work-first agency and tallied for
inclusion on the monthly report form. To complete this form, local work-
first administrators also retrieve the number of open TANF cases from
the Department of Social Services welfare office. Next they calculate rates
by dividing those participating by the total receiving assistance (minus
those exempt) according to the manner prescribed in the state manual,
and verified by state audits of local agencies.

The importance of this performance measure is acknowledged and
taken seriously by administrators at the local level. As one administrator

exclaims, "We are [very] . . . focused on participation rates since that is how we are funded." The attention such measures demand is punctuated by quarterly and annual county reviews by the state, state monitoring of the WMS computer system, and random state audits of in-house paperwork. As a result, task proficiency is given much attention. Training in work-first regulations and performance measures often takes several weeks, even for staffers with internal transfers. As one new trainee, who had transferred internally, remarked to me during break time in between training sessions:

> There is a lot to learn and people rarely get it right the first time; I guess that's why it takes a few weeks to train for a position.

Training often includes group sessions as well as days of shadowing the previous position-holder. As one administrator clarifies, "The money is federal, state, and local and we have to follow their standards very closely because we get audited quite often."

Within the work-first agency, there is a collective understanding of the way in which grant funding and performance are related. The employee training sessions that all new employees go through involve an in-depth description of the funding process that is in place as well as the vocabulary and criteria that are used for evaluation. This is supplemented with periodic "all-staff" training sessions (in which grant updates and new funding possibilities are presented and discussed). Participation rates are posted on the wall (on poster board with numbers marked in fluorescent highlighter). All of these practices maintain a strong sense of awareness about the performance measures by which the agency will be evaluated. As alluded to, these measures indicate a significant break from previous programs that TANF replaced, such as the Job Opportunities and Basic Skills (JOBS) Training Program initiated by the 1988 Family Support Act. As a training manual issued by the MDRC explains:

> The participation standards under the PRWORA are significantly more stringent than those in the JOBS program. Almost all adults receiving TANF assistance can be mandated to participate and are counted in the denominator of the participation rate. The numerator of the rate is also more difficult to achieve; the range of allowable activities is much narrower, the number of hours a person must spend in activities each week is higher, and the percentage of the caseload that must participate

is greater. At the same time, the provision in the new law that allows states to meet lower participation rates based on caseload reductions has generally made those rates much easier to meet, at least in the short term.[13]

Beyond highlighting the changes that PRWORA's standards invoke, this excerpt points to the coordination of caseload reduction with participation requirements. Local administrators must focus on the larger welfare goals of increasing employment and reducing welfare receipt, in conjunction with participation, in order to successfully do their jobs. Local managers are acutely aware that accomplishing these goals requires allocating their attention, not just among those already in the program, but also among those in various stages of the intake process. One administrator praises a section of the intake apparatus that accomplishes these goals particularly well.

> This room is very successful [she explains in an elated voice]. We have a very high success rate in this room. Many people find jobs before they even open a case file for welfare. . . . We have tremendous success here. It's great when people don't even have their welfare cases opened because the five-year limit is like a bank and if they don't use it up it's better for them, and it also keeps taxes down.

Stressing that this is a positive outcome for an applicant and taxpayers, this administrator only hints at the positive ramifications for her agency. When an applicant leaves the rolls or is diverted, the agency benefits in several ways. Most immediately, this is one less person that the local welfare institution has to pay for out of pre-issued block grant money. Second, lower caseloads have the added effect of reducing the required percentage of participants. According to the 1996 legislation, for each percentage point that the state's caseload is reduced beyond its figures for the 1995 fiscal year, the required participation rate is reduced an equivalent number of points.[14] Thus, moving people off assistance reduces the proportion of the remaining caseload that is required to meet participation requirements. Success at this task on the local level promises good standing with state overseers. Beyond these overt benefits to the agency, caseworkers save time on processing and avoid the stress of having overfilled caseloads. When caseloads decrease en masse, fewer caseworkers are needed and the county saves money. Finally, diverting

FIGURE 3.1
Federal, State and County ADC/TANF Caseloads Over Recent Years

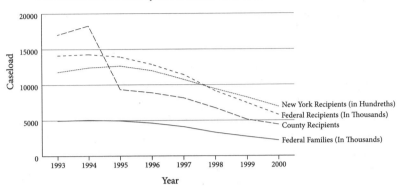

Sources: US Department of Health and Human Service: The Administration for Children and Families: Statistics http://www.acf.dhhs.gov/news/stats/caseload.htm as of 12/14/00. County Annual Budget 1990–2001

applicants from opening cases averts or at least postpones future fiscal liability for the county that is incurred as applicants exhaust their five-year federal time limit.

Figure 3.1 presents the overall pattern of caseload decline in East County as it mirrors that of the state and nation in general. Research suggests that such effects nationwide are largely due to changes of welfare processing (30-45 percent), in addition to an unusually strong economy, a massive expansion in aid to the working poor such as through the Earned Income Tax Credit (EITC), and a 5 percent increase in the minimum wage.[15]

Evident in figure 3.2, reducing caseloads has helped New York State to avoid federal penalties since the year 2000. Each year since then (data are only available until 2002), New York State's participation rates were below the federally mandated minimum, but the state and its counties were not sanctioned because of the 1996 legislation's allowance for participation rate requirement reduction by 1 percent for each percentage point the caseloads declined since 1995. This allowance, however, was modified when the PRWORA of 1996 was reauthorized on February 8, 2006, in the federal Deficit Reduction Act of 2005. Though the reauthorization did not change the list of activities that count as "work-related" or the rules for the minimum hours needed for a family to count toward these participation standards, it did revise the caseload reduction credit so that

FIGURE 3.2

Impact of Caseload on Participation Rate Mandate

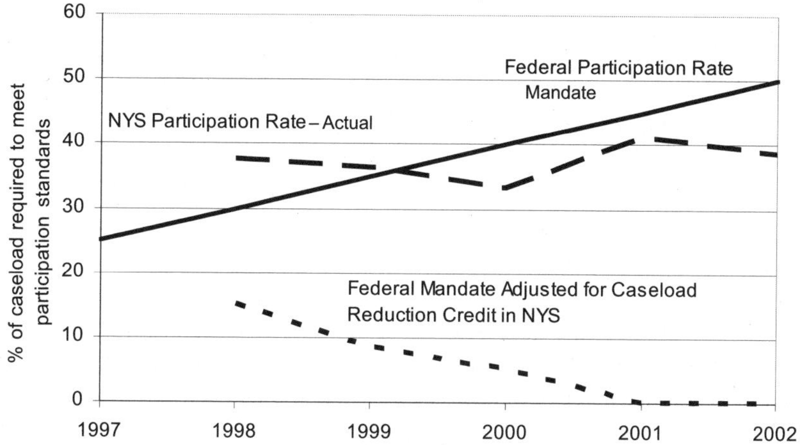

Sources: TANF Annual Reports to Congress, 2000–2004; http://www.acf.hhs.gov//programs/ofa/indexar.htm. Patel, Nisha, and Mark Greenberg. 2002. "Key State TANF Policies Affecting Micro-enterprise." New York, Washington, DC: Center for Law and Social Policy. Accessed online July 20, 2006: http://www.clasp.org/publications/welfare_policy.htm.

participation standards are reduced only for caseload reductions that occur beyond fiscal year 2005.[16] As a result, if New York State fails to significantly cut its welfare rolls further, it stands to face a challenging 50 percent work participation rate requirement (rather than its current adjusted rate of zero) which would likely be unattainable and would result in significant financial penalties.[17] As a result, caseload reduction promises to continue to be a primary goal among frontline administrators. Welfare researcher Yeheskel Hasenfeld notes that, through participation requirements, "states have a strong incentive to terminate recipients from welfare as a cheap way to meet the work requirements."[18] In the words of Trudi Renwick, senior economist for the Fiscal Policy Institute of New York, the state appears committed to caseload reduction:

Mathematically, there are two ways to increase the work participation rates: either increase the numerator (the number of cases in which the adults are engaged in work activities) or shrink the denominator (the number of cases). The Governor's proposals seem to focus almost exclusively on the second strategy rather than the first.[19]

Administrators are well-versed in the repercussions of caseload reduction, and it is among the ideals that they preach. As might be expected, pressure to reduce the rolls is also salient to the frontline caseworkers who become the targets of such managerial efforts. As one staffer explains in response to my question about whether she ever has trouble deciding what to do with applicants as they come through:

> Staffer: Well, yeah, like that lady that came through earlier today [who didn't have all the necessary paperwork]. I didn't know if they would see her or not. . . . Like with . . . assistance they're trying to cut it down.

In this way, institutional pressures focus on the immediate decisions of caseworkers with regard to applicants. Beyond reducing caseloads, caseworkers are also encouraged to promote compliant behaviors among their clientele.

As a how-to guide for welfare implementers explains, "Even in a well-funded and well-managed program, a substantial portion of a caseload will not be participating in a given month for unavoidable reasons."[20] The management strategy endorsed in response to this dilemma, as seen below, is to start early, prepping not only clients but also new applicants, to be the best participants possible:

> In order to have a given number of recipients count toward participation rates, programs must reach out to many more potential participants than those represented in the participation rate goal. Caseworkers' time is required to refer and orient people to the program, determine their initial and subsequent activity assignments, monitor their attendance, and initiate the sanctioning process for those who fail to participate without a good reason. As a result, caseworkers can spend almost as much time, and in some cases even more time, on nonparticipants as they do on participants.[21]

This insight, provided in a nationally available guide for local-level administrators, suggests the integral role of intake processing in grooming applicants that will count in positive ways toward the ultimate managerial aim of producing good numbers.

This connectedness of applicant and recipient processing, under the theme of performance measures, serves to instruct administrators and caseworkers alike as to the activities most worthy of their attention. Consequently, the work that is emphasized is reflective of performance measures, not necessarily of client success. As a database administrator explains:

[Beyond keeping records of applicants] the database only covers people as long as they are on Public Assistance and until they get a job. Once they get a job then we no longer keep track of them. Not even retention. If they get a job then we assume they're still hired and working unless they come back through the system [i.e., re-apply]. If they get a job but still need more money, they then go to CAP [child assistance] or something, but work-first is done keeping track of them.

As the maxim suggests, "If it was not recorded, it did not happen." The recorded and hence validated and rewarded work, caseworkers learn, is that which pertains to ensuring that clients will participate as required and diminishing the welfare caseload. It is not that which leads to client satisfaction, career advancement, or enhanced quality of life. In addition to workplace organization and instruction, caseworkers are motivated by the negative consequences of disregarding such institutional concerns.

Compelling Demands: Layers of Governance in the Enforcement of Work-First Work

The 1996 PRWORA took the first step in drastically re-ordering the service priorities of local welfare implementation. It required each state to pass its own welfare laws pursuant to its new standards. A cascading effect resulted in federal requirements and concepts in state and local laws and programs that were subsequently created to meet the requirements set forth by Congress. State laws and mandated participation rate schedules, such as that of New York State, reflect the importance that performance measures were given in this restructuring. A strong "work-first"/"labor force attachment" assertion that immediate work will lead to improved quality of life and self-sufficiency underlay this policy decision. The strict enforcement of participation rate mandates sent a clear message that the job of work-first was not just to ensure the welfare of the poor, but also to ensure that the poor are "working" (or at least preparing to work) in the paid labor sector to deserve their support. Through these mechanisms, caseworkers assembled to do the work of welfare reform find themselves compelled, through layers of accountability and enforcement, to do their best to achieve benchmarks of success that have been established for them.

Within work-first, an agency's funding is based on a series of complex relations that are tied very heavily to performance measures. As an administrator explains, "So our goal, in addition to preparing for the five-year limit, and dropping the caseloads, is to focus on participation rates." The link between funding and these measures, as well as the relationship of local, state, and federal governments to each other, is evident in the following section (§153 2. A. p. 107) from the 1997 New York State Welfare Reform Act:

> In the event that the federal government imposes fiscal sanctions on the state because of non-compliance with federal law, regulation, or policy relating to the temporary assistance for needy families block grant, other than sanctions relating to maintenance of effort spending requirements, the commissioner shall reduce federal reimbursement to each social services district in an amount equal to the proportion of such fiscal sanction that the commissioner determines is attributable to such district through review of relevant statewide and district-specific data or documentation. . . . The commissioner shall make such determination of district fault only to the extent that his or her review identifies specific district actions or inactions that resulted in the district's failure to meet the applicable federal requirement.

This excerpt clearly indicates that, if the state is sanctioned by the federal government for failure to meet specified performance benchmarks, it will pass on these financial penalties to the counties that it deems responsible for this outcome. It provides fair warning to counties that the state intends to use the county-reported data and documentation of performance as the basis for both assigning blame and assessing the magnitude of penalty. The collection of performance data is important, the law goes on to clarify, because if the state is "unable to identify which districts caused or contributed to such federal fiscal sanction, the commissioner, . . . shall assign the reduction in federal reimbursement to all districts."[22]

In accord with this layered hierarchy of penalty dissemination, the enforcement of the mandate to both meet legislated benchmarks and reduce caseloads is highly visible within state welfare reform legislation's discussion of ranking districts. This practice introduces a comparative dimension to performance measures that becomes visible in the following excerpt from state law (§153-k, p. 110).

> 2. Annually, the department shall rank each district based upon the percentage of its nonexempt public assistance caseload that leave assistance in the previous calendar year for unsubsidized employment without reapplying for public assistance within six months.

3. The ten districts ranked highest pursuant to subdivision two of this section shall be allocated pro rata share of the funds accumulated pursuant to subdivision four of this section and any other funds allocated for this purpose, based upon the number of recipients of public assistance in a district.

4. The twenty districts that are ranked the lowest, pursuant to subdivision two of this section, shall be required to pay to the department an amount equal to three percent of the district's state and federal reimbursement.

Such a ranking, combined with rewards and penalties for top-performing and lagging districts, respectively, places welfare districts in an adversarial schema that mimics private-sector competition. In addition to the financial teeth implied in these legislative specifications, comparisons between districts are further facilitated by the publication of rankings in the New York State Department of Labor District TANF and Safety Net Year to Date and Quarterly Activities Report. These reports are simple, yet the presentation of them, in a comparative context, leads to competition. When I asked if the presentation of all state counties in one book back-to-back leads to comparison between districts, one work-first agency administrator exclaimed, "Well, sure, it gets competitive!" One clear example of this is the state map that represents, via county border demarcations and a continuum of color shadings, the various participation rate ranges that each county achieved during the most recent evaluation period. This map not only provides a highly visible summarization of state district success rates, but it also facilitates the use of a comparative lens when measuring success within each district relative to others.

Unpacking Participation Rates

Looking at the participation rate report itself, that is, the actual form filed by the county for state review on a monthly basis, the high visibility of participation accountability becomes evident.[23] Clearly identified on the top left is the district or county that is filing the report, followed by the month it represents (the month is important because both TANF and SN—Safety Net is the general assistance program for people without children—are calculated monthly and averaged across months for final reports). Glancing over the report, one quickly notices the bottom line, a participation percentage for each of three groups: TANF all families,

TANF two-parent families, and Safety Net Individuals. These are the bottom line and the primary means of assessment used by the state and federal governments to evaluate the effectiveness of the program. These rates, in addition to being reported to extra-local state and federal levels, are also broken down to examine the performance of each of the local teams that works with the groups reported on (all families, two-parent, and SN) and the collective performance of the workers that are assigned to them.

In addition to these team-wide reports, a more precise accounting procedure is used to calculate participation rates for each individual job coach. Thus, the unit of analysis, and by extension the unit of accountability, extends through this accounting mechanism to the level of an individual employee. As one job coach described:

> Stan [one of the in-house data management staff] goes through on a monthly basis. He figures out the participation rate for each team and each individual team member. The team leader then makes sure everyone pulls their weight.

Doing this can make clear and visible who is fulfilling their requirements and which team members may be slacking off or failing to perform.

A layered hierarchy is thus present here in which the federal government may use its discretion to penalize states that fail to meet specified participation rates. These states may then exercise discretion in passing penalties on to delinquent counties that have failed to meet their mandated performance levels. These counties (represented by the local commissioner for work-first), in turn, can identify the specific teams that have not met their expected performance goals. Furthermore, the team leader can apply pressure to team members (specific employees) whose caseload participation rates are dragging down the average. This symmetry establishes a chain of passing on penalties and thus encourages a participation rate focus with the intent, at every level, of avoiding such negative repercussions. While this chain does not formally extend to intake (pre–case opening) caseworkers, the sensibilities behind it do. As Hasenfeld notes:

> There is a powerful bureaucratic imperative to enforce these rules because in the political economy of welfare departments, organizational survival is based on instituting a culture of eligibility and compliance with rules. This is because performance is measured by how well eligibility criteria

are enforced and cheating purged, by how quickly recipients are moved off the rolls and into work, and by how much welfare costs are reduced.[24]

It is clear that having clients who are not likely to comply with mandated participation activities will hinder the "performance" of the agency as a whole. The following section explores how performance pressures shape managerial efforts and, by extension, transfer institutional concerns to frontline and intake caseworkers. Subsequent chapters will explore the work of intake caseworkers as they attempt to reconcile these interests with the lowest layer of the hierarchy, the clients.

Performance Pressures and Managing Welfare Workers

The participation rate accounting system has powerful potential for organizing individual caseworkers as they go about their work. Through a layered structure of governance, a situation is created in which caseworkers at each level can be evaluated by pointing to the mandated participation rate and then pointing to the particular participation rate of their own client caseload, team, county, or state. This elicits both anxiety and caution. As one administrator remarked:

> The state places a high demand on us to meet participation rates. We have to meet them in order to keep our funding or else we get penalized. To give ourselves leeway we shoot for a higher level, 35 hours a week participation [even though the legal mandates don't require such a high rate until later on] just so when we fall short, across the board we are still above the minimum standards.

It is evident in this act that participation rates, as a powerful shaper of organizational accountability, place post-reform administrators in a new set of relations. In addition to supplying knowledge to senior county and state administrators about effectiveness of programs in attaining required benchmarks, the rates that are compiled and recorded also constitute a picture of managerial effectiveness and may have to be used to justify actions to senior case managers or to demonstrate managerial initiative. It is not surprising, then, that local administrators keep their own in-house records and databases, using them to report on optional performance measures as well as to meticulously weed through state-generated participation rate report estimates (generated through the WMS), to correct any errors before the final report is sent to press in the State Department of Labor (DOL) District TANF and SN Activities Report.

In addition to county work-first administrators, team leaders and frontline caseworkers, who are responsible for the actual day-to-day work of managing recipient participation, also show an interest in these reports. Although rates are worked out for the county/district as a whole and as the official responsibility of the commissioner, the team-by-team calculation and reporting of rates pulls team leaders and their teams into a microcosm of relations that reflects the larger social ordering. In printing out each individual team worker's rates, the caseworkers as a whole enact a context within which success or good work is to be read in comparison to the gold standard of the mandatory participation rate. Caseworkers are aware of this, as exemplified in a discussion with job coaches:

> Author: How are job coaches evaluated? How are you promoted or fired?
> Job Coach 1: Well . . . Participation rates, that's what really matters.
> Author: Really? Is that all, like when you're going for a promotion, that's all that matters?
> Job Coach 1: Well they also look at who on your caseload got jobs and what was your pay rate, but. . .
> Job Coach 2: Longevity! . . . Pay raises mainly go by time, longevity, how long you've been here.
> Author: Well what about being fired?
> Job Coach 1: Well that hardly happens, but if you fall below with participation rates . . . they will call you into their office and "counsel" you.

As expressed here, the emphasis of proficiency is not necessarily on what a coach may know or do but on the production of knowledge for their supervisor's reports. It is these reports, namely, performance measure reports, that gain the most visibility and for which administrators can be held accountable within the reform regime. The organizing power of these reporting mechanisms, however, does not stop at the boundaries of the explicitly mandated.

As a central organizer of local work, performance measures take on influence beyond their precisely stated concerns. This is evident in the situation one job coach explained to me following a discussion with another coach and a team leader. It illustrates the negotiation of performance measures that transcends multiple levels of agency hierarchy.

We all have to meet the state participation rates, but some people are exempt. Now we've been going above and beyond by trying to get exempt people to participate as well, but we're getting penalized for that. Our "hound dog" as we call her, [the one] who keeps track of all our participation and all here, just had a meeting telling us that we're being penalized because those exempt people who are participating are not meeting the minimum hours per week requirement, so that's being counted against us, . . . We just found this out because the lady from the state has been here doing an audit. . . She'll be back next week to finish it.

This job coach, who works at the intake level, a level not specifically scrutinized by participation rates, is taking an active interest in the participation rate process (brought to his attention by a team leader), responding personally and in an interactive manner to this measurement issue that reflects on his agency. As he argues his point, he simply asserts the question, "Why should we be penalized for being proactive and going above and beyond the call of duty?" The argument, importantly, is a rhetorical one, concluding for all intents and purposes in a resolve to more closely follow the rules of the state. This job coach's ardent concern for agency success is far from unique. Administrators and team leaders have succeeded in conveying to frontline caseworkers that meeting the goals set before the agency as a whole is in the interest of every staff member.

Local Fiscal Pressure: A Ticking Time Bomb

Interest in excelling at achieving the reform's goals is not limited to work-first caseworkers alone, but is shared throughout the agencies involved. As this eligibility intake worker, a recognizable remnant of the formerly existing welfare system, explains, fiscal sensitivity is a large part of this.

Now if the person has been in other counties we ask them, and we look up their information, which we can access in the computer for other counties in New York State. The other county is technically required to take care of them for the month that they move and the following month, so we often call and try to get a letter from the other county or look on the computer.

With other states, we have to call them since they're not on our computer, especially now we have to follow up to see how many months they have received assistance there, because with the federal limits, we have five years but other states have two, etc., and so if they come here after they run out of time there, their time there counts for their limit here as well. So if someone had three years somewhere else and then they came here, they would have two more years here and then they're done!

As she continues to explain, this can be a demanding task. This work, as described in the following excerpt, is neither straightforward nor simple. It requires skillful maneuvering such as listening for "what they're not saying to you." It is work that gets done, even if it is "a pain," because it is seen as important to the local welfare system.

> Author: How do you know what other state a person has been in other than them telling you? Like what if they don't tell you?
>
> Intake Worker: Well, we hope that they filled out a previous address and it's a pain if they don't know what county they were in, but we hope they put that down on the first page so that will tell us. Also we try to get their employment history as far back as we can . . . and from the addresses we can sort of tell what other states they have been in and we can check if they've been on welfare there. So you have to listen very carefully and always be listening. You have to try to pick up on what they're not saying to you. . . . You have to always pay attention to them, how they look, how they're sitting.

As the TANF caseworker implies, beyond the immediate need to meet participation performance measures, a time pressure has been added through the five-year (60-month) lifetime benefit limit (for each individual recipient) from the federal government. Following the depletion of this five-year bank, New York, like other states whose constitution guarantees aid to the poor, will have to compensate for the fiscal shortfall of lost federal funds for those who continue to need welfare assistance.[25] It is most likely to do this by increasing the financial burden levied on both the county and state in proportion to the loss of federal grants. This compounds the federal and state participation rate requirements with a local incentive to keep people off the welfare rolls and in the workplace as much as possible. This, in effect, makes diversion from long-term recipiency a central, if subtextual, goal. As an administrator discusses:

> Our focus is to keep, get the welfare rolls down to a manageable number, try to keep it to the five-year limit, since that is when the federal funds

cease and the state of New York, because of its Constitution which says that we must provide aid to the needy, in some form, must pick up the tab. After that, if the rolls are too big, who knows what will happen to the taxes. So we are trying to cut the rolls greatly.

Local administrators of work-first programs, like that of East County, now have a vested interest in dealing with chronic recipients. Funding is, after all, limited and increasing durations of recipiency are like financial time bombs, the fuses of which it is in the district's financial interest to extinguish. As one work-first staffer explains, "[we] try not to have any lag-time where people are just waiting [on us]. Work-first realizes that the clock is ticking and [we] don't want any time to be lost due to [us]." This concern over time limits has led to the targeting of supplemental programs to people with special needs. Subprograms have even been developed to assist in the rehabilitation of people with disabilities who would otherwise be exempt from mandatory participation in work activities, but who are not necessarily exempt from time limits. It has also prompted policies that are more stringent. As a welfare caseworker explains, while processing new applicants she now takes extra time to look up their names on the state-wide WMS database and write in the number of months that the person has received benefits in the past. While she could theoretically write in the total for all cases, she explains, she and her co-workers only write them in if the person's total is in the 50s, or more specifically 57 months plus, because their primary concern is with those approaching the 60-month limit. She continues:

> Welfare Caseworker: We put this down and once they reach the 60 months they are switched to Safety Net instead of TANF because Safety Net is not federal, just state and county. So with this they have to wait longer than the average Joe, 45 days instead of 30 and when they see that they are a 60-monther at work-first, they put them through a more rigorous and intense job search.

A work-first counterpart corroborates this, reporting:

> Job Coach: That's something new, we just started doing that maybe about a month or so ago.
> Author: Oh. OK. How come?

Job Coach: Because, so many people are, have been on for five years or so, and we call those people, those people who have been on for over 60 months, and for those people, their contacts have to all be verified. And all those contacts have to be, we have to find out whether they submitted an application or not, because of the length of time that they've been on public assistance so that makes it a little bit tighter on those people.

In this way, intake caseworkers look out for agency interests. A rigorous intake process is one way to discourage caseworkers from opening a case on long termers and those less likely to participate fully. In addition to less forgiving policies, the seriousness of concern over this time-linked funding arrangement is evident in the statewide chart created for monitoring these cases, which meticulously calculates the estimated arrival of current recipients at the 60-month limit.

This monitoring report succeeds in highlighting local concern over the 60-month federal lifetime limit. While keeping track of this information is not required for reporting to the federal government, the necessity for keeping such a record is implicit within the 60-month limit. In the inclusion of all state welfare districts, not only is the proportion of local caseloads that is approaching the limit framed as important, but also, once again, inter-county comparison is facilitated. Thus, via heightened public interest, financially backed performance demands, inter-district competition, and fiscal pressure, administrators are compelled to manage and caseworkers are compelled to perform in the interests of the reform regime.

This reconstructing of welfare implicates clients as much as, if not more than, caseworkers. The enactment of participation requirements is the direct mechanism by which welfare reform has withdrawn the right to nonparticipation in the labor market.[26] As Michael Brown argues, "TANF's fiscal structure undermines any possibility of building a viable work-conditioned safety net: it gives states powerful financial incentives to reduce caseloads and few incentives to reduce concentrated poverty in inner cities."[27] This enacts the portion of the welfare contract that ends "handouts." The replacement "hand-up" however, is not nearly as unwavering, as can be seen in the de-emphasis of client rights despite assuring clients that they will be supported in their efforts to take on greater personal responsibility.

Fair Hearings and the De-Emphasis of Client Rights

Accompanying the de-professionalization and contracting out of welfare implementation-related jobs, the daily tasks of frontline workers are characterized by a reinvigoration of the demand for frontline discretion. As eligibility determination is delegated to state and local levels, frontline workers are given administrative discretion in the processes of both changing client behavior and diverting clients from the system.

Historically, analysts have warned of both benefits and dangers related to discretion among frontline workers in matters such as eligibility determination.[28] Discretion is a vehicle by which caseworkers can use leeway to tailor services to client needs, but it is also a flexible source of reward or punishment, which, from time to time, has enabled caseworkers to be either excessively lenient toward or harsh on clients.

In response to these concerns, the federal government, prior to 1996, took affirmative steps to protect applicants from arbitrary and capricious actions by welfare caseworkers during eligibility determination. The Supreme Court's *Goldberg v. Kelly* (1970), and subsequent refusals to hear related cases, set a precedent for protecting applicants from frontline worker discretion and guaranteed applicants a "statutory entitlement" to AFDC to be protected through fair hearings.[29] When welfare was still a federal entitlement program, this and other rulings *(Shapiro v. Thompson* 1969; *King v. Smith* 1968) firmly established the U.S. Congress as the authority in charge of AFDC eligibility requirements.[30]

Although, prior to the passage of the PRWORA, Congress had begun to share some of this responsibility for establishing eligibility with states through demonstration Workfare and Learnfare projects, it was not until the 1996 welfare reform that a new precedent for local discretion was set. The reform's emphasis on, and indeed encouragement of, local administrative discretion rapidly trickled down from the state to the local level.[31] Not surprisingly, caseworker frontline discretion since the reform, as it is structured by administrative decisions, has also been identified as having a considerable effect on TANF caseload entries and diversion.[32] Far from being arbitrarily encouraged, however, this increase in discretion was introduced in the context of systemic work-first ideological restructuring.

In rhetorical terms, the 1996 welfare reform presents a new contract between the welfare poor and the government—the poor must strive for self-sufficiency and the government will offer a "hand up" rather than a "hand out."[33] However, the 1996 welfare reform is heavy on demanding accountability of the poor to this contract and very light on ensuring that clients themselves can hold the government accountable for its part in the bargain.[34]

The stark contrast between the reform's emphasis on work and de-emphasis of rights is illustrated by the fact that, in the midst of a considerable infrastructure of performance benchmarks for work-first activities, the reform created absolutely no performance standards for fair hearings. While the PRWORA legislation still requires states to implement fair hearings, there are no reporting requirements and no uniformed definitions for data categories.[35] There is prominent discussion and documentation on federal websites and in the pages of county budget reports that monitors participation rates, block grant funding, and caseloads on state and local levels. In contrast, information needed to monitor fair hearing proceedings pre- and post-reform are not even reported to the federal government and are available only in hodgepodge format to those who make specific requests to state bureaucracies. In fact, in New York State, as with many states, no pre-reform data have been publicly preserved which would allow for pre- and post-reform comparisons. Nationally, fair hearing officers in various states publicly debate whether the *Goldberg v. Kelly* Supreme Court decision that established fair hearings will even withstand legal challenges now that welfare is no longer an entitlement program.[36]

As a result of federal disinterest or silence and state uncertainty, we have very little knowledge about fair hearings and the disposition of client appeals in the time period surrounding the 1996 welfare reform. This lack of interest in client rights on the federal level trickles down to the state and local levels as well. Revisiting the data in figure 3.2, the governor has reported that New York State has consistently exceeded the federally mandated participation rates, and in so doing, has managed to avert the potential pitfalls of overextending block grant monies and having excessive numbers of clients exceed the five-year time limit.[37] This achievement finds a striking contrast in figure 3.3, which plots the rise in successful client appeals as a percent of fair hearing rulings that were brought against TANF agencies over the same years as the governor's reported success in reducing caseloads and reaching participation benchmarks.[38] These data reveal an increase in client wins from 73 percent in 1997 to 86 percent in 2001 and a subsequent win rate of 81 percent in 2002, suggesting a ratio of client wins to welfare office wins of 2.8 to 1 in 1997, 6.1 to 1 in 2001, and 4.3 to 1 in 2002.

FIGURE 3.3
Reversals as a percent of Fair Hearing Rulings (Affirmations and Reversals)

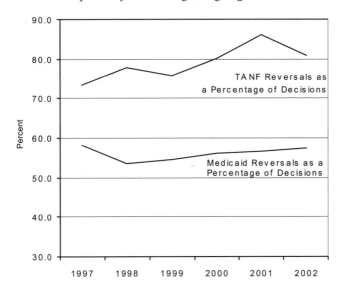

Similarly, less publicized New York State audits report that, as with other states such as Wisconsin, which loses an estimated 69.9 percent of appeals brought against its W-2 agencies, of the appeals that were audited, New York's counties lost roughly 78 percent of the appeals brought against them by clients in the years since the reform.[39] Successful client appeals in work-related hearings range from 53 percent in Texas to 52 percent in Wisconsin to 77 percent in New York.[40] Though some counties, especially outside of New York City, have increased efforts to intercept client complaints before they reach the appeals process, very little if any data are maintained and analyzed that would enable local administrators to fix the problems that cause clients to appeal and to address the underlying rights violations that cause these appeals to be vindicated.[41]

Such a high rate of successful appeals is indicative of a lack of attention to client rights. Also, as a caseworker-turned-hearing officer explains, there is a trade-off on the part of local administrators in which rights are intentionally subverted in favor of meeting performance measures.

[In my new position as a hearing officer], I read *Goldberg v. Kelly* [the Supreme Court case] which set up fair hearings and I learned that I was

being told [back when I was a caseworker] to do things against [clients']
rights. It depends on the attitudes at the top, are we trying to just get
people off welfare [by violating their rights] and for every 10 people that
ask for fair hearings there will be one that won't and [agencies will] get
away with it.

Such a trade-off exposes a Machiavellian approach to case management in
an era of fiscal stress that seeks to capitalize on the likelihood that clients
will be too lackadaisical, ignorant, or otherwise encumbered to effectively
pursue their rights.[42]

It is not only client shortcomings, however, that get in the way of clients seeking to assert their rights. Other factors also hinder the vast majority of clients from ever appealing in the first place. These include: first,
the institutional de-emphasis on welfare rights; second, power differentials between caseworkers and clients; and finally, lack of resources and
support (including textual literacy and legal aid). In contrast to emphasis
on work preparation, clients receive little if any coaching on their rights
within the system.[43] In the 1960s, massive protests and social movements
saturated welfare offices and poor neighborhoods with information, language, and support to ensure that government promises were kept. This
social movement activity has been lacking in the context of the 1996 reform. Rather, welfare rights have been mired in confusion that is partially
due to a lack of clarity about what the reform imperative to seek self-sufficiency through personal responsibility means once translated into the
complexity of bureaucratic processing. Speaking of this experience, a former TANF client explains, "[There's] more frustration in the area of . . .
the process, I call it jumping through the hoops. People are feeling like,
'I've done everything, now what's the problem?'" Another comment from
a welfare rights activist and TANF support group leader reveals that even
clients who want to be in compliance have difficulty understanding what
is expected of them, and as a result, they find their application for aid denied. The group leader explains:

There are continued calls from the community where they feel like they
are meeting the requirements of the work-first program, but when the
program finishes calculating and going over what their requirements
are, the way they perceive they should administer this, the clients are
coming up where they're denied. We've been having a lot of denials
coming in.

The complexity of increased local discretion in welfare administration and a need to balance budgetary concerns contributes to a lack of clarity over rights and responsibilities in the new welfare contract.[44] Promises made by welfare agencies to clients are constantly changing according to county needs.[45] One example of this is the extent of support that poor families can expect as they seek self-sufficiency through work:

> Hearing Officer: The counties are hurting. Like with the 1996 welfare reform the push was to get people into work so they increased childcare assistance for people up to 200 percent of the poverty level. Counties are now cutting; one is down to 140 percent and another 130 percent because of budget issues.

In addition to confusion over rights and responsibilities, due in part to the replacement of entitlements with sporadic supports, the increased local discretion brought about by the reform has enhanced the power differential that caseworkers have historically held over clients.[46] Staff members, by virtue of their street-level position within the welfare-state structure, exercise the power of discretion. Welfare policy manifests itself, ultimately, in the specific ways that these individuals implement it on a daily basis.[47] As one worker explains, "This is a powerful position; you have power over people, their lives, their livelihood." From the perspective of clients, the outcome in East County is not a "user-friendly" one. Applicants see workers as condescending, scrutinizing, and unsympathetic to critiques of low wage working life. In the words of one client, "How are people greeted at the welfare office? There are times when they are rude, obnoxious, condescending, treating people like they are less than them because they are there for need." A support group leader commented, "People call in tears because of the way they were treated." Another explains, "You know, you have to work with people, it's not like you're the judge and the jury, and that's how they act."

The discretionary power that allows caseworkers to wield these prerogatives also shields them from retaliation. Complaints from applicants must be in writing if TANF administrators are to take action, yet individual applicants are wary about making such a formal report. One former applicant explains:

> Folks are not willing to [put a complaint in writing]. They're afraid of repercussions from the worker in the form of well maybe losing paperwork or not entering the information in the computer in a timely manner, which will result in them not being able to access the benefits.

As a result, very few clients file an appeal.[48]

Finally, those clients who do file an appeal face yet another set of barriers due to a lack of resources. Many do not have the technical literacy needed to challenge the evidence brought to bear by county officials. As Sarat has documented, fair hearings are a site of power and resistance. They are a "foreign terrain of the lawyer's office" in which "the welfare poor seem very conscious of the fact that neither here nor in their dealings with the welfare bureaucracy are they able to find a 'place that can be delineated as their own and serve as a base from which relations of exteriority can be managed.'"[49] In such an environment, it is difficult to navigate if one lacks legal aid resources, and in New York State an estimated fewer than 10 percent of fair hearing appellants have legal aid representation.[50] This is due in part to a shortage of legal aid resources and a lack of awareness about these resources. As one appellant remarked at the conclusion of a hearing, when it was mentioned that she could have enlisted the help of a legal aid attorney, "If I had known I could have a legal aid representative, I would have done that first."

The fair hearing process in general is a confusing and disorienting one, regardless of whether one is appealing TANF, Food Stamps, Medicaid, or another program, and regardless of whether or not legal aid is present, though legal aid does seem to make a notable impact. Hearings are extremely rule-bound and follow a set legal protocol that can become a barrier to appellants as they attempt to state their claims. One appellant expressed frustration, making the following clarification during her hearing: "I don't even know what I am allowed to ask here, due to the way you present yourself." According to hearing officers, this disorientation is quite common. One officer explains, "Often times appellants keep interrupting and I have to ask them to wait over and over." Even with attempts to make the proceedings more accessible, such as one hearing officer's directive to a county representative to "Please explain in language she will understand," the content of hearings is complex and confusing. This is largely because hearings are grounded in complex rules and regulations rather than appellants' real-life concerns. In the words of a hearing officer to an exasperated appellant, "You can only have a hearing on the things in the regulations." Another hearing officer explains:

> Hearing Officer: I understand they are issues that caused a lot of problems, but I cannot address them.
> Appellant: Why not?
> Hearing Officer: Because it's not in the regulations. I won't.

While staying within the parameters of the regulations may seem straightforward enough to state and county representatives, the situation is rarely so simple for clients who have a great deal at stake and only marginal understanding of complex institutional rules. To the extent that clients are unable to make their voice fit within the institutional language of regulations, they and their concerns are silenced. As I will explore in the following chapters, the language of both fair hearings and the wider welfare institution emphasizes some aspects of clients' lives and de-emphasizes others. It is a language that translates broader institutional concerns to the local level. In so doing, it shifts the risks of the global economy, and policy adaptation and enforcement, to the county and individual client level. Thus, the policy contradictions and assumptions that state and federal actors ought to address are shifted to local actors. In the words of a state hearing officer who mediates the resulting disputes between counties and clients, "There is a lot of conflict [here]. Here they're in conflict, but with each other, not me."

Conclusion

The welfare reform created a situation in which "states now had tremendous incentive to remove people from the rolls and little oversight to prevent them from doing it by any means necessary."[51] In this chapter, I have examined how the sentiment behind this broad statement becomes concrete in the restructuring of the welfare state according to principles of accountability. This restructuring, however, has created new forms of worker vulnerability as well. Not only are new social service positions created within a framework of de-skilling and deprofessionalization, but they are also set within a context of rising contingent work. Recent research by Barley and Kunda asserts that contingent work does not necessarily equal low-skilled work, but there are two tiers of contingent work such that some high-end workers find contract work suited to their needs and preferences.[52] These workers are often located in technical fields and serve as "independent contractors" or "temporary professionals" who work under contract for employers as needed. The contingent labor constructed for work-first caseworkers appears to be of this sort and differs in marked ways from the contingent labor that many clients will engage in. They often cycle through menial and temp positions that require less skill, pay low wages, are episodic in nature, have little chance for advancement, and offer few or no benefits. Though the work of these two groups is characteristically different, the PRWORA has nonetheless had a parallel impact in eroding worker protections for both groups. In the case of welfare employees, this comes in the form of nonunion, contract status. Clients find they are no longer entitled to a safety net, and there is no longer comprehensive oversight of the promises that have replaced it. Both forms of erosion are related to an outsourcing or downloading of risk.

Both accountability and vulnerability are hallmarks of a neoliberal reconstruction of the Keynesian welfare state. Where the Keynesian state relied on federal leverage to weather economic risk en masse, the neoliberal "work-first" welfare state decentralizes and downloads economic risks of the global economy to states, agencies, individual workers and, eventually, welfare recipients.[53] This is evident in the delegation of administrative responsibilities and financial burdens to local counties. The de-emphasis on guaranteed rights alerts individuals to their need to fend for themselves. The hiring of caseworkers on a temporary basis and outside of civil service and union protections normalizes contingent employment. The performance measures imposed on local managers foster local competition, both economically and in terms of policy performance. In this context, the reorganization of the welfare workplace and the de-prioritization of government guarantees engender the inter-scalar relations by which actors on the local scale are brought into sync with neoliberal interests on the extra-local scale of the global economy.

4

New Technology
and New Customers

The 1996 welfare reform act has been regarded as perhaps "the first large-scale 'information age' social policy in the United States."[1] The federal government expects and demands that local work-first offices develop the information technology (IT) necessary to collate and pass on performance reports. By the same token, local administrators find themselves in need of a steady flow of information in order to monitor their progress and to ensure that the links they have made with collaborating agencies are functioning as planned. The role of IT in reinforcing work-first goals, however, extends beyond the passive recording of performance measure data; it serves to structure and to frame the thinking of caseworkers. This chapter explores how work-first IT is an active force in the construction of a common sense that sees employers as the logical customers of work-first. I argue that this corporate-centered approach to welfare is built into the paperwork, forms, computer interfaces, and data that give structure to caseworker decisions. As such, the daily work of monitoring client motivation and ability to work becomes complicit with a politically neoliberal approach to poverty. It fosters low-wage worker attitudes among poor families that are conducive to employers and the extra-local interests of the national pro-business lobby. In effect, daily casework begins from the point of reference of neoliberal work-first common sense to the extent that caseworkers rely on IT and comply with its prescribed uses.

An Information Age Social Policy

TANF has combined many of the record-keeping requirements of its predecessor program's income maintenance focus with a host of new work-first surveillance needs. As a result, states and localities, such as East County, have had to scramble to re-assess and expand their information

technology capabilities. This has not been undaunting. Shari, a TANF intake worker with 15 years under her belt, has worked in her office since
before the 1996 reform, when the cases they processed were AFDC. An art
major in college who found herself sidetracked into the human services,
Shari retains an eye for aesthetics. She explains that many of the old state
data systems are archaic, ugly, and are supposedly in the process of being
redesigned. But the reporting needs of the reform won't wait and local
agencies have had to develop their own internal databases and record-
keeping mechanisms to make sure that accurate information is kept. They
need to track not only error rate-related data regarding eligibility determination as was stressed under AFDC, but also client progress through
work-first processing, participation in required activities, compliance with
work-oriented policies and time limits.[2] With this increased complexity
has come a heightened dependence on information technology. In the
midst of a system crash, she explains:

> When the computer is down, we're shut down. We can't do anything. We
> make a quick call to have them fix it. We can't do anything till it's back
> up again.

Shari's comments not only underscore the vital importance of information
communication systems in the post-welfare reform age; they also identify
IT as crucial to understanding the construction and maintenance of common sense in processing decisions at the welfare office.

With the 1996 PRWORA, case management across the nation was
forced to change to incorporate work-first goals. With any such change,
new points of institutional emphasis emerge and others fade. The case
management system that has come about in East County is one of several possible alternatives adapted nationally to address work-first requirements. Nevertheless, it is indicative of new case management priorities
that are consistent with the broader neoliberalization of the public safety
net. In reinventing welfare, the neoliberal agenda de-emphasizes structural bases for inequality and instead focuses attention on the individual.
The individualized theme of "personal responsibility" has emerged as an
increasingly acceptable value in debates on such welfare components as
personal retirement accounts to replace social security and individualized
medical savings accounts to replace Medicare.[3] The common thread is a
championing of the free market and a loss of focus on, or even denial of,
the potential exploitativeness of the market.

This chapter begins with an overview of changing work-first technology and case management priorities. It then examines how caseworkers routinely deploy this technology to scrutinize clients with regard to motivation and ability to work. I contrast this adversarial stance toward "clients" with work-first's embrace of employers as "customers." I examine how local aspects of technology are molded to cater to employers through inculcating them as gatekeepers. In essence, case management technology is structured less around "creating jobs for people who don't have them" and more around socializing "workers for jobs that nobody wants."[4]

Technology and New Organizational Priorities

Technology, defined in scholarly literature as "the process whereby organizational inputs are transformed into outputs through the application of tools, techniques, and actions," has been characterized in the human services as being "inherently indeterminate and ambiguous" largely because, unlike manufacturing organizations, the raw materials (namely clients) vary, and the outputs are more difficult to enumerate.[5] Nevertheless, the "tools, techniques, and actions" that human service technologies employ in their typical work of "processing people or changing people" have been known to function in accordance with underlying institutional imperatives.[6] With the 1996 welfare reform, the mission of the welfare state shifted away from focusing on eliminating poverty and toward functioning as a labor market intermediary. As with other labor market intermediaries—temp agencies, job training programs, labor market exchanges, and employment services—work-first attempts to regulate or moderate connections between potential employees and employers; here specifically by mandating that all welfare clients prepare for and attempt to work in any job offered to them and by encouraging employers to hire clients.

Enforcing this mandate requires significant modifications of welfare's safety net function. The new priorities of the welfare institution as a labor force intermediary are evident in the emerging technology of work-first that has developed to coexist along side pre-reform technologies. Though caseworkers in both the welfare and work-first office share data on a daily basis, they work in very different contexts. Their database systems both keep track of clients, but they are a contrast in material technology and the focus of this technology.

The welfare office WMS—welfare management system—database system has existed for many years and is set on a black screen with digital-looking orange lettering, reminiscent of the rudimentary graphics of "pong" and other first-generation computer/video games. It is constructed on a hierarchical database model which relies on preconceived categories and subcategories that are inflexible, though able to handle large, statewide information traffic patterns. The current Windows-based drop-down menu database of the work-first office presents the starkest of visual contrasts with what caseworkers call the "antiquated" WMS. Able to support all the fonts and coloring of desktop computers, this database is adorned with photos of individuals "working" in various fields and theme-appropriate clip art. As caseworkers explain, this system is so new that "they are still working out the bugs," and it is thus susceptible to nearly weekly system "shutdowns" and/or crashes. Despite the inconvenience of growing pains, there is also considerable excitement about the organic nature of this locally created data management system. Because it does not need to handle the volume of the state WMS system, the local work-first database system is not bound to state-determined reporting categories and functions, although the lineaments of these are certainly present and heavily influence the data collected. Beyond this, however, it is capable of incorporating new questions and retrieval strategies as the need arises—evidenced by the flurry of macro programs written at the request of caseworker teams with differing interests in order to "query" the growing data repository. On-site database programmers are employed full time learning new strategies and creating automated push-button report-creating codes with such descriptive names as: "what are my jobseekers' current activities," "job skills data entry status," "employment history," "people waiting to be scheduled for an orientation," and "daily changes in employability code."

The databases of the welfare office and work-first office are different not only in appearance and structure, but also in function. The welfare database has incorporated basic post-reform fields such as records on sanctioning, but for the most part it handles the pre-reform task of managing information on eligibility and need. Fueled by a series of paperwork documenting rent, heating, income, assets, and other means-tested criteria, the central capability of the welfare office data system is managing documentation of need and calculating an appropriate amount of public assistance. In contrast to this eligibility and budgeting function, the work-first data system performs the task of managing data on compliance and job readiness. Fed by paperwork such as attendance sheets and faxes, forms from employers and job search verification phone calls, the work-first database structure is built to serve the function of recording compliance or lack thereof. Reflected in the computerized forms that a job coach fills out, this monitoring function is often as simple as binary records of whether a client complies or not.

> Job Coach: Then by their name [we] mark one of three options, incomplete, failed to report, or showed and fulfilled requirements.

Applicants can act in only so many ways according to the workplace technology displayed on this networked computer screen, one of many like it. Furthermore, each scenario has been thought out beforehand and has its own prescribed responses for caseworkers. Another job coach describes a similar relationship and the contingencies that are paired with each client action in his site of processing. He explains under which conditions he would mark the various categories on his computer screen—a clear example of how technology used for screening clients is also related to diversion.

> Job Coach: [1] They could not show up [and be denied].
> [2] They could show up and have an incomplete job search, which in that case we would take the job search from them and tell them to go back and re-apply because their case is going to be denied.
> [3] They could hand in a complete job search where we'd verify their job search contacts to make sure they had handed in applications. If those come back negative, then the following week, when they come back in and show up, we tell them, "Your job contacts are 'bogus' and we sent you over as not complying."
> [4] The [fourth] thing would be someone could have come through the three or four weeks that they are normally required to do, and their case opened up, which in that case we schedule them for the next phase of work-first activities. . . or
> [5] [He explains in a more positive tone] a person could come in and say they got a job!

As this coach describes the contingencies, it becomes evident that finding a job is framed as the one clearly successful outcome of processing. It is also clear that clients can be denied aid via multiple technology-reliant pathways that are only hinted at here, such as attendance records and job search verification information pathways. Three of the five options involve screening out clients who are seen as insufficiently motivated to work and furthermore not likely to be "good" employees. Through such mechanisms, work-first technology allows caseworkers to systematically purge those who do not show up, have incomplete paperwork or have not fully completed required job search activities, or have submitted job search paperwork that surveillance networks have identified as falsified.

Though clearly functioning with different priorities than the welfare office computer system, the two databases are far more collaborative than competitive. This is evident in the following example of recording client compliance in the work-first office and digitally transferring this information to the welfare office. The institution-wide integration of work-first technology assists not only in monitoring clients, but also in linking collaborating agencies as members of the same team.

> Job Coach: Now if they don't show [to work-first orientation] we put down "No Show" and under final outcome we put down "other," since we don't know why they didn't show up today. For the "final outcome" we put down today's date and this closes their screen and so the information goes back to the welfare office and the person gets mailed a letter [by the welfare office] saying they didn't show up and this is what they have to do, re-apply all over again.

In this way the collaboration between old and new technologies link collaborative agencies and monitor clients—the two central needs of work-first.[7]

Though it is informative to analyze various database tools in East County, perhaps it is more important to study the patterns by which caseworkers deploy the hardware. Some locations may not have invested in such expensive hardware, and indeed we know that, even given the same policy objectives, human service agencies will often go about things in different ways; "devolution of programmatic authority, limited scientific knowledge of program efficacy, and unavoidable discretion of frontline workers creates variation in the technologies employed by human service organizations, even when they are charged with carrying out the same public policy."[8] To understand the role of technology within work-first philosophy, the remainder of this chapter will concentrate on the ways in which caseworkers think about and use technology to affect work-first case management. This is particularly important given the ability of technology to outlast the original intents of its creators:

In human service organizations, technology is crafted from daily experiences and shared beliefs that staff develop about clients' abilities and needs. As other scholars have noted, this is a moral task that involves exertion of power (Handler, 1992; Hasenfeld, 1992). Yet once established, the service technology assumes larger proportions. It actually creates structures that direct staff actions, reinforces their beliefs, and shapes their interpretations. It defines what is rational and socially acceptable within that organization.[9]

In East County, such technology organizes common sense and the actions that derive from it. Most prominently, it fosters a radical shift from focusing on poor families as welfare's major constituency to an emphasis on employers as customers of the program.

Employers as Work-First Customers

Though never officially calling employers the new customers of welfare reform, work-first's focus on immediate employment for TANF clients has led to a broader recognition among caseworkers that this involves catering to those who hire their clients. This aspect of the reform dynamic has not been lost on employers, who have also come to see themselves as beneficiaries of the work-first welfare system. In the words of the U.S. Chamber of Commerce, "Changes to the law should continue to focus on workforce development and productive employment for welfare recipients and include . . . [r]ecognition given to the role of employers as *customers* of the program."[10]

As the chamber further explains, it sees work-first as an ally in the quest to secure workers in the forecasted "tight labor markets" to come.

> By 2010 the labor force will fall short of meeting the demands of an estimated 58 million job openings by more than 4.8 million workers. In addition, over the next 15 years 40 million workers will be retiring. Employers are faced with the challenges of future tight labor markets and increasing demands for higher skill levels. The key to business success is hiring and retaining qualified workers. The question is however, where will employers find these workers?[11]

Though the 1996 reform was heavily work-oriented, it was not as much so as its business-minded advocates had hoped; caseload reduction credits, which reduced the number of clients that states must transition to the labor force by the number of clients removed from the rolls, meant that only 34 percent rather than the benchmark rate of 50 percent of adult TANF recipients were actually working as of 2002.[12] The 2006 reauthorizing legislation addressed this problem, and in the process appeased its new customer base, by re-setting the caseload reduction credit at 2005 caseload levels, applying local pressure to bring participation up to 50 percent or to even further reduce caseloads within a year. This promise of still more low-wage workers has met with the approval of business interests, as evident in the U.S. Chamber of Commerce's official position on TANF reauthorization:

> We supported the restructuring of the welfare system in 1996. A key element of that support was that the welfare system help recipients transition into work, not serve as an ongoing support system. The restructured work-first program has successfully opened a new source of workers for employers. . . . Reauthorization of the welfare reform act should build upon the positive impacts of the 1996 law.

Business approval of welfare reform is not surprising. Through recruiting and monitoring workers for employers, work-first welfare essentially functions as a state-subsidized temp or screening agency to produce compliant and sorted applicants for low-wage jobs.[13] Assisting with work-first attempts to reach out to the larger business community are not only links on the work-first website to "outsourcing" firms and "temp agencies," but also a specific portal dedicated to employers which promises that:

> Our professional Job Developers will pre-screen candidates according to your company's specifications. [We] can also provide on-site facilities for job interviews.

Furthermore, the website informs:

> Work-first invites employers to conduct job interviews on site. Many local employers have taken advantage of this service. If you are an employer seeking to expand your workforce, we would be able to pre-screen candidates and set up an interview schedule convenient for you.

Though employers are clearly beneficiaries, they are not the only ones who see this state-business partnership as positive. Among caseworkers, collaboration is justified as a means toward ending dependency and promoting personal responsibility by asking community members to pitch in to help. As one East County administrator explained in a public interview, the perspective of work-first involves seeing welfare dependency as a problem not just for government officials but also for local businesses. "I really think welfare is not just a government problem. . . . It's an issue the community, businesses, and employers must address together." Far from re-casting employer involvement as charity, however, she is quick to clarify, "We're not asking any business to take someone on who isn't going to meet their expectations. That's not the purpose of [work-first]. We're working to place people at real jobs where they can do meaningful work." In this way caseworkers come to see encouraging employers to use their services as being in the interests of both employers and the state.

As evident in newspaper clippings and press releases, the overtures made by East County welfare administrators have been met with pleased employers. One news article reports:

> The personnel coordinator at [Heroy] Corporation says there are definite benefits from working through [work-first]. She emphasizes that the service is completely free to the company. Also, the program already has qualified candidates listed. By working with [work-first], [Heroy] can quickly find an employee for a clerical position that previously might have taken a month or longer to fill.

In the enthusiastic words of Heroy's personnel coordinator:

> In our experience, no extra training is required. These [people] are very motivated. They want to get right back into work.

A local representative of Manpower, the nation's largest temp agency, also had positive things to say about East County's work-first program from an employer's perspective.

> Manpower has had a great relationship with [work-first]. . . They've been able to make the requirements of whom they recommend to us more strict and they're very good at pre-screening for certain types of skills.

TABLE 4.1
Summary of Types of Jobs Obtained by Welfare Clients
Between January 1, 1985 and November 30, 2000 (n=5978)

Occupational Category	Percent of Clients in This Occupation	Percent of Those Obtaining These Jobs that Are Women	Average Hourly Wage	Standard Deviation of Hourly Wage	Average Weekly Hours Worked	Standard Deviation of Weekly Hours	Average Annual Salary Based on 50 Weeks Worked
Clerical	9	95	6.79	1.56	32	9	$10,880
Construction	1	11	7.05	1.43	37	5	$12,981
Critical Care Tech.	0	0	8.11	0.00	23	0	$9,124
Education	1	90	6.19	2.19	30	10	$9,394
Food Service	15	80	5.56	0.82	28	9	$7,790
General Laborer	11	47	6.05	1.14	33	9	$9,859
Health	0	100	5.15	0.00	35	0	$9,013
Healthcare	9	94	7.22	1.68	31	9	$11,105
Laborer	0	100	5.15	0.00	40	0	$10,300
Maintenance	9	73	5.75	0.94	30	10	$8,653
Managerial	1	72	7.16	2.32	33	8	$11,892
Manufacturing	10	67	6.12	1.24	38	6	$11,534
Misc.	5	60	6.02	1.78	31	9	$9,408
Retail	17	88	5.56	0.77	27	9	$7,603
Security	1	48	5.53	0.69	33	9	$9,062
Services	8	81	5.85	1.34	29	10	$8,577
Technical	1	51	7.83	3.21	35	9	$13,828
Woodworkers	0	0	7.56	0.00	40	0	$15,120
Grand Total	100	76	6.07	1.41	31	9	$9,347

Source: Agency records compiled by the author.

Manpower has hired work-first referrals to be receptionists, administrative assistants, and technicians as well as to do data-entry and some industrial and electronic-assembly work. These jobs are generally consistent with the type of jobs that East County's clients have ended up in.

Among all East County welfare clients who found jobs between January 1995 and November 2000, 58 percent were in the service sector (including clerical, food service, healthcare, retail and general services) and 10 percent were in manufacturing. Nationally, approximately 46.2 percent of welfare leavers have been concentrated in the service sector and another 14.0 percent in manufacturing, almost all of them at near poverty wages.[14] The average hourly wage for those who found employment through work-first in East County was $6.07, producing an average annual salary of merely $9,347 based on 50 weeks of work and an average of 31 hours worked weekly. This is well below the poverty line for any family with more than one individual—but such low wage conditions are highly favorable to businesses. Coordinated with the reform's promise of workers, the low wage economy generated a 40 percent job growth figure nationally in the two years immediately following the reform (1996–1998).[15] Nationally, as a result of reform-related policies, an estimated one to two million low wage workers will enter the workforce between the years 1993 and 2008.[16]

In addition to providing prescreened and motivated workers for low wage jobs, East County work-first, consistent with national trends, has also offered to subsidize low wage work directly by offering to underwrite the costs to employers of hiring clients who successfully make it through the intake process and are now on the welfare rolls.[17] Similar programs exist in New Jersey, Georgia, Mississippi, Salt Lake City, Baltimore, and New York City.[18] Through such programs some of the biggest companies in the nation have become involved as corporate sponsors of welfare, including Bell Atlantic, Federal Express, United Parcel Services, National Telecommunications, and Marriott.[19] An online brochure in East County explains:

> [Work-first] offers a great incentive to employers who would like to take a chance on hiring someone with potential but who may have limited skills. On-the-Job Training is one of the best ways to assist recipients of temporary assistance who need training to transition off the welfare system.
>
> In exchange for hiring one of our participants, East County can help by paying up to 50 percent of his or her gross wages for up to six months. We find that this arrangement offers an easy transition to the work place with limited risk on the part of the employer.

Another alternative for employers is to volunteer to serve as a work experience site where work-first clients will labor for free as part of their job training. A local hospital, having taken up this offer, explains how they have found it mutually beneficial:

> The [work-first clients] the hospital accepts are in effect assigned a work site (at Grant Hospital) in exchange for continuing the public assistance they're already receiving. The individuals get valuable on-the-job training. Some graduates go on to other jobs, some stay with the hospital, and others decide they will return to school. One volunteer has decided to enter an LPN program in the fall.

Through such arrangements, "welfare now functions as a temporary subsidy to businesses and consumers, in the form of unemployment insurance for temporary workers and wage supplements for low-paid labor."[20] A hospital representative continues:

> To our benefit . . . a [work-first client] is with us three to five days a week. Volunteers not from [work-first] may only work half a day. The continuity in the workplace we get with [work-first clients] is important to the hospital and it's important to the volunteers. They get more training.

This rosy picture, as we are reminded by a caseworker, is built upon a foundation of coercion, "[when you are] on TANF and if you don't do what or go where you are assigned, you can be sanctioned . . . You do, however, always have a chance to explain yourself in front of the judge."[21] In contrast to the courting of employers, caseworker relationships with clients are considerably more adversarial. Caseworker relationships with clients are furthermore built upon emergent work-first technologies that are based on the premise of serving employers as customers. In East County, such technology organizes and empowers caseworkers to investigate applicants to screen out those who are unmotivated and unable to work.

Surveillance of Motivation to Work

Case management has for some time included activities such as intake, assessment, monitoring and case closure. Now these activities are focused as tools of screening clients according to standards of motivation and ability to work.[22] One caseworker explains, "Of those who come to work-first, some really want to work . . . [and] some are just going through the motions." Sorting the two is a central function of the work-first system. Not only do employers seek motivated workers, but welfare reform's emphasis on personal responsibility now presents those motivated to work as the only ones truly deserving of aid. Accordingly, caseworkers of the work-first system have developed and deployed case management technologies that enable them to differentiate among clients.

> I won't know [what to do with them] when they walk in but when I go in their file and see the number here [indicating how many weeks of job searching they have completed], . . . [I look at] information on the WMS [the statewide database system], and their job search contact forms

[including carbon copies from verified job searches and their attendance record computer printout] . . . then I know what to do with them.

Information gleaned from their computer screens guides caseworkers in their initial meeting with clients. Personal discretion is still relied upon, though it is heavily circumscribed by technology. Another caseworker explains her judgment of client motivation.

So, basically, from that information that we get from these sheets, and, like I said, just the impression of the person that we get, we can usually tell.

Her "impression of the person" indicates a substantial element of discretion blended with information provided by IT. As another explains, technology provides access to the clues or cues that "give a person away":

So it depends on the information that's on the sheet. It depends on what we're picking up from the person, you know? I mean I can't honestly say that I'm a perfect judge of character, or anything like that, but there are certain things that give a person away.

These "things" or clues may come from the computer more than from the live client sitting there. Offering an example of one such clue, a caseworker conducts a database search for the name of a woman who just handed in an application:

Caseworker: [reading from screen] Denied, see case narrative. [Reading Case Narrative] No show. Work-first, the third time. See? She doesn't want to go through work-first.

Although the database does not actually say that she "doesn't want to go," this caseworker is accustomed to reading between the lines of case records to determine what meaning they hold for screening clients. By relying on this textual narrative of the past, she makes an assessment and then conveys to me what this implies about her that can also be verified thanks to technology.

Caseworker: She doesn't want to go to work-first. I wouldn't doubt it if you look up her case and you see she's got 61 months! [This would mean that she has been on and knows the system and has exhausted her lifetime limit.] . . . [looks up the woman's case in another database query] Look here! Her record goes back to 1989.

This hardly visible mental work of spotting such patterns is made possible by a linking of welfare and work-first office databases through a complex matrix of records, referrals, and outcomes. Having such information at one's fingertips allows a caseworker a certain degree of confidence in determining whether or not a client is sufficiently motivated to work—since, "if they don't show up to work-first, they don't really want to work."

> Author: So what can you tell from this person's records going back to 1989?
> Caseworker: Well it's just a flag to say she's not a newcomer . . . More than likely they don't have files that go back to 1989, but they may combine older files with the newer ones and ask, "Why is she here again?" A lot of these people have patterns . . . looking at their history. Work-first is concerned because they want her to be able to work.

Though many work-first reporting mechanisms are computerized and networked and are interfaced daily with welfare office databases, not all work-first technologies aimed at determining work motivation make use of such advanced hardware. A simple fax can be just as effective in weeding out those who don't show up to orientation sessions, and are thus considered unmotivated. One such example is the faxing of attendance records back and forth between welfare orientation, work-first orientation, and TANF caseworkers. The welfare orientation worker begins with the blank sign-in sheet that originates in her office.

> Welfare Orientation Worker: With this [sign-in] form, it is easy now to fax the names over to work-first. It also has a column for sign-ins over at work-first, or for "No Show" to be written in place of the signature. After orientation, this sign-in form is faxed back to us and the TANF worker appointments next to the "No Show" names are now cleared and opened up for other people since the appointment is automatically cancelled with a no-show.

Failure to show up is perceived as a fairly straightforward indicator of lack of motivation: "Hey, if you can't bother to show up for some free money, well that's too bad for you." Absences could also be due to the illness of children or a bus that did not show up, but these are the responsibility of the client.

In other instances, however, caseworkers ascertain lack of motivation by using cues other than a simple "no show." Textual records are central to such caseworker assessment of client deservingness.

> Caseworker: They have to fill this out. . . . it gets done in orientation with the TA and again you can see this person cared. And you can tell because . . . she filled it out. You know she's looking for work, she filled it out. A lot of people don't even fill this out . . . At least if she didn't find a job you could say, "Well, she was serious because she did all the stuff she was required to do and she filled it all completely in."

As another job coach explains, the routine scrutiny of agency forms submitted by clients provides clues as to when something about a client seems "wrong."

> Caseworker: Usually, based on the information that's on the sheet. O.K. now if this information was written in with three different colored pens, something's wrong. Or if all the dates were on a Sunday, something's wrong. You know what I'm saying?

Suspicious behavior is a clue that a person may not be motivated to find a job. For instance, she explains:

> Caseworker: If their contacts . . . have not been done properly . . . And that's one of the reasons why everything has to be completed because, usually if you're interested in a job, you need to know the phone number and the address, so that you can follow up on it. If you don't have that information, then it doesn't really appear that you really want that job.

From this textual work, caseworkers are not seeking to ascertain whether or not clients have access to a phone. Rather, their intent is to assess what type of person an applicant is. A caseworker explains this.

> Caseworker: For some people, that's [collecting welfare] a way of life. That's all they know, that's all they've ever done. Some just want a little help. Some don't want to work, you can tell them. The ones that want to work, they get a job and sometimes just want Medicaid or need extra money.

> Some just go through the motions, put down applications right out of the phone book.

This coach's comments imply that she sees her work as bringing her into contact with different types of people, including, at a minimum, ones who want to work and ones who do not. She also implies that, using her own judgment, and the technology in front of her, she can make a quick determination between the two types. She is not alone in this. Assessing clients' motivation to work is a central function of work-first technology. It is fundamentally linked with assessing ability to work.

Surveillance of Ability to Work

Having identified clients who are motivated to work, caseworkers must then be sure that the clients are truly able to work. Various means are used to determine the ability to work, and malingers are often exposed. The following orientation statement implies clients must be ready to work. If they say they are not, they will need to take further steps to address their inability.

> If you feel you can't comply with anything here . . . you can meet with a specialist and you will have to prove it.

Work-first is committed to moving as many clients as possible into the labor market; at the same time, however, it has a reputation to maintain among its employer customer base. It promises employers, "We're not asking any business to take someone on who isn't going to meet their expectations. That's not the purpose of [work-first]. We're working to place people at real jobs where they can do meaningful work." Admittedly, a considerable number of clients carry baggage, or in the words of caseworkers, have iceberg issues, i.e., unacceptable behavior that is just the tip of a larger iceberg of issues. These issues would likely keep them from meeting the expectations of employers. Chief among these are limitations related to physical disability (including pregnancy), drug and alcohol abuse, domestic violence, and mental illness. Given the problems these issues can create for employers, it is not simply the clients that caseworkers are looking out for. Since work-first promises to screen their clients for employers, the responsibility to sort out those who cannot work falls to East County's caseworkers and the technologies they have established.

This process commences with the use of paperwork technology, through which applicants begin by pre-sorting themselves. This is seen in the following field note excerpt:

> Sandy distributes a required form: "This form is being used to determine if you're going to work-first or the Hospital, etc." (Applicants claiming a disability preventing them from working are sent to the hospital for evaluation. The paperwork completed by the physician then determines what level of workforce engagement is appropriate.) The applicants must then indicate the employability status for each person in the household. The listed statuses include "employed," "able to work," "disabled," "enrolled in high school full time," and "due date if pregnant." For those family members who are employed, the applicant must fill in employer information, rate of pay, and number of hours worked per week.

With the assistance of this form, those who claim they can work are sent directly to work-first. Those who indicate a reason that they are in some way inhibited from working are given a medical appointment form and referred to one of a list of collaborating physicians and health professionals. Simply asserting disability is not good enough, as the following applicant finds out.

> Applicant: I'm disabled, waiting [for disability pay]. I don't want to waste the county's money. They [doctors] get paid $100 per hour.
> Interviewer: Oh, you asked? [She quips, a bit tongue in cheek.]
> Applicant: No, but. . . . Well [She flounders a bit.]
> Interviewer: O.K. I'll send you to the Medical Examiners . . . I think they get a flat rate anyway.

As is evident in such exchanges, the referral infrastructure of work-first allows caseworkers to maintain a suspicion of low motivation to work and essentially outsource the potentially challenging task of determining work ability. Clients receive forms stating the following to bring with them to the medical examiners' office and to complete in order to grant consent to the sharing of medical information with the welfare office:

> _____Name_____ has indicated to the Department of Social Services that they may have a medical, drug & alcohol or mental health limitation. In order for us to make a determination of eligibility for temporary assistance

the following appointment must be kept . . . I, the undersigned, give my permission to the [county-contracted] Hospital and/or my personal treatment provider to release medical and/or psychiatric information in their possession to the East County Department of Social Services.

Through such mechanisms, work-first enlists the assistance of a network of county-contracted physicians, mental health and substance abuse professionals. It activates the professionalism and technologies of the health professions to determine work ability.

When you go to your doctor appointment, bring any papers you have with you. This doctor doesn't know you. It's not a full physical exam but more of an oral exam, but he will decide whether you are able to work or not, so bring prescriptions, etc.

As this caseworker explains to clients, several kinds of input will be used to screen them; the report of the health professional they visit, and also the broader network of providers who have already given them prescriptions and diagnoses.

Caseworker: When you go to your exam at County Hospital it is like a 5-10 minute oral exam so you must be under a doctor's care and have the paperwork showing you are disabled.
Applicant: But I am in physical therapy and will be in it for 6 weeks longer.
Caseworker: You're not able to work?
Applicant: No, not now.
Caseworker: Do you have paperwork verifying this?
Applicant: Yes.
Caseworker: OK, then you can mark disabled and bring these papers with you when you go to see our physician who will decide whether you are able to work or not.

Since county physicians, like other work-first caseworkers, only see clients for a few minutes, it is clear that their contribution to surveillance is based on a form of meta-surveillance of the work done by other physicians—essentially their 5-10 minute interviews involve reviewing the work of their colleagues. Thus, not only are clients under scrutiny, but so are other physicians, who may be persuaded by clients to exaggerate disability. One caseworker explains the reasoning behind this double check: "These doctors, I'm not sure if they're intimidated by clients or what, but they're not doing their jobs. . . . Work-first is concerned because they want these people to work." Another caseworker explains:

> A lot of these people are lying, they don't want to participate in the [work-first] program and it's supposed to be mandatory . . . like this lady says she has depression . . . [this one] she's claiming she's disabled.

In essence, it is the role of surveillance technology to determine the difference between "those trying to get by and those who are legit."

Such concerns are evident in the following case narrative:

> TANF Worker: So then, after the form verification, I write up the narrative . . . So I write down who is applying, where they live, where they last lived. Look here. I wrote down that she lost her job because of poor attendance and in parentheses, I wrote, "Had been warned," so that's important to the case. Then look. She had been receiving unemployment for two to three months, and then it looks like they found out that she lost the job because of her own fault and they stopped the payments. Then look. I said, "Sent to Medical Examiners and found to have no Drug and Alcohol Problem." So I sent her to work-first, and then her seventeen-year-old son moved back in with her from living with a foster family out of state and, since he wasn't going to school, I sent him to work-first too.

Embedded in this narrative are surveillance-generated cues to this applicant's tendencies that this caseworker deemed to be important enough to take account of in this concise narrative. These include the fact that she lost her job due to poor attendance, and furthermore that she did this despite being warned. The medical examiner's opinion that she was not suffering from addiction further serves to frame this picture as that of a person who deserves to be sent to the work-first program despite her claims that she has a drug and alcohol problem. Such notes become a permanent part of an individual's case history, available for future use by caseworkers who want to know what "type" of person they are dealing with. In the words of one caseworker: "Well, it all depends on what kind of TANF worker you are, like I like to know what I'm up against so I review the client history before meeting with them." Case notes are examples of how technology designed to determine ability to work becomes meshed with other sources of surveillance to further sort clients and ensure that as many workers as possible are motivated to enter the labor force and subjected to the screening processes of work-first. IT has evolved to focus not only on such tasks as screening clients on the basis of motivation and ability to work, but furthermore on incorporating employers as gatekeepers and deploying technology to foster low wage worker attitudes.

Employers as Gatekeepers

Via information technologies similar to the pathways described in the previous sections, work-first surveillance can be seen as it "radiates" beyond the walls of the welfare office.[23] Surveillance has existed for some time prior to the 1996 reform, and continues to involve such things as contacting landlords, the Department of Motor Vehicles, and a plethora of other government agencies. Unique to work-first, however, is a new emphasis not only on serving employers through screening and motivating workers, but also by collaborating with them in surveillance. As evident in the following situation, a general suspicion of work motivation, and the role of employers as customers of welfare, combined with use of technology enables a multifaceted surveillance system that would otherwise not be possible.

> Caseworker: I had a person the other day who provided me with verification in a medical statement verifying that she had to stop work, based on a doctor's recommendation. So I called the employer and the employer indicated to me that that wasn't true at all, that the person actually stopped working so that she could go back to school . . . [Then, contacting the doctor, he gathered more information.] The doctor had recommended that she could return to work on 5-8 but she turned that 5-8 into 8-8 . . . So, I mean there's a situation where I could have just dealt with it, you know, on the spot and probably, . . . given it [the benefits] to her right there, but the whole story just didn't seem, something just seemed wrong, so . . . You make a few phone calls, you pend ["Pend" refers to placing an application's processing on hold until requested information is brought in] her for some information. You look over the information that they provide.

Within such work-first surveillance, employers emerge not only as customers, but also as gatekeepers of welfare.

As with other forms of community-wide surveillance, employers, the quintessential members of this network, are routinely contacted to verify the details of clients' applications for aid. In some instances, such as the following one, letters are solicited from employers.

> Caseworker: OK you're a two-parent case . . . What's Roger [her husband] doing? . . . Working part time?
> Applicant: No, full time.
> Caseworker: What we will need is a letter from your and his employers saying how many hours a week you are working and what the normal hours are.
> Applicant: It's 10 to 5 everyday [volunteering her information].
> Caseworker: OK we need his too, on something with letterhead.

In other cases, contact with employers is made via the phone, such as the following mock phone call simulated by a caseworker.

> Hello, I am Alice from social services and Joanna has informed me that she has found work with you. That's great . . . I was wondering if you could help me verify some information. How many hours a week is she working/going to be working? . . . Well on average? . . . And the salary is?

In still other instances, caseworkers employ standard forms to gather alternative perspectives on events in the lives of clients.

> Caseworker: Why are you no longer working; what happened, did you quit or were you fired?
> Welfare Client: I had a problem with my manager. She was always yelling at me for things that were not my fault and I said that I'm not going to take it anymore and she told me to leave, I was fired.
> Caseworker: Oh, I need this filled out by the employer.

As with other forms of surveillance, the technology in front of caseworkers routinely trumps the words of clients. Caseworkers such as the following even go so far as to warn clients of this:

> On this form place the number of hours of work you do per week, on average. Please be accurate, when we get back the verification from your employer, if that shows less than you marked you can be denied for noncompliance.

In the following processing event, a caseworker handles a discrepancy between an employer's and a client's report by relying on the employer, even though this results in added participation requirements and even though the client was present and the employer was not.

> Caseworker: This [form completed by the employer] says she is working 22 hours a week, but this [form completed by the client] says 30. According to this [employer form] she still has to do a job search.

Privileging the word of employers over clients is especially consequential in cases where clients quit jobs or refuse an offer, both of which render them ineligible for aid. The pairing of work-first rules and the authority employers are given within the surveillance system create a situation in which worker maneuverability and bargaining power are severely hampered—especially if employers are familiar with work-first policies and use them to their advantage.[24] As one former client explained:

> Take the abuse because if you don't, public assistance will kick you off because you quit the job. It's called a voluntary quit.[25]

This dilemma harkens objections of welfare rights groups and labor unions that, "because employers know that welfare recipients are legally obligated to take any job offer, they are decreasing their entry-level wages and increasing their use of part-time and contingent labor."[26]

Much of the surveillance that involves employers, however, occurs out of sight of clients. In the following excerpt, a job coach exemplifies the commonplace use of surveillance (in this case write-ups of phone calls used to verify applications) as evidence in confronting a "noncompliant" applicant. The textualization of these verification phone calls, via caseworkers writing notes from the phone conversations on the form that was handed in by the applicant herself or himself, adds information to the authority of the job coach that she uses in exposing and penalizing what she, on behalf of the institution, considers to be the applicant's effort to get by without fully complying. While she uses this encounter to enforce the rules of the program (and interactions such as the following are commonplace), her displeasure with such a duty is also evident.

> Caseworker: Mrs. Tate, I'm just looking at your stuff right now. . . . These are contacts that have been called.

Here the caseworker shows the applicant the highlighted lines on last week's search form, the one that the applicant had filled out during her job search two weeks ago and had handed in last week (when she picked up the two blank forms that she had to fill out for this week). The marked-up sections on the form (in red) represent contacts or places where caseworkers called employers to verify that the applicant had indeed submitted the applications for employment that she indicated on this very form. The highlighted entries signify employers who had been called but who did not corroborate that the applicant had applied for work there. The caseworker then gives the applicant two sheets stapled together. The half sheet in front explains that, because of her incomplete job searches, her application is being denied and she must re-apply.

> Caseworker: Read that thing [handing the sheets to the applicant].
> Applicant: [She looks at the sheets, skimming over them.]
> Caseworker: Did you read this? . . . Did you understand?
> Applicant: [She utters a hesitant and almost inaudibly low] No.
> Caseworker: [She opens last week's contact sheet and asks] Did you put in an application at all these places? [Her body language suggests she is half expecting the applicant to admit that she didn't.]
> Applicant: Yeah. [She says in a meek voice.]
> Caseworker: [Indicating a few employer names highlighted in bright yellow, she continues:] These said you didn't. [She points to one non-highlighted and then a highlighted one in particular and says:] There they said you did, but there they said you didn't have an application with them. . . .
> Applicant: [She remains silent, just listening and watching, serious.]
> Caseworker: [She continues.]. . . You can't have any on here that say no . . . You have to go back and re-apply. [Her tone is matter of fact, calm, clearly siding with the logic she presents.]

Often a confrontation will end at this point, with applicants accepting the authority of this textual knowledge and leaving the office, presumably to re-assess their next move. This applicant, however, persists:

> Applicant: [In a disbelieving and slightly louder astonished tone she utters:] Are you serious?
> Caseworker: [A bit lighter in tone, she addresses herself, the whole room, anyone listening.] Why does everybody say that? . . . Why would I make this up?

Applicant: [Recapping the caseworker's message, she asks:] So, because one
employer said I didn't apply, I have to go all the way back and start again?
[The process is now at least two weeks under way.]

Caseworker: [She continues matter of factly:] Actually there's three [out of
10].

Applicant: [Weakly defending herself]: If I didn't do it, I wouldn't put it on
there.

Caseworker: [She just looks at her sternly. She has said all she will say.]

At this point, the message is clear. It is the applicant's word against the word
of the person at the respective employer's office, be it McDonald's, a gro-
cery store, who answered the phone caller's questions about the applicant's
applications. The information produced from this interaction appears tex-
tualized on the desk in front of the caseworker. While the applicant is the
most obviously upset by this encounter, the caseworker is not unshaken.
As the applicant mumbles to herself, turns toward the door, tears up her
forms (two rips), and storms out quietly, mumbling to herself under her
breath, the caseworker also mumbles to herself. She takes a deep breath, as
if she just did something tough that she didn't really want to do. As seen
here, though caseworkers such as this one take an active role in creating
and constantly refining casework technology, "once established, the service
technology assumes larger proportions. It actually creates structures that direct staff actions, reinforces their beliefs, and shapes their interpretations. It
defines what is rational and socially acceptable within that organization."[27]

In this instance, the surveillance used to divert this client from the application process was gathered through a simple phone call such as the
following.

Hello. Can I speak with the manager? Oh not there, well supervisor, etc.?
Well I'm calling from the Department of Social Services and I was won-
dering if you could tell me if Malika has placed an application for employment with you.

Though such practices are straightforward, they are also susceptible to
potential errors. Oftentimes the manager will be unable to answer the
phone so other employees with questionable levels of regard for nosy call-
ers may be the source of the surveillance. Whether or not the employer
who is contacted treats the surveillance efforts of caseworkers seriously,
their outcomes are consequential to clients. As a job coach explained, it is

not only the actions of clients but also sometimes the inaction of employers that can lead to rejection from the welfare application process.

> They send them some paperwork. "Here [applicant name], bring this to your employer and tell him he's gotta fill it out." You have ten days to get it back in, so if you don't have it in within ten days, oh well they do something to your case. And then you have to come back and you gotta do this all over. And people come through here all the time, we see them over and over and over.

In addition to routine surveillance, caseworkers sometimes involve employers in their efforts to go above and beyond in investigating clients. In the following section, a job coach discusses how he has used basic technology (i.e., phone calls and recorded contact information) to investigate a male client who was allowing his wife to complete his job searches for him. After the wife brought in completed Job Search Contact forms for herself and her husband, the coach noticed that they were identical and completed in the same handwriting. He then called employers to verify that the applications indicated on the form were on file there.

> Job Coach: Well I called [the potential employer] and asked, well "Did . . . John Smith have an application?" You can hear her looking through the applications and she says, "Oh no, Mary Smith has the application, she, oh wait a minute! Oh John's is right underneath it." "Oh really?" And then she'll say, "Oh well, they must be married." "How do you know this ma'am?" And she says, "Oh because they're all written in the same pen and the same handwriting." And then when I call to verify the other applications, I ask the question, "Are they written in the same handwriting?" "Yeah." "O.K., thanks very much." . . . You can see that she does that because she wants her damn case to open up because she's got children and he don't want to do anything. So she's fudging . . . the process so that her case opens up.
> Author: Is that valid? Does that count as his application?
> Job Coach: [He definitively states,] No. I had to go to a fair hearing to testify that they didn't do an independent job search. And you know, that was . . . they lost.

As seen here, this job coach, consistent with his co-workers, takes the initiative to investigate textual "cues" that look suspicious to him, rather than just accept and record them as if they were completed as required.

Such investigative work also serves another purpose in deputizing certain members of the community to honorary positions as overseers of the poor. In essence, these workers and, most prominently, employers become recruited as gatekeepers to aid in the work-first system. In the process, caseworkers become aligned with employers more so than with clients. Accordingly, a large portion of welfare's technological restructuring has coincided with a new effort to court and serve employers, even at the expense of clients.

Fostering Low Wage Worker Subjectivity

The central way in which work-first technology is structured in order to serve employers as customers (in addition to screening motivation and ability, and deputizing employers as gatekeepers) is by fostering low wage worker attitudes. Through maintaining close surveillance of work-first participation, caseworkers compel clients not only to immerse themselves in the labor force to their full capacity, but also to see themselves as their employers see them and to adopt a submissive stance in order to get ahead in the low wage, contingent, and unstable labor market. This process begins on the first day of processing with the use of a film that resembles an emotionally charged commercial. This film is designed to confront client resistance to low wage unstable work. It does this by valorizing menial labor on ideological grounds of personal responsibility and self-sufficiency and the contention that "every job is a good job." By contrast, critiques of contingent and low paying work are dismissed with the concessions that "not every job is glamorous" and that sometimes it takes "lots of little steps," or persistently advancing through "lots" of menial jobs before work is able to make one self-sufficient. The following field notes reveal this message:

> This orientation session is led off by a video intended to present the "state's message." This video, entitled "Working for Self-Sufficiency," begins by documenting the new law established by the 1996 PRWORA and the 1997 New York State Welfare Reform Act. It then goes on to stress the message that work is your first responsibility. Although some jobs may not be "glamorous," it concedes, "every job is a good job." Forward-looking behavior is encouraged; "You'll never get a promotion on welfare," the video explains. At its conclusion, the video summarizes the two important goals of this new program: 1. Personal responsibility—each person must

find a job that fulfills household needs; and 2. Self-sufficiency—everyone should work towards being able to live without cash assistance. "Even if it takes you lots of little steps," the woman in the video explains, "the reality is that we all have to work to be self sufficient." Then she adds, "For some people this is a change." After watching 10 minutes of happy laborers, shown as proud construction hands and dedicated service workers, the climate in the room is such that few, as I judge from my own reaction, want to be lumped into the group for whom "work" and efforts to become "self-sufficient" are much of a "change."

The message conveyed through this video technology carries with it not only the authority of a film that matches television quality production standards, but also the imprimatur of "the State of New York" on whose behalf it claims to speak. As such, it lends legitimacy to the message far beyond that which might be accorded a caseworker delivering the same message without a soundtrack and on-site footage.

The work-first video uses its authority to set a foundation for work-first attitudes by neutralizing dissent. The master narrative of this video silences clients who would object to menial work by painting them as self-important by virtue of their desire to enter the labor force with a "glamorous job" rather than start at the true bottom rung of the labor market. It furthermore undermines those clients who would criticize the work-first agenda on the grounds that low wage work is insufficient to lead one out of poverty. In effect, the video presents a counterargument to what some scholars have identified in the United States as a "labor market [that] appears to operate in such a way as to 'trap' many of these individuals in the lower reaches of the job market, where real wages are static or falling, career ladders are truncated and employment insecurity is a common characteristic."[28] Counter to this, the video presents an alternative allegation that those who do not climb out of poverty have simply failed to take enough "little steps" up the career ladder. Thus, responsibility for contingent employment and insufficient wages is shifted to clients as opposed to structural problems of the labor market or of local employers. This neo-liberal framing of the problem of poverty, as based in individual responsibility, also lays the foundation for further use of technology to monitor acceptance of personal responsibility and to reinforce placing the onus of labor market success on the individual. As one caseworker describes, it is really clients who must take responsibility to "step outside of the box" and leave their comfort zone to assume personal responsibility and keep taking little steps until the jobs they find allow them to survive without the various welfare supports on which many low wage workers rely.

> Caseworker: Most of them, you're asking them to step outside of the box, go beyond where they are comfortable—and they are not used to work. We're asking them to be responsible for themselves, we're asking them to be more than responsible, we're asking them to take the jump from point A, unemployed and on welfare, to point B, employed and on welfare, to point C, employed and on reduced welfare assistance, to point D, employed and off welfare, or self-sufficient.

Not only is surveillance technology actively used to monitor clients through each of these steps in the manners already described, but the brief windows that this technology allows into clients' lives enable caseworkers to prod clients along at each of the various stages.

For instance, routine queries into employment status and history as a term of work-first compliance yield opportunity for caseworkers to offer pro-employer advice on how to deal with problems of insufficient pay or employment hours.

> Caseworker: Some come and say, "Well I left my job. I wasn't getting paid enough for the amount of work I do." Or, "I was working but I wasn't getting enough hours." And I'm like, "Well work the hours you are getting! And then look for another job for the rest of the hours!"

Such advice not only encourages clients to stay in poorly or incommensurably remunerated positions, but it also encourages clients to adapt their behaviors to accommodate common cost-efficient employer practices of underpaying employees and keeping weekly work hours low and unpredictable to avoid paying benefits and overtime and to avoid having to staff and thus pay "excess" employees during nonbusy down times in the workday.

Keeping active surveillance over an applicants' work status permits work-first to monitor and enforce a policy that compels mothers to engage in work to their full capacity—30 hours a week. Once a person is working 30 hours, they are exempted from the job searching requirement of work-first. Accordingly, caseworkers urge clients to offer themselves to their employers, or even plead or ask for special consideration, to work as much as possible.

Job Coach: How many hours you doing?

Applicant: Twenty-six to twenty-eight.

Job Coach: If you can squeeze in two more hours, you won't have to do a job search. Do you think you can do maybe half an hour more a day?

Applicant: I will check with my employer.

Job Coach: OK . . . twenty-eight is pretty close to thirty.

Offering such encouragement to increase hours is common. A Job Coach explains:

Job Coach: So if they're working 25 hours a week we always, you know, encourage them to try to get their employer to give them an additional five hours so that, . . . at least they don't have to continue doing the job search portion.

In other words, dealing with the unreliable and variable hours assigned to them by their employer is their problem, not that of their employer as seen below:

Caseworker: Because you are employed [the interviewer can see this from the grid in front of her] but not regular, steady, full time, available work to you, I'm sending you to work-first. . . .

Applicant: Thirty hours isn't? [She challenges the interviewer's assertion, as if to say, "Are you telling me that 30 hours isn't full time?"]

Caseworker: Well that was back in the beginning of May . . . Based on this here you would be eligible, but to be eligible, because you're not employed to your capacity . . .

Applicant: [She cuts in.] But I got full-time sometimes . . . but when it's full-time you don't help nobody.

Here the applicant points out that the logic of the interviewer and the system suggests that, to avoid the remediation work involved in work-first participation, applicants must be working to their "capacity." Yet, working to one's capacity would often diminish one's eligibility for aid. The worker agrees. Below, this conversation continues.

Caseworker: So that's what you need, because then you help yourself. If you had 30 hours in the past four weeks, you wouldn't have to go to work-first. You'd see a TANF worker and then maybe we'd make a one-time payment.

Applicant: But if my rent is $500 and half my income goes to that . . .
Caseworker: [Cutting off the applicant's sentence, the interviewer points out
what she sees as a flaw in the applicant's logic.] If you're working full time
then you're getting more money than Public Assistance alone. . . . [In clos-
ing she reinforces] So to be eligible [for assistance without having to go to
work-first], you have to work to your full capacity, 30 hours a week.

The underlying message delivered is that, although the welfare state has
invested vast resources in developing work-first surveillance technology,
the purpose is not to fix labor market problems such as unsteady jobs that
pay below living wages. Rather, the end to which surveillance is deployed
is to ensure that both clients and employers understand that the neoliberal welfare state seeks not to replace but to reify the labor market as the
predominant mechanism of subsistence. As seen in the following excerpt,
clients are expected to do whatever it takes to succeed in the market.

Applicant: How long do I do these? [She is referring to Job Search contact
forms.]
Caseworker: Till you find a job.
Applicant: I could do 500 of these . . . This is getting tougher and tougher. I'm
running out of places to go, and I walk to all of these.
Caseworker: Keep trying.

In essence, it is not the state that sets the standards for behavior but the
market—the state is merely a labor market intermediary that socializes
and prepares clients to satisfy the demands of employers. Conditioning
therefore involves getting clients to think in terms of their employers. One
caseworker's comments make this connection clear.

Caseworker: So any excuse you can think of, we've gotten. What we really try
to get to is if you had to give an excuse to your employer, what would you
tell them.

In the following example of an argument over how to fill out a digital attendance sheet, a job coach also makes plain that this involves submitting
oneself to "the habit of doing whatever is expected of you." She attempts
to prepare an applicant for expectations of employers that are typical
to hourly wage positions that demand punctuality more ruthlessly than
higher paying jobs do (such as the job of the coach herself).

Job Coach: I had one lady ask me yesterday. You know she came in well after twelve [This is the deadline] and she said to me, "Haven't you ever
been late to work?" or you know and the answer is "yes." "I have been
late to work, you know, but there are also jobs where if you arrive late
for work you won't have a job." You know? So yes, some of them get kind
of bent out of shape over the fact that um, if they arrive late we don't see
them. But the whole message that we're trying to send is, "You have to be
on time because some employers will not tolerate you being late". . . You
know, at all. You know? So you have to get into the habit of doing whatever is expected of you on time. So that's the message that we're trying to
send.

Getting applicants to accept such messages and "get in the habit of doing what is expected of them" by employers is a large part of the remediation work that caseworkers do. Beyond its apparent uses in screening
and conditioning low wage workers to be docile employees, it is part of
what Anna Korteweg describes as a "discursive strategy" for constructing
"women's future subjectivity as workers."[29]

On the base level, caseworkers equate working with being "moral" yet,
in order to comply with this taxonomy in the given contemporary economic context, Korteweg argues that a second level of pressure is applied
advocating for "an effacement of self in order to gain access to work that
pays a living wage and for active self-exploitation in order to climb the
job ladder."[30] Epitomizing this approach, a caseworker delivers a motivational speech during orientation intended to inspire clients to submit
themselves to work realities in which poor mothers as workers are so devalued and without bargaining leverage that "sometimes you have to work
for free first" and prove yourself to employers who may then be willing to
pay you.

Many of you have been here before, that's fine, gotta go from job to job,
there are layoffs, employers leave, but the Bottom Line! [Hilda raises the
tone of her voice for emphasis] is to Get You Out Of the System! . . .
Do you know that 20 percent of all employed people do not like their
jobs? . . . But you have to work hard to climb that rung to where you
want to be. . . . Welfare reform is not big on education because people
would go to training and then change their minds! Often you have to
work for free first! but then you do a good job and you take your good
work and attendance record and the new skills with you and you use it

to get another job . . . [She speaks from her own experience.] I walked to
work while saving to buy a car, and now I work two jobs! One here and
one at the mall!

From this perspective, those clients who embrace work-first sensibilities
anticipate a high likelihood of not liking their job, don't complain about
employer instability, are not encumbered by juggling both work and
school, and are willing to work for free just to prove themselves. As far as
serving employers as customers of work-first is concerned, this is a dream
come true.

Asserting the Interests of Employers through Technology

The work-first approach to welfare not only impacts clients and caseworkers but also employers since it serves to regulate both low wage workers
and the unstable labor markets on which they depend.[31] Though on the
surface, welfare is a policy directed at poor parents, it amounts to a with-
drawal of the right to nonparticipation in the labor market. It has eliminated entitlement to aid and it requires that the parents be work-ready
in order to be eligible. This is, in effect, a supply side intervention in the
labor market that serves the interests of employers in several ways. First,
it promises a greater number of workers will enter the market. In fact,
estimates suggest that approximately one to two million additional workers will enter the workforce due to the welfare reform between the years
of 1993 and 2008.[32] Second, an increase in labor supply serves to reduce
the bargaining power of all workers in the low wage secondary labor market (regardless of whether or not they are welfare clients) and it exerts a
downward pressure on wages and working conditions.[33]

Third, in conjunction with lowering wages, the flooding of the low wage
labor market increases the substitutability of workers, encouraging employers to hire new workers and thus displace others at the slightest of provo-
cations. In one estimate for New York City, Charles Tilly estimates a wage
reduction of 26 percent or the displacement of 58,000 workers, or some
combination of the two.[34] This flooding encourages a churning of workers
that decreases long-term job security for the working poor and reduces the
need of employers to invest in training, benefits, improved working conditions aimed at employee retention, and other resources that would assist
employees in building long-term careers. Instead, employers are encouraged and enabled to treat workers as contingent, expendable workers.[35]

In addition to these boons to employers, the work-first approach, by requiring applicants to be job-ready and to accept any job offered to them, and quit none, subsidizes the social costs of producing a contingent labor force. In East County, this worker socialization is enabled in large part by the surveillance work of caseworkers. In addition to urging clients on with maxims such as "Often you have to work for free first!" "You have to think of what an employer would say," and "You have to get into the habit of doing what is expected of you," caseworkers add to the bargaining power of employers by incorporating them as gatekeepers who are consulted as clients seek to both attain and remain eligible for aid.

Though on a local level, work-first in East County appears as a welcomed effort of welfare administrators to reach out to the business community, such a local perspective overlooks the integral role that employers have had in ensuring that their interests were represented in the national welfare policy in the first place. As Holloway Sparks reports, 100 of the nearly 600 witnesses testifying before the 104th Congress as they deliberated how best to reform welfare were business representatives.[36] In its 1996 testimony before Congress, the U.S. Chamber of Commerce, the nation's largest business federation, reported that not only was welfare reform second (behind unfunded mandates) on its list of 64 priorities, but also that 99 percent of its membership "advocated an overhaul of the current welfare system," 98 percent believed that welfare recipients who received welfare related education and training services "should be required to work," and 94 percent "supported placing a limit on the amount of time that one can receive welfare benefits."[37] As Ellen Reese has argued:

> Business support for restrictive welfare policies, most concentrated among low-wage and ideological conservative business elites, is linked to the rise of neoliberalism, economic restructuring, and economic globalization . . . In response to rising international competition, falling profits, and the wave of environmental and labor regulations of the 1960s and 1970s, the corporate rich increasingly invested in right-wing think tanks.[38]

In 1996, the year that welfare reform was passed, she further documents, such "conservative think tanks were cited seven times more than progressive think tanks by the mainstream media" thus enabling business-funded conservative ideas to claim the dominant middle ground of public debate.[39]

The strategy behind this business interest and activism in welfare reform was the maintenance of a steady and readily available supply of cheap labor. "Rather than taking the 'high-road' strategy for economic growth by investing in technological innovations and skilled labor, American business leaders have pursued the 'low-road' strategy of deregulating the labor market, cheapening labor, and making labor contracts more 'flexible.'"[40] The propulsion of hundreds of thousands of women from welfare into the less skilled and low wage sectors of the labor market was projected to suppress wages in these sectors of the labor market by as much as 12 percent.[41] Corporate-sponsored think tanks, such as the American Enterprise Institute, have publicly acknowledged that they see the purpose of welfare reform as increasing the supply of low wage laborers.[42] The work-first approach to reform has not left them disappointed, creating workfare mechanisms that provide "'a continuously job-ready, pre-processed, 'forced' labor supply for the lower end of the labor market' where turnover rates are high."[43]

When we look closely at welfare mechanisms such as those in East County, we see that the story of motivating low wage labor according to neoliberal design is also the story of work-first technology evolution. Liza McCoy notes the importance of examining the ways in which power dynamics exist within institutional forms of knowledge and information sharing.

> When we look in this way, texts and representational practices come into view as key constituents of the restructuring of institutional relations. Since contemporary "ruling" depends in a large way on documentary forms of knowledge that construct in texts the objects of managerial or professional decision-making, changes in relations of ruling are likely to be evoked and driven through changes in the kind of documentary knowledge produced and the uses to which it is put.[44]

Morgen and Maskovsky argue that the 1996 "welfare-state restructuring can be seen as an important moment in the reshaping of social citizenship through the reconfiguration of state, market, and family relations."[45] Not only is citizenship now defined in terms of nondependence due to labor-force-based self-sufficiency, but employers are recast as the ultimate citizen since they are the stakeholders on whom the status of nondependence is dependent. They provide the means for those without capital of their own to enter into the labor market and sell their labor, and thus the deference given to employers and mobile capital within global neoliberal restructuring is reproduced within the U.S. welfare state. This re-ordering of citizenship is visible in the new surveillance infrastructure and practice, through which the interests of clients, the state, and employers have undergone a reprioritization in welfare state activities.

5

"We Are a Thorn in the Side of Those Who Won't Change"

Buying in to Work-First

The common sense of work-first is socially constructed in a multitude of ways: Institutional entrepreneurs advocate new ways of doing things. Performance measures redirect the attention of local implementers. Technology hardwires common-sense rules into work practices and record keeping. In accordance with all of these changes, caseworkers rearrange their strategies for interacting with clients. Finally, clients who wish to make it through the new welfare system rearrange their family life to accommodate institutional values. The success of each of these elements, both individually and as a whole, however, depends on whether caseworkers and clients buy into the ideology of the institution. If either of these groups resists the assumptions of work-first, its power is diminished. The strength of common sense is, after all, the fact that people hold its premises in common. If caseworkers did not buy into work-first they would likely find ways to undermine and subvert it, as caseworkers have done with previous welfare reforms. Similarly, clients who do not buy into work-first have at their disposal a multitude of forms of resistance, ranging from passive inaction to political mobilization. Notable about the 1996 reform, however, is that there is relatively little evidence of such resistance when compared with the past.

Some previous welfare programs have met with hostile political attacks, as in the 1930s and 1960s when vast coalitions of the public demanded more generous benefits. Others have been undermined by caseworkers who did not believe in what they were told to implement. Neither is the case with TANF. National research finds that both caseworkers and clients are in general agreement with the goals of the program, even if they have concerns over the details.[1] This chapter explores both local and extra-local mechanisms that contribute to this ideological buy-in to the common sense of work-first and to the neoliberal values that they represent.

The chapter begins with a description of what ideological buy-in looks like on the front lines of work-first, particularly in the case of clients who later become caseworkers. I then analyze how national dissatisfaction with the AFDC program that preceded TANF set the stage for a change in approach and justified a tough love strategy. I trace this way of thinking as it emerged among local innovators in East County and as it was conveyed to caseworkers through administrative efforts to coordinate caseworker discretion. I explore how work-first appealed to caseworkers because it empowered them to take a stand against perceived dependency. Despite widespread acceptance, however, I also find work-first to be in need of continual re-affirmation; maintaining widespread buy-in to work-first common sense requires ongoing emotional effort on the part of clients who participate and caseworkers who implement it. Those clients who most effectively perform this emotional work of reaffirming the values of work-first are sometimes offered positions on staff at the welfare office. Even then, however, they continue to be engaged in a dynamic by which caseworkers police each other's behavior to ensure that it remains consistent with work-first values.

Buy-in on the Front Lines

Caseworkers in general tend to harbor a sense of empathy for those whom they see as making the effort to change their behavior in conformity with work-first requirements. Nowhere is this more visible than among caseworkers who were once welfare clients themselves. Clients turned caseworkers present themselves as "success stories" that current clients would do well to emulate. Their concentration in highly visible processing sites such as orientation sessions provides them an opportunity to share their personal tales and to suggest to new clients that "you too can do what I did!"[2] Holding such job titles as technical assistant and information aide, more junior positions than job coaches and case managers, clients turned caseworkers account for approximately one-third of the 100 or so staff at work-first in East County. These clients turned caseworkers represent not only behavioral modification but also a transformation of client attitudes in conformity with work-first ideology.

Commitment to the work-first agenda is clear in the comments of Kyle, a black father of two who has been employed by work-first as a technical assistant for three years. Though he barely completed high school, he carries himself with an air of having graduated cum laude from the school of hard knocks.

> I was where they are now a few years ago. But now I'm here. They [the applicants] need to change. We are a thorn in the side of those who won't change.

With commitment such as this, the aims of work-first ripple through the welfare institution to the front lines. Kyle's words place the onus on individual clients who must internalize an ideology of individual responsibility and then act on it. He represents the ultimate manifestation of institutional efforts, since Kyle himself is a former welfare recipient turned caseworker. Though it is hard to say to what degree he really believes the work-first mantra, or is simply "playing along" with the moral code to which he now owes his livelihood, his reputation is one of being strict. He explains that he is not alone in his tough love approach: "Some past recipients who are now working for work-first are the hardest on applicants."

To some observers the existence of clients turned caseworkers is living proof that the welfare reform is working. Clients are assumed to have seen the error of their ways and bought into the work-first agenda. As I will explore in this chapter, however, buying into work-first requires effort and personal adjustment for clients as well as administrators and caseworkers. It involves replacing and/or melding previous beliefs with the neoliberal philosophical foundation on which work-first is based. This transformation is not only personal, however. It is in many ways catalyzed and cultivated by popular sentiment of a need for change.

The Need for a Change

The 1996 welfare reform was widely embraced as a change for the better. "Indeed, by the mid-1990s, both policy elites and the public believed that anything was preferable to the status quo of AFDC."[3] Public opinion polls in the wake of the 1994 election indicated a popular consensus such that "the public preferred *any* possible package of reforms" over what was in place.[4] An increase in employment among women and the association of welfare with Cadillac-driving black welfare queens made AFDC "politically indefensible at worst, unattractive at best, even among many committed to women's equality (or racial justice)."[5] AFDC's unpopularity presented a conundrum for many who entered the human services line of work in order to make the world a better place by directly improving the lives of those they served. The 1996 PRWORA offered a way out of this predicament and a new direction.

The legislation, set in a broader context of "the neoliberal thinking in favor among political elites," presented caseworkers with a revised understanding of poverty as stemming from personal rather than structural or social weaknesses.[6] The legislation also reframed the labor market, which had previously been seen as the source of exploitation of the poor, as the solution to ending poverty and thus "ensured that welfare reform would encompass some shift of responsibilities from state to labor market and tie assistance to work activities or to employment—so as to support, rather than undercut, the low wage labor market."[7] Beyond this general redirection of welfare philosophy, the PRWORA allowed local administrators and caseworkers to fill in the blanks. The result has been the emergence of new patterns of discretion that caseworkers have cultivated in order to respond to the reform's demand for behavioral change.

"A Thorn in Their Side"—Justifying Tough Love

The 1996 reform eliminated the federal entitlement to aid and set out to dramatically reduce welfare caseloads. Rather than do so under the banner of a reduction in help, the rhetoric of welfare retrenchment in public debate justified it in terms of giving or returning to the poor a sense of self-sufficiency and personal responsibility that they had lost or been denied under the previous welfare system.[8] Indeed Charles Murray, widely considered a catalyst for the 1996 reform, argued, "the welfare state has artificially, needlessly created a large dependent class. At the bottom is the underclass, stripped of dignity and autonomy, producing new generations socialized to their parents' behavior."[9] Newt Gingrich, then Speaker of the House and architect of the Republican "Contract with America" that brought welfare reform into the legislative spotlight, similarly argued: "The welfare state reduces the poor from citizens to clients. It breaks up families, minimizes work incentives, blocks people from saving and acquiring property, and overshadows dreams of a promised future with a present despair born of poverty, violence and hopelessness."[10] Adapting an even more brazen approach, Representative John Mica of Florida likened welfare recipients to alligators, who, though independent in the "natural order" become dependent when fed by welfare-doling well-wishers.[11] His conclusion was similar to one that might be encountered in a zoo—"don't feed the alligators."[12]

Although it was conservative thinkers and politicians who called for welfare reform legislation, the sentiments were by no means limited to Republicans. By the 1996 signing of the legislation, this thinking had captured the middle ground of public debate, including the Democratic President Bill Clinton, who declared substantively similar reasons for signing the legislation: "A long time ago I concluded that the current welfare system undermines the basic values of work, responsibility and family, trapping generation after generation in dependency and hurting the very people it was designed to help."[13] The shared political consensus thus emerged that "People are better off . . . thinking of their welfare as their own responsibility rather than as the government's responsibility. They are better off living (and their children are better off growing up) in communities where people take responsibility for their own welfare."[14] Casework in welfare offices across the country was consequently reorganized to bring about what was considered a radical change in the thinking and behavior of poor parents and to be a "thorn in the side of those who won't change."

The Role of Local Buy-In

Defining what some have labeled the "devolution revolution" House Budget Committee Chairman John R. Kasich (R-Ohio) declared that Congress wanted to "return money, power, and responsibility" to state and local government.[15] In the process, a new federalism emerged to replace the "cooperative federalism" that had dominated since the 1950s. This "cooperative federalism" had taken social equity as its primary objective in response to such policy challenges as market failure, racism, urban poverty, and individual rights.[16] In its place the new federalism has substituted local discretion. However, as David Ellwood has argued, particularly in the case of welfare reform, even though significant devolution seems to have occurred, it is far from a complete delegation of authority. The discretion Congress allotted localities to design and implement welfare programs is severely restricted by regulations involving work requirements, time limits, and pressure to reduce caseloads (see also chapter 3).[17] The 1996 welfare reform reintroduced familiar pre-1960s themes such as diverting applicants, withholding information, elongating the application process, and exhorting families to find help elsewhere, such as with relatives or in soup kitchens. It is unique to the present moment, however, in that it paradoxically both decentralizes welfare through delegation of authority and centralizes welfare discretion in moral terms. It creates stiffer national eligibility standards based on both performance measures and "personal responsibility."[18] In this way, local efforts to move from AFDC to TANF vary with regard to specifics but conform on the whole to the ideological framework that circumscribes them.

Moving Beyond AFDC in East County

Though welfare had long been considered safe from conservative efforts to reduce or dismantle it because it fell under the protection of liberals, by the 1990s "many liberals, too, came to agree that creating dependency was the problem with welfare."[19] As one staff member recalls, "I used to be a hippie, but we needed a change." Among those advocating change were welfare administrators who felt that previous attempts to revise welfare, such as the 1988 Family Support Act, had not really made the improvements that were needed. One TANF administrator who had led previous welfare programs explained:

> We saw all the things we did in which we tried to be helpful to clients and in some cases it worked but we just really didn't believe it was working, because the caseloads just kept getting higher and higher. Why are they getting higher and higher if we are successful in helping people? That's not right, something's wrong, we're doing something wrong. So that is kind of the way we went at it.

As another administrator remarked, previous policy did not sufficiently take into account that poverty was to some degree an individual's responsibility.

> It overlooked the fact that there was a generational aspect to poverty in many instances. It overlooked the fact that at any given point in time in this city there were hundreds of jobs available for people that people just weren't accessing.

Voicing similar concerns, a veteran caseworker explained her dissatisfaction with the status quo that AFDC perpetuated:

> If there's anything I would change, it goes back to that whole thing about helping people change their mentality about work that work is a good thing, that work is better than assistance, you know I'd definitely try to change that if I could.

Such comments are instructive of the neoliberal shift in thinking that took place. According to a neoliberal ideal, the purpose of welfare was no longer seen as providing shelter from the labor market so that poor mothers could de-commodify themselves and focus instead on raising their children, as was the initial intent of the program and as has remained a central goal in many European nations (see chapter 8). Instead, welfare came to be seen as more of an unemployment insurance that should only be paid when mothers cannot find work—not when they choose to focus on caregiving work instead. Work-first thus represents an effort to shift welfare toward a liberal free market ideal; "welfare reform aimed to extend the compulsion of the market to welfare recipients."[20]

Though consistent with the broader neoliberalization of welfare policies, the discretionary leeway afforded in the PRWORA also allowed implementation to be responsive to local concerns. As one administrator in East County explains, the mistakes of the past offered lessons that could be incorporated into work-first programs.

> I completely believed in the concept [of my former program], we should definitely make sure people should be able to get a job and get off welfare [by sponsoring college training] and we did everything we could and we were quite frankly very successful, but on the other hand it opened my eyes. A lot of the people we were putting in this program we were setting them up for failure. . . . We had been assuming they were ready to get an education. There was so much else going on in their worlds and they were not ready for it. I began to think that perhaps they could benefit from learning workplace behaviors first in unpaid work experience [i.e., workfare].

Following from reflections such as these, work-first was slowly, yet deliberately, assembled in East County. As another administrator describes, incorporation of experiential lessons and the creativity that local discretion allows is an ongoing process:

This program has changed over time, there is a lot of innovation. Having an idea years ago you keep working the problem, and saying is it still relevant today?

In addition to fostering the collusion of experience and inventiveness, the local discretion of work-first allowed administrators to selectively recast work-first in a manner aligned with their own public-service and social justice concerns. As an administrator told me, the intent was to avoid becoming punitive like programs that emerged elsewhere.

> Local Administrator: The [criticism] was that this was just such a terrible punitive system. And in some places it might have turned out to be that way. We were adamant that it would not be that way, and probably of all the things that we did related to this whole project, that is the thing I am most proud of. We were not perfect, I will not say that at all, but the vision behind it always was that we are going to help people on public assistance make their lives better. . . . So we felt like we had the right way to look at it. We weren't just looking at it like we were going to have a great participation rate and we were going to reduce cost. Now that did happen! That did happen. But that wasn't our goal. It might have been the county's goal; it might have been the state's goal. That wasn't our goal.

Reaffirming this concern for salvaging and retaining the human service ethic within the work-first system, another administrator asserted:

> Employment is the center of our system, but it is much more than that. It is really about getting kids and families out of poverty. . . . The reality is that, given the skill sets they have, something like 20 percent of the caseloads have 12 years of school. Their skill set isn't great. So if someone does take something along the lines of an entry-level job, is it enough to get them out of poverty? If the answer is no, then in our minds equity and fairness dictate that we need to step up to ensure they have access to ongoing supports to get out of poverty. If they are doing all they can, if they are doing the right thing, I think we owe them, I think society owes them to support them to get their kids out of poverty. . . . We tried not to approach it in a punitive model but to offer real opportunities, if you work with us some really nice things would happen. So I think we try to be a lot more positive than I think a lot of other jurisdictions have approached it.

Such comments reflect a mixing of sentiments within East County's welfare system. With the 1996 welfare reform the problem of poverty was publicly redefined as one of dependent behavior among the poor. In the words of social critic George Gilder, "the key problem of the welfare culture is not unemployed women and poor children" but rather that these women "have the income and the ties to government authority and support."[21] Though the 1996 reform emphasized anti-behavior rather than anti-poverty objectives, the social justice interests of local administrators, at least in this case, were able to offer a discursive counterbalance to the federal emphasis on cutting caseloads and meeting participation rates.

As Morgen and Weigt note, "today's political rhetoric is vastly more concerned with ending welfare dependency than with ameliorating poverty."[22] However, in East County caseworkers were also faced with a countercharge of anti-poverty which emanated from senior administrators and came to be seen as coalescing with work-first rather than contradicting it. A staff member explains how she rectifies local administrative concerns with that of the broader work-first paradigm:

> As our commissioner says: we are not anti-welfare, we are an anti-poverty program. We try to enable them to work so that their standard of living increases while taxpayer contributions decrease. We see this also as a way of breaking the cycle of poverty.

As the following sections explore, local discretion is affected both by individual caseworkers' assessment of whether applicants are "doing everything they are supposed to" and by broader efforts of administrators to coordinate the use of discretion in accordance with work-first and local goals. An administrator recalls:

> The vision behind it always was that we are going to help people on public assistance make their lives better. Now whether everybody always *"bought into"* that I don't know, but that was our vision.

Coordinating Discretion

The coordination of frontline discretion in East County was a process rather than an event. In its early days the staff consisted of a bricolage, or rearrangement of caseworkers who had been transferred or borrowed from other departments. As one administrator recalls, "there wasn't a lot of buy-in." At this time the welfare office employed approximately 200 people and only four were dedicated to work-related activities. An administrator recalls, "There was a big culture change, we really couldn't hire more yet so we worked with the people we had." However, as work-first began to take shape and new hires were added, the number rose from four to nearly 100. As a new, non–social services agency, work-first was able to hire for mission, ensuring that those who were hired bought into the goals of the reform.[23] In addition, much of the training focused on providing enough background information so that caseworkers could "believe in" the mission of work-first. In the words of one administrator, "There is no profit motivation here, so you do things because you believe in what you are doing."

Drawing many staff members from preexisting social services agencies also presented another problem of having to re-teach staff to use discretion where they were used to following bureaucratic regulations to the letter of the law. As a work-first administrator in East County explained, it was a drastic change from what existed before:

> There was an organizational culture that was not flexible. You just didn't do anything without going through the exact proper channels and doing everything exactly by the regulations. . . . And I think they were very afraid to do what they were not used to doing, and I am saying use your best judgment. This is what we are about. This is what we want to accomplish. . . . Make a decision on it and go forward and if there is something we need to change on it afterwards we will. . . . The big change was we were going toward being more intentional about requiring people to participate.

In addition to encouraging discretion, administrators had to actively assist in the calibration of that discretion. Team meetings were utilized to discuss such things as defining and redefining what a job search actually entails, coming to consensus on when it is reasonable to give clients a "second chance" and developing rules of thumb for whether a client can reschedule and for how long. As an administrator recalls, this use of discretion followed a logic in which one thing led to another:

> We were saying that we believe that people will ultimately be better off in the workforce. And if we are saying this we need to try to do our best

to get them into the workforce. But this was such a huge change and the questions were like, "This person has to reschedule, should I do it for two weeks or four weeks?" and "This person says she can't do this type of job but her past work history suggests that she can. What should I do?" Before [as caseworkers in AFDC and other programs] they were told that what you should do is help make sure people get their benefits and get out of the way. We had never had to enforce anything before; it was a huge change.

Though many staff members eventually bought into the work-first approach, this involved a culture change that was not always easy to achieve. An administrator recalls that staff members were sometimes slow to accept the new direction of the reform:

> The culture of the staff was an issue. I remember one of the staff saying my job is to get these cases off my desk. I said, sitting back, aww, yikes this is going to be tough. . . . There were individuals who very much disagreed with this, but we went out all the time and explained what we were doing.

With persistence, administrators and staff were able to overcome the inertial tendency of organizational culture to resist change. Administrators repeatedly shared their message and reiterated it in different ways. They were aided by the incorporation of work-first aims into performance monitoring (see chapter 3) and new technology (see chapter 4), both of which helped to send the message that work-first was here to stay. The strategy was not to steamroll those who resisted but to "massage" them.

> Local Administrator: There can be a zillion obstacles from staff culture to technological issues, to regulatory issues, interfaces with other divisions that might not see the issue the same way, it might be a community agency, so it's trying to massage all of those relationships and interfaces and that sometimes is a real, real challenge.

Through such efforts at "massaging," caseworkers began to actively assume their new role as mediator, and protector, of a new philosophy of welfare in an age of work-first.

From Structural to Individual "Philosophy"

The 1996 welfare reform was as much a political reform as it was a new strategy for program implementation. One local administrator remarked, "As politics changed, funding from the other program I was running disappeared and money for this one appeared." Though local administrators and caseworkers are sure to credit broader political changes with the rise of local welfare reform, they also tend to understate the extent to which their daily actions are connected with these broader politics. The concrete work in which they engage, and the new manners in which they deploy discretion, are the product of extended political logics. An administrator reflects on this connection while describing the difference between AFDC and TANF.

> [Under AFDC] there was so little attention placed on employment and that wasn't an oversight, it was based on the philosophy of welfare at the time—the definition of poverty at the time. It really starts from a simple question, why are people poor? And the organizational answer flows from that. And the belief that the whole system was based on was that people were poor because of society and structural issues beyond their control. People were poor because of structural imbalances in the capital economy. People were poor because of racism, sexism in our society. People were poor because of loss of spouse, loss of job. It was very situational.

For administrators and caseworkers, then, what changed was not their mission to serve, but the "philosophy of welfare" that prevailed. As a job coach of the new work-first program explains:

> Motivating them to get a job and to want to really work and improve themselves, [is] what we . . . really do here.

One local administrator reminded me that "the pressure is [still] to do the right thing"; the difference now lies in the philosophy that guides what "the right thing" is. As another administrator explains, the "right thing" according to work-first is motivating people to make their behavior congruous with the demands of the labor market.

> We make no bones about it. We want to change behavior. We want people to work. People who are not working, to work. . . . If I want to

change behavior, it takes a relationship; it takes humans interacting with humans.

As this administrator alludes to, changing behavior is a much more involved task than simply assessing financial eligibility. It requires relationships of "humans interacting with humans." This relationship, however, is very different from supportive social work relationships of the past. Whereas welfare efforts of the 1960s had sought to address structural issues of racism and sexism, and in the process ameliorate structural issues of social and economic inequality, the TANF approach is much more individualistic, and much more punitive.

Carrots and sticks work together such that both punishment and reward are needed to change behavior. An administrator explains:

> They need to learn to take personal responsibility for working. . . . And you don't do that just by punishing them when they don't do what they need to do; you do it also with offering rewards and helping people understand why ultimately their lives will be better.

Justifying her daily case processing with an understanding of behavioral pop psychology, a caseworker explains, "It's like that [B.F.] Skinner said . . . the only two things are punishment and reward and everyone's preferences for rewards are different." Accordingly a caseworker explains, "When you are on public assistance if you don't do or go where we tell you, you will be sanctioned." Alternatively, during the application process a caseworker states, "If you don't do this you'll be denied!" Within these parameters, caseworkers readily wield case denials and sanctions as a form of punishment.[24]

Though diverting clients is heavily tied to performance measures and technology, discretion weighs heavily in the final decisions. A caseworker explains that attitude can be as important as paperwork in ending a client's application unfavorably with a denial.

> I don't just go by the paperwork. I really go more by . . . is this person willing to cooperate and do what's expected of them. Or are they, you know, very upset and not wanting to do it. Um, because technically [if they don't cooperate] in the end it's not going to be favorable [for them].

Caseworkers attempt to be cordial when they have the opportunity. Nevertheless, their task of enforcing personal responsibility is largely adversarial in nature: "We give them bad news about half the time," "We are a thorn in their side," "I read their files because I like to know what I am up against," "I tell them, 'shame on you!,'" "I'll embarrass 'em, why not?"

For compliant clients, their case is more likely to open, but caseworkers stress the rewards of work as an end in itself; "That's what you need to do, help yourself." In addition to being cast in the light of being responsible, and doing what one is supposed to, applicants who find formal employment are also compensated with material perks such as reimbursed childcare and transportation, exemption from job searching activities and sometimes job retention bonuses. For instance, a caseworker explains that certain programs and extra resources are available only to clients who are deemed compliant.

> Now if you just applied, you're an applicant, you don't get a whole lot, but I will give them the driver's education depending upon their job search. If they come to me for driver's ed, I say, "Did you complete your first job search?" Yes, OK, then you can do it.

Similarly, caseworkers explain, there are computer classes and other "extras" such as bus passes that, like driver's education, are made available only upon request and only if the caseworker judges the client to be deserving of the benefit. Many of these rewards or carrots are advertised and touted to clients by caseworkers, as in the following instance where a caseworker urges an increase in work hours to meet the cutoff for reduced job searching requirements:

> If you can squeeze in a few more hours, you won't have to do a job search. Do you think you can do maybe an hour more a day?

Explaining the logic behind this reward system, the coach shared:

> We always encourage them to try to get their employer to give them additional hours since part-time is anything less than 30 hours a week. If they have no job they do 10 job searches a week. If they are working but less than 30 [hours], they have to do five job search contacts per week

and bring them back every week. If they hit 30 they don't have to continue doing the job search portion.

Policymakers have described such discretionary encouragement and punishment as the hard to measure "suasions" that caseworkers exercise over clients. In the words of Lawrence Mead, an architect of the 1996 legislation, "suasions tied to benefits that today often try to change lifestyle" include, among other things, "pressure to work or pay child support."[25] So the goal is broader than simply ushering clients into jobs. A fully successful attempt at behavioral change would involve fostering a lifestyle of long-term work, even if this requires recycling clients through low wage jobs until they get it right. A job coach explains:

> See because the trick here, that I've learned at work-first, is not to get them the job, it's to keep it. That's the hard part for our people, it's that they have a hard time keeping it. So you see a lot of repeaters . . . But in order to get something right you have to keep doing it.

In the words of an administrator, the new approach is to "see you as a person rather than a label." Articulating this line of reasoning on the front lines, one caseworker explains, "It's like quitting smoking; different things work for different people, but since the system is now temporary, we are trying to get you out of it."

Casework as Behavioral Conditioning

In the context of national discourse, the work-first approach has painted poverty as an individual rather than structural dilemma to be solved on the local level, by poor families themselves, as government weans them off its corrupting largesse. This approach is indicative of what Nancy Fraser describes as a therapeutic approach to governance that corresponds with a medicalization of poverty.[26] Sanford Schram, like Fraser, draws critical attention to the medicalization of poverty as if it were a personal vice such as smoking, alcoholism, or drug use that is in need of a cure.[27] The mission hence is to get clients to change by first coming to understand themselves as deviant.[28]

As Marchevsky and Theoharis observe, "The medicalized lexicon of welfare dependency locates the causes of poverty in individual characteristics and failings of poor people, while tying the personal health of the poor to that of society by turning welfare dependency into a social disease that must be aggressively diagnosed, quarantined, and treated."[29] As another commentator argues, "All of our other social ills—crime, drugs, violence," are seen as derivatives of welfare dependency.[30] Under the "new paternalism," the new mission of welfare is thus "to supervise and recondition the behavior of welfare recipients, who as 'sick' and 'damaged' people cannot be entirely trusted to act as responsible adults."[31] The resulting task for caseworkers is to develop a routine that enables them to first construct a line of distinction isolating or quarantining this dependent underclass, and then to act to re-condition their behavior.

Within the medicalized-therapeutic paradigm, casework is less an offering of shelter from poverty and more an offering of "tough love" or "get tough" attitudes and actions that demand penitent and rehabilitated behavior of clients. By extension, any resistance by poor parents becomes psychologized as personal weakness: denial and an unwillingness to participate in necessary therapy.

Taking a Stand against Dependency

Caseworkers are encouraged to buy into the work-first approach because it is perceived as a response to a dependent mentality that has developed among clients under AFDC. As one caseworker explained, she would like to end the feeling of "being owed things":

> People come through thinking that they're owed something . . . that well you're supposed to do this for me. I'm supposed to be able to get food stamps and you're supposed to take care of my kids and you're supposed to pay my rent and you're supposed to, you're supposed to, you're supposed to you know, and if I die and go to hell it's your fault! And I think if anything I could change I would change that whole attitude about that, you know and try to help people be more responsible for their own well-being, and see work as better than assistance.

From the perspective of caseworkers, there is no reason for such an attitude; "I don't understand it, like how can you think that way."

Though some critics assert that the problem lies more in the complexity of client lives, caseworkers maintain that something must be done.[32] Work-first's requirement to show compliance provides such a mechanism, even if it is a long and difficult process. In the words of one caseworker, the road from dependency to self-sufficiency is a challenge.

And this is what [policymakers] don't understand. It's hard for someone who has always relied on government assistance to be able to learn to be self-sufficient. It's kind of hard.

As this job coach explains, however, he intends to effect a change in applicant behavior by stimulating thinking:

Author: And do you use that [form] at all?
Job Coach: I do . . . mostly to get them to think, you know.

To explain what he means, he then presents an exemplary conversation:

"Have you applied for Temporary Assistance before?" . . . "Yes," . . . "How many times?" . . . "I don't know how many." . . . "Well you should know how many because you have a five-year time limit." . . . "How much time [do] you have left?" . . . so it's. This, I think, is not mostly for us, I think it's mostly for them.

Pushing clients to answer questions about their situation is part of the conscious efforts that caseworkers make to prod applicants toward a particular way of thinking about their situation. In addition to creating and using specialized forms and protocols for this, caseworkers take impromptu opportunities to send the message that clients should be moving away from a dependent mentality. One caseworker recounts:

This person working one month comes in for another 30-day bus pass. I say, "We only give one." Invariably the next question is, "Well then how am I supposed to get to work?" . . . [I say,] did you never think you would have to ever buy your own bus pass?

In another instance, a caseworker berates a client for asking the government to pick up the tab for her mistake.

I said [to her], "It's our fault that you lost it [a bus pass]? We should pay? I mean, where is the responsibility?"

Under TANF, clients are expected to gradually move toward taking greater personal responsibility in all things, including not only managing income but also such things as paying rent. When it seems this is not happening, caseworkers such as the following take notice:

> TANF Worker: This form for vouchers is more paperwork for us, but some people prefer it to getting the cash. So they choose this even though they could do the cash because they are just like, "Oh you're going to pay my rent, that's one less thing I have to worry about." If we just pay their rent, though, we're not teaching them responsibility.

In such cases, caseworkers imbue the choices that they make in daily processing with didactic value. Avoiding doing things for clients that would make it too easy for them, caseworkers also sometimes adjust their services to make things more difficult than they have to be in order to discourage what they see as poor, or as the case may be, dependent behavior. In the following instance, a caseworker explains how she modifies the recommendation of her colleagues who assess level of need in order to ensure that she is not giving the client too much.

> Caseworker 1: They told me $80 but I only gave $60. She could make it on $60. She didn't need $80 for those things.
> Caseworker 2: Yeah, it depends on where you shop. You could go to Aldi's.

Together they banter about ways to do it the cheapest. Interviewer 2 closes with, "We don't want to be enabling."

This logic extends also to efforts in the job market. Rather than "enabling" excuses, caseworkers such as the following refuse to accept certain excuses that are indicative of a "dependent" frame of mind.

> Author: So are there ever not good reasons that they may call with that you won't re-schedule them for?
> Job Coach: Oh yeah, plenty. Like for example, "I have an appointment for a job at 1 p.m." Well, you had between 8 a.m. and 12 to come here, so you could have done both. Not going to fly. And when you're working you're going to have to schedule appointments around work hours. At least that's the whole premise. We try to get them to that frame of mind.

Recognizing the importance of frame of mind, one orientation leader explains, applicants often must do a considerable amount of mental preparation in order to accomplish what caseworkers demand of them.

Orientation Leader: I say, "Listen, have you taken time to mentally prepare yourself for work?" You have to take time to mentally prepare yourself, so I say, "Listen, take today, and go home. Go home, and get yourself ready, then start tomorrow."

As another coach explains, it is clear when a client is in the compliant frame of mind.

Job Coach: You know, we've been doing this for so long. We can sort of gauge how they handle and you know how they present themselves, how they, come across, their attitude basically. We can sort of gauge, you know, the kind of person that we're dealing with. . . . So we can tell right away sometimes, if a person is really going to be very disagreeable or if a person is, you know, going to say, "Well, OK, I made a mistake." That makes a big difference for us too.

Client Emotional Work

Clients who wish to rise above suspicion of dependency—and thereby avoid further scrutiny that could lead to diversion—must make a concerted effort. In other words, in order to be a successful work-first client, one must learn to conduct "emotion work."[33] Emotion work is a gendered concept, since historically emotion management is something required of women, particularly women in home life and face-to-face service professions. It involves harnessing mind and feeling and subjugating these private aspects of self to the scrutiny of others, in this case actors in the welfare institution. Frame of mind and commitment to work cannot be communicated via compliance alone, as one caseworker reminds us: "I don't go by what's on the sheet so much. I really go more by what I'm getting from this person. Is this person willing to cooperate and do . . . do the work that's expected of them." In the words of another caseworker, the power dynamics between caseworkers and their clients are such that applicants will be able to access more aid from the work-first system if they learn to act more like "sugar" than like "vinegar."

Job Coach: If I have something that you want, why would you berate me, give me a hard time about it, call me names and cuss me out? . . . Just because some people don't have the social graces or whatever to uh figure out that uh I got something you need and you need to treat me decently to get it . . . and it's usually the younger people. It's usually people who are 18, 19, 20, maybe 22. They seem to be quickest with the short temper and attitude, just probably not worldly wise enough to figure out that, we have something you want; you get more flies with sugar than vinegar.

Given the importance of caseworker impression, clients who wish to be successful are thereby compelled to do emotional work; they must suppress their feelings "in order to sustain the outward countenance that produces the proper state of mind in others," to manage the image they project in the presence of caseworkers.[34]

For instance, applicants must recognize caseworker views and act on their perception of these views, to make sure that caseworkers do not think of them as trying to get out of welfare requirements for responsibility. Sometimes this involves a straightforward declaration of one's intentions whenever there is possibility of doubt.

I'm not trying to get out of work-first. [This applicant's tone suggests that she is insulted by such an insinuation.] It's my job hours. I don't want to lose my job by going to work-first.

Other times this emotional work reaches deeper and applicants may judge that an appeal to their very nature as a person is needed.

I would be working; I'm not a lazy person. If they can help me out with a job or whatever.

As seen in the following interaction, even applicants who are already working in some recognized capacity may feel forced to manage their image actively for fear of being categorized as irresponsible. This exchange begins with a TANF interviewer probing an applicant to decide whether she should send her to work-first or not.

Interviewer: OK. Your doctor said that you're totally disabled? Or just this job? Just for the purposes of the job you do now?

Applicant: Well he just wants this to heal. He could put it in writing, but I'm sure if I push him, he'd let me go back earlier.

Interviewer: But when you go back, it will only be for 16 hours? [Her tone of voice suggests that this is not enough to constitute a full work week.]

Compounded with the suggestion that her work status is inadequate, the caseworker's use of this line of questioning triggers a response in the applicant that involves her turning up the throttle on her image management. She sits up straighter and seems to focus her attention more acutely on the matter at hand, and the urgency of her performance. She then responds, speaking energetically, and proactively re-asserting herself:

> Applicant: No. More if I can get childcare! . . . See I'm behind on my bills right now . . . [She launches into a discussion of her long-term plan.] See, I want to switch to days so if I can work then, at that time, then I can see my school-age children. Since my husband left, he used to take care of the kids. But now I'm working nights so I want to switch to days, and I just want help in catching up on my bills.

The importance of such eagerness to represent oneself in a positive light is evident in the actions of caseworkers who scrutinize what applicants say, and later, among themselves, may comment on what they perceive to be the "real story" of an applicant. From these "real stories," they infer applicants' desires—"Oh, she just didn't want to go to work-first" or "She's just lazy, doesn't want to work." Although applicants are not privy to these after-hours discussions, those who are familiar with the system and its ideologies do pay careful attention to the implications of what they say.

It is never in an applicant's interest, as this woman who apparently regrets having volunteered information reveals, to be associated, even by implication, with those who characteristically rely on aid services or are dependent on the system in any way.

> First Applicant: [A TANF interviewer is interviewing her.] If they can't do it [she refers to her request for a non-food voucher], can I have a referral to go to that church thingy? That one that gives out things?
>
> TANF Interviewer: Catholic Charities?
>
> First Applicant: Yeah, I guess. I don't know what's out there. I haven't done this before. [She distances herself from those who consistently rely on public and private charity.]
>
> Onlooking Applicant: [She is seated nearby, waiting to be helped by the next free interviewer. She hears and responds to the first applicant's question.] Oh, they're only open on Thursdays.
>
> First Applicant: Oh.

Onlooking Applicant: [She smiles bashfully, in contrast to her assertive in-
terjection seconds earlier. She seems a little embarrassed that she knows
this information. She then clarifies as if she doesn't want the interview-
ers to think that she is on assistance too often.] I only know [she directs
her explanation at the Interviewer who has just finished with another applicant in time to overhear this exchange, and is now about to begin her
interview] because my brother had needed help and I had to bring him
there. [She smiles, visibly trying to express that it wasn't she that needed
the help.]

Here, overt knowledge of the system and tangential services is recognized
as a liability. The impulsively helpful onlooking applicant quickly assesses
that she must do some image work to repair the damage that her comment may have done. While the specific clues and cues that applicants use
to alert and shape their presentation of self may vary among applicants,
consistencies among caseworkers suggest that applicants are sensible to
pay attention to this work. As one caseworker explains, "If there's something that I have, and you want it from me, I'm not saying that you should
kiss my butt, but there's definitely a way to present yourself that, you, you
know get the things that you need."

Under this new system the means test of income and resources for eligibility still exists, but, as the following caseworker explains, it has been
augmented by a "sincerity" test. As caseworkers explain, successfully representing oneself as an earnest job seeker pays off.

Work-First Staff: We have so many people come through the doors where
the perception is that they're not really trying. So from, throughout any
department here, I would think if . . . anybody who is sincere . . . , they
would make themselves known and people would bend over backwards to
help them.

For instance, a coach explains;

A lot of people [are] just going through the motions coming through. . . .
So if an individual is, well let's say they're working. They're working part
time. They come in. They have their job searches and they're not going
to be able to get back here until the following week. They need a bus
pass for transportation. I'm not going to just not serve somebody because
someone is at lunch. That doesn't make any sense to me, especially if that

person has done all the stuff that they're supposed to do. You know? Why penalize somebody for, no, no reason at all? So I go snatch, if I can find one, I'll go snatch or steal a bus pass and do it up and make sure they have a bus pass.

Another coach explains that she will meet sincere and motivated clients halfway by facilitating their efforts to acquire a job.

> We make copies of [their resume] for them and I will e-mail stuff for them, or not e-mail stuff, I'll fax stuff to employers, um you know mail their letters for them. If they don't have stamps, fine, bring them in; we'll put them in envelopes for you, you know. Anything that we can do to help them, you know, get hired, fine. Why not, and you don't really mind doing that for these people because you know that they're sincere in what they're doing.

As they attempt to coach clients toward work-first behavior and attitudes, caseworkers tend to see themselves as providing a service to the deserving poor, which they clearly distinguish from the nondeserving or dependent poor. This sensitivity toward using discretion to reward "sincere" applicants who put forth the right kinds of effort emanates from the upper levels of management, as we see in this explanation from a caseworker.

> Job Coach: Judy [a senior administrator] has always instilled upon us that the people who come through here are our customers. Maybe not in the traditional sense that they're paying for whatever service you're providing, like when you buy something you're a customer, but they need to be treated like customers. If you can help them do something or get something accomplished, that really, that makes more sense than shuffling them off to the next person or having them wait. So I think, for people who have been here, [they] can understand that mandate, [they] . . . would try to make sure that person got what they needed before they left here. Just to make it easier for them. You know, like I said, If they're doing everything they're supposed to do, why jerk them around?

Key to this special treatment of applicants who are "doing everything they are supposed to" is that they have, in some way that caseworkers recognize, shown themselves worthy—whether by finding a job, completely filling out paperwork, or by doing something "extra" or not required, such as making a resume or asking for help faxing things to employers. Clients who are able to master the skill of "emotion work," in addition to complying with all work-first requirements, are likely to be successful at negotiating the work-first gauntlet. Some who excel are even invited to join the work-first institution as caseworkers.

Clients Turned Caseworkers

In the midst of daily confrontations between clients and caseworkers, former clients turned caseworkers hold a symbolic status as both enforcers of reform policy and living proof of the outcomes that are possible when clients embrace and internalize the reform ideology. Approximately one-third of work-first caseworkers were formerly welfare clients who were placed at the work-first office as part of a workfare assignment (i.e., work in exchange for TANF benefits). Later they are hired as an official staff member after proving themselves. In the minds of other caseworkers, they are cast in stark contrast to the majority of clients.

> There is something like probably 50 percent of the people who come through here don't want to find a job. You can tell by their job searches. Go to the mall. If they really wanted to work there I imagine they could find a job. They don't have to come here to do this. There are some people who have come through, like ones that work here, and something changed, now they're working. They want to improve themselves, I don't know what changed.

Clients turned caseworkers embody a sense of pride in their employment status and are featured prominently in high-visibility locations. Usually hired on as TA's (Technical Assistants) as opposed to higher paid job coaches, they dominate the reception area, serve as the majority of work-first orientation leaders, and handle the bulk of the auxiliary services such as arranging childcare, bus passes, and work clothing vouchers.

Becoming a caseworker entitles former clients to inclusion in an exclusive group. While co-workers in both major sites of intake processing (the welfare office and the work-first office), regardless of job title and pay, generally treat each other as colleagues, it is clear that this level of esteem does not extend to clients. Evident in speech patterns, such as the use of inclusive and exclusive phrasings, caseworkers tend to draw a line of distinction between themselves and those they serve. As this line is drawn, it is clear that clients turned caseworkers are on the caseworker side of this boundary. This distance is clear in the way a technical assistant describes how she became a caseworker:

> Client turned Caseworker: They need to assess themselves before they come here, ask "Why am I applying for assistance?". . . I did Work Experience here [this is the workfare internship that applicants whose cases are opened are required to participate in following job club training], and then I was hired on. What changes is the way your job makes you feel about yourself, like a human.

In describing her transformation, from one who needed to be taught personal responsibility to one who now teaches it herself, the trajectory of this TA parallels that of what Pierre Bourdieu describes as "oblates" of an educational system. Bourdieu adapts the original meaning of an "oblate" as "a child from a poor family entrusted to a religious foundation to be trained for the priesthood" as a means of analogy to "the intense loyalty felt by the teacher of humble origins who owes his whole education, culture, training and career to the state educational system."[35] There is a cyclical nature to this loyalty. Oblates feel positive about their institution in large part because it has invested in them; likewise, this TA attributes her newfound self-esteem, that enables her to feel "like a human," to her interaction with the welfare institution. Due to this loyalty, "they offer to the academic institution which they have chosen because it chose them, and vice versa, a support which, being so totally conditioned, has something total, absolute, unconditional about it."[36]

Welfare oblates cast their lot with the work-first institution they serve and its overall missions, interpreting their work contribution within this paradigm. We saw this in the opening words of Kyle that applicants need to change and that "we are a thorn in the side of those who won't change." As with Bourdieu's oblates, they come to see their position as "a form of symbolic remuneration, comparable to a rise in salary," which further contributes to a sense of satisfaction with their work.[37] As one technical assistant explains:

> I like my job, it's not bad. I used to be one of them, [welfare recipients], but now I'm working here and something changed. I feel great about myself. I try to get them to see that they can do it too.

In the case of work-first oblates, as with Bourdieu's oblates, "The agents themselves have a psychological stake in becoming party to the mystification of which they are the victims—according to a very common mechanism which persuades people (no doubt all the more so, the less privileged they are) to work at *being satisfied* with what they are, to love their fate, however mediocre it may be."[38] Through this work, welfare oblates, as evident in the TA's assertion that "I try to get them to see that they can do it too," come to see themselves as role models. Another caseworker similarly comments, "They should all be working like us." Remarks such as these make it clear that caseworkers in the newly configured work-first office and partnering welfare office accomplish more than just an implementation of policy requirements. They also consciously endeavor to provide a model of the types of workers that they feel their clients would do well to emulate.

Caseworkers who were formerly clients also hold a reputation for being "among the toughest on applicants." Their actions reveal a confidence that "we did it so we know how hard it is, but we know that it can be done." A former client turned technical assistant explained that he has integrated such a message into the mandated orientation session that all applicants must attend:

> It is tough, but as I tell them in my orientation, "I was sitting in your seat a few years ago. I know what it is like, and if I, a single father with three kids can make it, so can you with one or two kids or a partner and three kids . . . It ain't easy, it sure ain't easy, but you can do it."

Presenting themselves in this assertive and self-assured fashion also garners good relations with better-paid caseworkers who have never been on welfare, and who thus hold a less tenuous position within the organization. Maintaining a hard-line reputation is a way of showing they belong in their position, and thus of keeping their job by impressing the job coaches who supervise them. It also serves to help former clients distance themselves from current clients who are generally perceived as "others" whose will must be broken and whose lack of good work ethic must be reformed. Former clients who have become caseworkers also serve a broader institutional function as an affirmation of the work-first enterprise as a whole. In the reasoning of caseworkers who have not been on welfare, the presence among them of former clients who have converted is a morale builder and a symbol that they are doing the right thing, despite what frustrated current clients assert.

The gruff exterior presented by former clients who are seen as being the strictest with applicants, however, is not the entire story. Their understanding of the real-life messiness of clients' lives impacts their efforts to reconcile reform ideology with reality. One former client caseworker explains her approach:

> If it's serious enough, there's ways to make it easier on them like getting them exempt. This lady comes to me and says I want to do all the things you tell me to but when I go outside, he'll see me, so I tell her here's the name of the person at the welfare office, go and tell them just what you told me, and they can decide if you have to come back over here for job searches or not.

Similarly, former clients are attuned to the concerns of their counterparts and are thus able to allay their fears with levity, as in the following instance during an orientation session.

> TA: Federal laws have changed and now they really want you to try and get a
>   job rather than public assistance, and we do too.
> Applicant: But you can't negate the factors!
> TA: Oh, kids? We understand it may be tough with childcare and transporta-
>   tion, now we're not asking you to work miracles, just do your best.

Exuding a sense of understanding, clients oftentimes seek out these supposedly harsh party-liners. One former client admits that applicants will sometimes make requests:

> So you know at that point they'll say, well you know I don't want to see him, can you help me? You know, or they'll even ask for [another co-worker who was a former recipient] or who was in the orientation that they dealt with; they'll want to see that person.

This popularity of former clients among current clients is in part a function of knowing the community through living in it. Similar to the community workers described by Nancy Naples in *Grassroots Warriors*, former recipients offer an ease of communication and a form of feedback loop with community members.[39] One such connection is made below as one applicant comes back in the door, apparently remembering something he wanted to ask, about 20 seconds after leaving. He walks directly to a client turned caseworker and he asks:

> Applicant: I heard some friends are coming here three hours a day for some class.
>
> Client Turned Caseworker: What friends?
>
> Applicant: Homies. [As he says this it visibly clarifies the question for the client turned caseworker, who then directs the client to the appropriate place.]

Reflecting on the ease of communication oblates have with clients, a job coach teases a technical assistant who is a former client: "Oh but they all have good rapport with you, because even when we give them grief, they go to you." As a result of these open lines of communication, it is not unheard of for informal complaints to reach caseworkers through the extended communication networks of clients turned caseworkers.

> Client Turned Caseworker: [Client Turned Caseworker gets off the phone and says to Olivia] Did you see someone named Maplethorpe? She says she came in here the other day and saw you. . . . I went to school with her and she was a little weird back then too. I think she just needed to vent. . . . She called me to complain that you were mean to her. [She said] that you were cold . . . .
>
> Olivia (Job Coach): [In response, she asks interestedly] She called you to tell you that I was cold to her!? [Visibly agitated at such an allegation, her face becomes pinched as she replies]. . . I was not. I did not say anything to her. . . . I'm chilled, I didn't say anything to her. . . . I never said a word to her.

While some interactions among caseworkers bolster support for being unyielding toward applicants, this one clearly strikes a nerve in Olivia. Her desire to set the record straight among her co-workers, overtly defending herself against what she works up as slander, shows her displeasure at the fact that someone would say such a thing. Not opting for a terse rebuttal, however, Olivia makes a point of re-telling the entire story several times (paying no heed to applicants who subsequently arrive and look on), to be sure that her side is represented, ultimately summarizing her quandary as:

> Olivia: Vent back with them and they get upset, you don't say nothing and they get upset.

Despite conciliatory comments from her co-workers such as "I think she just needed to vent" and "We have the hardest job," Olivia's disquietude with this incident remains transparent in her unprompted comment later on that day:

> Olivia: [Speaking to Client Turned Caseworker, another TA, and me.] You know, it would be good to invest in one of those hidden cameras and just hide it up in that corner. [She motions to the far corner of the ceiling.]
> Client Turned Caseworker: Yeah.
> Olivia: Because today I was in here all by myself.
> Author: Why would that be good?
> Olivia: To back you up, show what really happened.

In this comment, it becomes clear that, although hours have passed since the discussion, Olivia is still thinking about the alleged incident in which she was accused of being "cold." Her suggestion shows that it is important to her that she not be thought of in that way (by her colleagues and by clients). Furthermore, by advocating for a video camera, she implies that, if one had been installed, she would be vindicated.

Evident in another instance of feedback through clients turned caseworkers, the following conversation reveals not only a check on caseworker behavior but a preference for dealing with former clients turned caseworkers:

> A Client Turned Caseworker: She says that Ferrina [the receptionist in front of the building, a former client] is the nicest person, that she saved her life, and that Joanna . . . she is mean, she said that Ferrina should be back in the job search office helping people instead. She said that Joanna called the police on her.
> Joanna: I did not. She said she wanted to see a supervisor [now more forcefully defending herself]. So I went to get one, then when I was out of the room I realized that everyone was in training. I was cool with her. I did go out to reception and say if she comes back in here please let me know. I did not call the police on her. [A sheriff officer is stationed out by reception on a daily basis, perhaps this led to some of the confusion.]

The appeal of former recipient caseworkers to current applicants seems to stem from an ability to empathize. A former recipient explains that being able to really listen is a sought after skill, one that those who have had similar experiences tend to possess.

TA (Former Client): I was sitting in [their] seat a few years ago . . . So I really listen to them.

Author: Is that part of your job?

TA: No, actually it's not in my job description, I just, people find me.

Author: Where do they find you? In orientation?

T.A.: Yeah, in orientation when I run those and when I'm in here, I rotate in here to do bus passes and childcare. And they see me then, then they come to talk with me.

The work that former clients turned caseworkers do to listen to, empathize with, and at times intervene in the cases of current clients are a reflection of their understanding of the challenges that exist in bridging policy and the reality of everyday life. As in the case above, doing this work often leads former clients outside of the parameters of their official job descriptions. The result is a broad array of work roles aimed at reconciling reform ideology and their knowledge of client lives. A former client turned caseworker explains:

So I do everything, there is no limit to what I deal with, childcare, bus passes. I'm a social worker, I do emotional stuff, how will I get my kids to school, domestic abuse.

As oblates of the work-first system then, clients turned caseworkers are part of an exchange in which both they and the institution of welfare benefit. By epitomizing the extreme of client conversion to the mind-set of the reform, the institution simultaneously gains fierce champions and public witnesses to the validity of its enterprise. The presence of clients turned staff members serves an institutional function, even if welfare reform itself is not something to which they ideologically ascribe. Though one comments, "I'm not in this business for the welfare reform; I'm in this to feed my kids," the underlying reasons for her participation are of less institutional relevance than her behavior. By simply playing along, welfare oblates become exalted in status, rising not only out of the depths of deplorable dependence and un-deservingness to the ranks of the worthy employed, but even further into the echelons of the institution that has invested in them to the formerly quite distant and seemingly unattainable status of a "social worker."[40] Even with this elevation, however, clients turned caseworkers are still not free of institutional efforts to manage their attitudes. In addition to endeavoring to change client behavior, caseworkers routinely act to police each other's use of discretion.

Policing Colleagues' Remediation Work

In the midst of prodding, pushing, rewarding, and confronting applicants, caseworkers act collectively to police each others' performance. This takes form along a continuum ranging from helpful advice to sarcastic scrutiny. For instance, Joseph offers consoling words to Alyce after having observed her confrontational encounter with a client:

Joseph: You know, you did that very well . . .
Alyce: [She exhales deeply, mumbling to herself.]
Joseph: [He explains empathetically toward Alyce in a clear effort to console her.] It's not fun.

Such unsolicited commentary from co-workers is common following encounters with clients. However, while typically offered in familiar tone, such comments are not always reassuring. Caseworkers are just as likely to mock each other for being "a softy." In the following extended interaction, for instance, two co-workers, Caroline and Ed, interact to give each other critical feedback following their respective confrontational interactions with clients.

Applicant: [Hands in a Job Contact sheet] Is that good?
Caroline: Where are the phone numbers?
Applicant: Oh, I have to have them filled out too?
Caroline: Yes.
Applicant: So what does that mean? Is it complete?
Caroline: The phone numbers are missing.
Applicant: So what? Does that mean that I have to go back to the mall and ask people their phone numbers?
Caroline: Did you go to the mall to fill these out?
Applicant: Yes.
Caroline: Well . . .
Applicant: So I am supposed to not only fill out all of these forms and get the person's name but also get their phone number when they're all busy doing things? [She asks this question in a manner that suggests that this expectation is ludicrous.]
Caroline: It needs to be filled out to be complete. The people who check up on these and call employers aren't going to take the time to look up the

phone numbers. We just had a meeting about this the other day and they have to be filled out.

Applicant: So what will happen? Are they going to deny my case? [Nervousness becomes evident in her voice.]

Caroline: If it's not complete.

Applicant: Can I go look them up or something?

Caroline: [She points to the form.] All of these must be filled out—employer, name, phone number—for it to count. Starting next week, when you come in, all of this must be filled out.

In this fairly typical interaction, like previous examples, the job coach relies on textual information to confront the applicant and push her to comply. Also, consistent with caseworker efforts to turn confrontations into teaching moments, Caroline ultimately decides to give the applicant a break as long as she fully complies for the following week. As the applicant leaves, Caroline realizes that the applicant was not the only person in the room paying attention. Ed, a fellow job coach who was also in the room and apparently observing, remarks:

Ed: Getting tougher, but still not that tough.

Ed's comment, while chiding, is also spoken within the context of Caroline's reputation for being lenient with clients, although she has also been known to be demanding of them.

Without further observation, this isolated interaction might simply suggest that some coaches are tougher than others. More accurately, this interaction provides a window of insight into a broader picture in which this type of criticism is mutual among caseworkers. Indicative of this dynamic, these two coaches swap roles in a subsequent scenario later in the day. As Ed sits at a table talking with an applicant who has come in for a weekly job search appointment, there is an outburst of arguing and the conversation suddenly becomes audible to the rest of the room.

Applicant: [In a raised voice, so most in the room can see she is upset, she demands] So what am I supposed to do?

Ed: [Using a calm voice, he says] I don't know. I'm just saying . . . [The applicant cuts him off mid-sentence.]

> Applicant: No, maybe you should listen to me. [She commands.] How are
> they supposed to make sure that my kids are getting to school? Tell me
> how?
>
> Ed: [Maintaining a calm voice, he begins to respond] I am not sure but what
> I am saying is . . . [The applicant once again cuts him off.]
>
> Applicant: [She demands] I got Social Services on my ass because my kids
> are missing too much school! How are the people who are watching my
> kids supposed to get my kids to and from school if they are busy watching
> other kids?!
>
> Ed: [He tries to calm her down, but she remains angry.]
>
> Applicant: How are they supposed to do that?
>
> Ed: You're upset. How about I handle your case on another day? How about
> you come back on another day? I'll help you another day?
>
> Applicant: [She says nothing.]
>
> Ed: I will reschedule you for tomorrow.

At this, the applicant storms out of the room. It is unclear if she intends
to return the next day or not, but everyone in the room, including other
coaches and waiting applicants, are staring at Ed after having watched the
applicant walk out. Ed walks over to his desk, next to Caroline's. Caroline,
who had been previously scrutinized by Ed as being "not that tough," then
says to her co-worker whose applicant has just walked out the door:

> Caroline: If that was me, she wouldn't be coming back tomorrow.

In this statement, made to a grimacing Ed, who acts as if he knew he had
it coming, Caroline declares that she would have been tougher on the applicant than Ed was.

While this swapping of positions, from critiqued to critic, is ironic, it
is also very telling of the liberty that caseworkers exercise in comment-
ing on each others' work. Far from following lines of management, caseworkers of lower rank freely engage in these forms of cajoling each other
with caseworkers higher in the hierarchy as well. It is part of the behind-
the-scenes "emotion work" that caseworkers do in order both to maintain
consistency and to keep each other in line with institutional ideology. By
participating in this reinforcement of tough love on clients, clients turned
caseworkers learn to act in a manner consistent with the ideological attitudes that both enabled and brought about the enactment of the 1996
reform.

Examining how routine actions "inflected with ideology and culture" give "overarching meaning to certain practices" allows us not only to see where national discourse enters into frontline work, but furthermore, to see what Louis Althusser describes as the role of ideology in the reproduction of relations of production such that "ideology constitutes subjects, while subjects in turn constantly reproduce the ideology that constitutes them."[41] Understanding this relationship between ideology and its reproduction in the attitudes of local people helps us to understand the mechanisms by which work-first common sense is continually constructed and reconstructed.

6

"Not Everybody Fits into Their Box"

Work-First, Gender, Race, and Families

Work-first common sense is constructed through the efforts of numerous people and at numerous levels, but at its heart, it is an approach to family life. National entrepreneurs sold the ideas of reform to local innovators, who in turn have passed it on to caseworkers, but it is poor families that are asked to adapt their lives to the values and goals of work-first. TANF implementers attempt to sell families on the goals of "personal responsibility" and "self-sufficiency" in the labor market. The logic behind this approach is one of empowerment. Poor people who work will be better off; they will have higher incomes and more self-esteem than those who do not work. What this logic does not emphasize, however, is that poor people who turn to TANF for assistance are predominantly mothers and disproportionately of color. This chapter examines how work-first interacts with family life and in particular the nurturing and reproductive care work of mothers. As this chapter unfolds, it becomes clear that the common sense of work-first is one in which families are expected to prioritize paid labor market productivity over the reproductive work of raising a family. In particular, TANF in East County urges restructuring of family such that those who satisfactorily limit reproduction, contract out childcare, and tailor relationships with men are favored in receiving welfare aid.[1]

These policy changes come as families in general face pressure to transform and conform to new rules of a global community. The vast labor pools available in the global economic network have altered the productive-reproductive balance of families. Households have historically been valued not only for their market production capabilities but also their capacity to reproduce society, including the labor market, by bearing and nurturing competent offspring.[2] At times reproduction has been considered a primary asset by pro-natalist national policies, and in some instances women who concerned themselves with matters outside the home, such as women's suffrage, have been chastised for diluting their capacity for reproduction and thereby engaging in "race suicide."[3] For certain racialized groups, such as African Americans during slavery, women were actively encouraged to "breed" since each successful occurrence represented an increase in units of "property" and "labor"; intrusion into women's fertility decisions were thereby justified on the basis of the needs of "a changing political economy."[4] Worker expendability in the global market, however, has given the productive power of families clear priority over their reproductive functions; global capital is less inclined to invest in the family- and community-building required for long-term local prosperity than to use its mobile capital to move its investments to locales with cheaper and less-organized labor.[5] In this climate, not only is unpaid care work devalued in comparison to paid market labor, but structural inequalities of race and class are reproduced.

Nonwhite and poor women historically have had to work in addition to parenting, while wealthier and whiter women to a larger extent have been able to not only avoid paid labor by virtue of their husbands' privileged labor market placement but also reduce their unpaid and family caregiving work by hiring nonwhite and poor women as housekeepers, maids, and nannies.[6] Transnational portability of workers has expanded these class and race differentials on a global scale with the emergence and acceleration of imported domestic and care work laborers.[7] As Leith Mullings writes, "Household structure in both developing and industrialized countries is shaped by global as well as local processes, as policies implemented at national or international levels increasingly mold reproductive experiences."[8] She further explains, "These processes form the context for stratified reproduction, whereby 'some categories of people are empowered to nurture and reproduce, while others are disempowered.'"[9]

The analysis that follows explores these new neoliberal imperatives at the front lines of the reinvented welfare state as a site of state regulation of the needs of the poor that also requires a transformation in clients and the ways in which they relate to their families and the labor market. I first present a framework for understanding who work-first clients are in terms of their gender, race, and family obligations. I then examine how the implementation of work-first, as a program that serves primarily women and children, involves not only diverting families from aid but also provoking changes in reproduction, childcare, and the role of men within these families. Finally, I critically assess how explicitly stressing a color- and gender-blind work-first model and implicitly devaluing family and care work in work-first processing forces poor families to conform to a new model of family life. This model is based on a fusion of classical liberal individualism and liberal feminism that has been tweaked to accommodate a neoliberal demand for flexible and unencumbered low wage workers.

Embodied Clients

Writing around the time of the last welfare reform, Nancy Fraser discussed "the coming welfare wars" as wars "about, even against, women."[10] "Because women constitute the overwhelming majority of social-welfare program recipients and employees, women and women's needs will be the principal stakes in the battles over social spending likely to dominate national politics in the coming period."[11] Though she was largely correct in this assessment, she could not have known that much of the 1996 welfare reform's "battles" would center around the framing of women's needs and responsibilities. Nevertheless, it was a safe bet since welfare policy in the United States since colonial times has focused on women and their care of children.

Since its inception, ADC, AFDC, and now TANF has been a portion of the federal safety net that has concerned itself with the needs of poor families. As a result, the people whom intake workers nationwide serve are largely mothers (90 percent of adults are women and over 70 percent of the entire caseload is comprised of children).[12] As seen in figure 6.1, next to their children, adult women compose the majority of TANF recipients in the site of this research, East County, New York, as well.

Women's receipt of TANF at a rate seven times that of men highlights the fact that a majority of cases are made up of groupings of women and children. Figure 6.2 provides some insight into the size of these groupings, suggesting that over 50 percent of these applicants have either one or two children and nearly a third have three or more (the family count includes the mother as well) in East County.

The TANF family characteristics for fiscal year 2002 indicate that the average number of family members nationally was 2.4 with an average of 1.9 recipient children per active case family.[13] (The average household size in the United States in general is 2.59 and the average number of children

FIGURE 6.1
County TANF Totals by Age and Gender

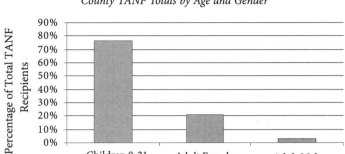

Source: Data Collected from the County Department of Social Services, 1999

FIGURE 6.2
County TANF Caseload by Number of Family Members in Case

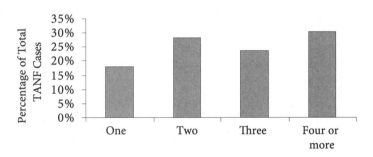

Source: Data Collected from the County Department of Social Services, 1999

per family with children in the United States is 1.86.[14]) The average age of TANF mothers is 31 and the vast majority of these are single (over 66 percent). Furthermore, though slightly over half have completed 12 years of schooling, most of the rest have not made it that far, leaving approximately 94 percent of TANF mothers nationwide with a high school education or

FIGURE 6.3
Comparison of County Population and County TANF Caseload by Ethnicity

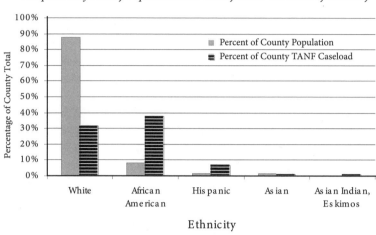

Source: Data Collected from the County Department of Social Services, 1999, and the U.S. Census Bureau, 1990

less in a day and age where nearly all employers in good-paying jobs are demanding more.[15]

There is also a racial component to the demographics of poor families in that blacks are disproportionately poor and therefore comprise a disproportionate percentage of the welfare rolls. In East County, as in the nation, African-American and white clients comprise similar proportions of welfare recipients, but whites comprise the majority of the population.[16] African Americans account for 38 percent of TANF caseloads and whites account for 31 percent in East County (as opposed to 38.3 and 31.6 nationally), indicating that African Americans are disproportionately represented in East County as they are in the nation (see figure 6.3).[17] Nationally, African Americans or African Americans in combination with one or more other races comprise 12.9 percent of the population while whites comprise 77.1 percent.[18]

This is significant not so much because African Americans represent a slightly higher proportion of the caseloads than whites, but because it is indicative of a disproportional representation of blacks in poverty. While the poverty rate overall fell in recent years to 10 percent for all families in 2003, it has remained disproportionately high among blacks as compared to whites (28.7 percent versus 8.9 percent among families with children under 18, and 42.8 percent versus 28.1 percent among *female headed* families with children under 18).[19] This widely recognized overrepresentation of blacks in poverty at the national level leads to higher rates of welfare participation and thus welfare reform has a higher rate of impact on these families.[20]

The concept of intersectionality recognizes that social patterns of inequality not only appear along the lines of gender, race, and class, but that these dynamics often intersect to bring about complex scenarios of political economy that cannot be adequately understood by looking at matters of gender, race, or class in isolation. Considering these dynamics in concert as they permeate the welfare state on the local level in obvious and subtle ways offers a complementary lens of analysis that adds critical dimensions to our understanding of global restructuring and labor relations as they affect poor families. In this case, intersectionality emerges as a useful lens for understanding the ramifications of TANF diversion and new work-first expectations for reproduction, childcare, and gender relations among parents.

The Weeding Out and Diversion of Families

Within the context of welfare reform, the nurturing work of parenting is not valued as producing a commodity. Only the sale of paid work in the formal labor market context garners the definition of "work" that is represented in the term "employment." In the course of processing applicants, caseworkers pair self-sufficiency with the responsibility to participate in this particular kind of work in a way that sets it in binary opposition to the notion of "dependency." Fraser and Gordon suggest that "dependency" has historically referred to all who depend on another for their livelihood (a definition that would include both wage and salaried workers who have an employer), but in modern times this older meaning has been replaced by a reference to only specific types of dependency that are typically experienced by women who are dependent on men or the government for finances needed to underwrite their parenting work.[21] This juxtaposition of working versus nonworking, and self-sufficient versus dependent, emerges within work-first as a reinvigorated version of coding for deserving and undeserving—a practice that has historically focused scrutiny on innate characteristics of the poor, rather than the environment in which they struggle to survive.[22] In this way, the processing work of work-first caseworkers serves to orient applicants to an individualistic, internal-focused way of thinking about their situation that discounts parenting work as real labor.

This way of thinking is both enabled and reinforced by institutional means of record keeping. As Barbara Cruikshank argues, the uniformity of numbers in the welfare state "does not represent the realities of poor women's lives."[23] Griffith and Smith similarly explain:

> [In] calculations of paid work, the hours and effort oriented toward earning a monetary reward are not applied to and seem incompatible with mothering. Yet the taken for granted dimension of mothering identified as caring somehow obscures the fact that what mothers do for their children involves time, effort, thought, and planning, and that it is done as other work is, under definite material conditions and with definite resources.[24]

Reflecting on the devaluation of care work in the market many years earlier, Senator Daniel Patrick Moynihan's comments remain accurate today: "If American society recognized home making and child rearing as productive work to be included in the national economic accounts . . . the receipt of welfare might not imply dependency. But we don't. It may be hoped the women's movement of the present time will change this. But as of the time I write, it had not."[25] As a policy reliant on an economy and labor market that renders such work invisible, work-first participates in devaluing the caring work in which many applicants take part. This collusion materializes in the culling function of the work-first gauntlet.

Evident in table 6.1, there are numerous potential reasons for being diverted from TANF. This summary indicates that intake practices—such as orientation meetings stressing new requirements, independent searches for work, and monitored/assisted applicant job searches (AJS)—are all indeed critical sites of diversion. From the perspective of work-first, compliance is a public act, while the reasons for noncompliance are often relegated to the private sphere: "You do whatever you need to in order to be prepared for work." On further introspection, however, the frequency of family-related complications appearing as typical reasons leading to diversion (over 50 percent of the reasons listed) suggest that diversion is also at least in part a function of conflict between the overarching market orientation of work-first and mothering responsibilities.

Since the sexual division of labor in contemporary U.S. society continues to designate women as primary caregivers for those who cannot care for themselves—children, elderly, the sick—not only are women more directly affected than men by government programs to help those in need of care, but women who seek out TANF assistance must balance care work for their families with "work" as defined in the ideological categories of the work-first approach. [26]

Reflecting the prioritization that emerges to reconcile this conflict, Frances Fox Piven has argued that neoliberal welfare restructuring has reframed welfare receipt as a market relationship in which families must exchange labor for benefits. [27] However, and critical to understanding work-first's capabilities for diversion, the work that is required is not flexible or even accommodating to family life; rather, it is family life that must, if families are to be compliant, adjust to low wage labor market demands. Since clients are required by work-first to accept any offer of employment made during their ten weekly job applications:

> Mothers who are mandated to leave welfare for employment in the low-wage labor market do not simply contend with the difficulties of combining the low-wage labor market with family needs, they must also cope with the conditions brought on by their (oftentimes) involuntary entry into the low-wage labor market. This shift constitutes a particular social relation that bears attention. For instance, a mother may have to adjust to caring for very young children differently than she intended, with little say over the conditions under which she cares for those children or in ways that create lasting familial and/or financial instability. [28]

The committed follow-through on the part of caseworkers to ensure that processing threats of denial and sanction for noncompliance are not hollow, despite family encumbrances, creates a stern institutional configuration of demands and repercussions by which paid work is prioritized over family and caregiving work. Those who fail or refuse to subject their families to this paradigm are exemplary candidates for diversion.

Through its ready use of diversion, work-first serves as a model and a mechanism for the neoliberal restructuring of poor families. While not explicitly aimed at such restructuring, welfare reform requires women to devalue the work of family reproduction and nurturance in favor of labor market productivity. They must become "unencumbered clients" in order to successfully navigate work-first processing. This process individualizes mothers by defining children and kin not as societal assets or values in

TABLE 6.1

Major Events and Reasons for Application Denial or Closure

The Stages of Intake Processing	Major Events Leading to Application Denial or Closure	Typical Reasons for These Events
The Application	Did not fully complete application	Unable to understand legal and technical writing (or illiterate)
	Did not wait to be called up for prescreening interview	Childcare responsibilities that conflict with long wait in the waiting room
	Accepted a diversion grant	Needed immediate and very short-term help for one-time financial emergencies
Prescreening	Did not complete drug and alcohol screening	Childcare or transportation problems, family emergencies
	Another adult in the household did not complete drug and alcohol screening	Difficulty getting other adults to comply
	Fail to sign a form such as identifying an absentee parent so child support can be enforced	Difficulty balancing relationship with child's noncustodial parent
	A staff member finds an error in reported information	Staff usually consider this purposeful deception to gain benefits
	Late for appointment	Childcare or transportation problems, family emergencies
	Did not show up	Childcare or transportation problems, family emergencies
Welfare Orientation	Late for orientation, locked out	Childcare or transportation problems, family emergencies
	Did not show up	Childcare or transportation problems, family emergencies
WTW Orientation	Late for Orientation, locked out	Childcare or transportation problems, family emergencies
	Did not show up	Childcare or transportation problems, family emergencies

The Stages of Intake Processing	Major Events Leading to Application Denial or Closure	Typical Reasons for These Events
Family Assistance Interview	Did not successfully complete WTW orientation or other location referred to	Childcare or transportation problems, family emergencies
	Missing a form of verification	Waited too long to request documentation of landlord or employer, etc. Or overlooked a needed form
	Welfare investigators visit home and find inaccuracies in application	There is often confusion as to how to list and update rapidly changing household arrangements
	Unable to document a claim	A landlord or other did not submit it or not in possession of evidence of a need
	Did not show up	Childcare or transportation problems, family emergencies
Applicant Job Search	Found a job	May no longer need assistance, or forget that employment needs to be documented
	Did not fully complete a job search: May have forgotten to record employer phone number or may not have filed enough job applications	Transportation issues, lack of good jobs, childcare issues: difficulty juggling job searching and family responsibilities, including emergency situations
	Incorrectly completed a job search	May have failed to do an independent job search, i.e., someone else such as a family member filled out the application
	Employers fail to confirm that an application was filed	Usually claim that an application was filed and that the employer is mistaken
	Did not show up or was denied a rescheduled appointment	Childcare or transportation problems, family emergencies

themselves but as commodified liabilities; getting through processing successfully is in large part a matter of ability to manage barriers in the form of children and adult kin.

Since many women on welfare are quite accustomed to work, welfare versus work is a false dichotomy; diversion becomes not merely a measure of compliance and willingness to work but a measure of ability to modify family structure to meet the work-first paradigm.[29] In the words of a former client, it becomes a measure of ability to fit into a box.

> Not everybody fits into their [work-first's] box. . . . You've got women out there that are being abused . . . and you've got children out here that have got juvenile delinquent problems and no one wants to keep them. And then you want to take away their food? . . . Because first of all, you're not going to keep your job having to run around and see about your child . . . When people are dealing with family emergencies [work-first] is not a priority on your agenda. You're dealing with your emergency situation at that time and other things become secondary until that crisis is handled.[30]

"Fitting into their box" involves coming to see reproduction, childcare, and relationships with men—in short, reproductive functions of family— as a lower priority than the value women can assert through participation in labor market production. It involves approximating a work/family balance that, in part due to significant differences in workplace demands and flexibility as well as childcare resources and marriage markets, has largely worked for the middle class. In the words of one caseworker: "We all have to balance work and family and now so do they." The work-first approach has declared as defunct a history of providing special social supports for poor women and their children. "Welcome to the new world," a caseworker exclaims. In the following pages I explore how the gendered assumptions of this "new world" intersect and interact with racialized and impoverished mothers and their families—particularly with regard to reproduction, childcare, and the role of men.

Poor Women's Reproduction As Problematic

Though bearing and raising children has traditionally been viewed as a public good for society—since families who do this shoulder the cost of reproducing society by raising future workers and taxpayers—this is not universally the case. The 1996 PRWORA makes a clear distinction between families whose reproduction produces a public good, and those whom it sees as producing a public cost. In praise of the first type of families, the legislation makes the following statements:

> The Congress makes the following findings: (1) Marriage is the foundation of a successful society. (2) Marriage is an essential institution of a successful society which promotes the interests of children. (3) Promotion of responsible fatherhood and motherhood is integral to successful child rearing and the well-being of children.[31]

In stark contrast to praiseworthy functions of family, Congress outlines another type of family—poor, and particularly single-mother families which are characterized as producing crime-prone and maladaptive children that are more of a public cost than a public good.

> The negative consequences of an out-of-wedlock birth on the mother, the child, the family, and society are well documented as follows. . . . [the mother is] more likely to go on public assistance and to spend more years on welfare once enrolled. . . . [the child has a] higher risk of being born at a very low or moderately low birth weight. . . . low verbal cognitive attainment, as well as more child abuse, and neglect. . . . lower cognitive scores, lower educational aspirations, and a greater likelihood of becoming teenage parents themselves. . . . [it] reduces the chances of the child growing up to have an intact marriage. . . . [they are] more likely to be on welfare when they grow up. . . . Between 1985 and 1990, the public cost of births to teenage mothers under the aid to families with dependent children program, the food stamp program, and the Medicaid program has been estimated at $120 billion.[32]

Continuing with a list of potential problems for children of single-parent and teenage parent families, including, "more likely to fail and repeat a year in grade school," "more likely to be expelled or suspended from school," and "higher rates of violent crime," the Congress concludes with a declaration:

> Therefore, in light of this demonstration of the crisis in our Nation, it is the sense of the Congress that prevention of out-of-wedlock pregnancy and reduction in out-of-wedlock birth are very important Government

interests and the policy contained in part A of title IV of the Social Security Act (as amended by section 103(a) of this Act) is intended to address the crisis.[33]

Rather than address these issues structurally as manifestations of the feminization of poverty, the Congress set out armed with statistics, ghetto ethnographies, and individualizing discourse that have served to "reinforce the idea that the family, not public or political institutions or the workplace, [is] the primary institutional location for intervention into poor life."[34] Buying into a neoliberal discourse that places the ultimate blame for such problems on the most local of sites, the family, Congress seems to absolve government and the economy of responsibility; it commits itself to the contention of columnist William Raspberry: "I submit that all of our other social ills—crime, drugs, violence, failing schools— are a direct result of the degradation of parenthood by emotionally immature [welfare] recipients."[35] In response to the contrasting types of families that it defines in the findings of the legislation—good and bad for lack of better terms, the Congress set out in the PRWORA to conduct a targeted anti-natalist project to discourage reproduction in the case of unmarried poor women.

> IN GENERAL—The purpose of this part is to increase the flexibility of States in operating a program designed to . . . prevent and reduce the incidence of out-of-wedlock pregnancies and establish annual numerical goals for preventing and reducing the incidence of these pregnancies.[36]

As part of this plan, PRWORA requires that teen parents who receive aid attend school and live at home in an effort to curb childrearing among adolescent women.[37] Beyond advocating reducing reproduction through federal restrictions, the PRWORA furthermore offers fiscal incentives to states to reduce out of wedlock births via local innovation by awarding $20 million "illegitimacy bonuses" to the top five states annually that reduce the rate of illegitimacy among women (including those collecting aid and those not).[38] Though such legislative declarations and incentives make it clear that "the major goal of some welfare reformers is to reduce the number of children born to women receiving public assistance," the exact means by which this takes place in local work-first offices such as East County varies considerably due to the delegation of responsibility to the states.[39] At its most controversial, some have advocated requiring birth control for all women on welfare.[40] Less controversial and enacted in over one-third (34 percent) of states is the movement to cap family benefits, disallowing additional aid for children conceived while their mothers are on welfare.[41] In the words of Donna Shalala, then Secretary of the Department of Health and Human Services, "We're sending a clear message that we will pay for your first kid for a short time while you get ready for the work force. But we will not pay for a second kid."[42]

While neither New York State nor East County has enacted these policies, both have responded to the call with programs and policies designed to reduce pregnancies among the poor. Given the state's "interest in reducing long-term dependency on welfare," it focused its efforts on teen pregnancy and childbearing rather than nonmarital childbearing among adults.[43] In hopes of winning an illegitimacy bonus, New York State, under Governor George Pataki's direction, transferred $7 million of fiscal year 1998 TANF funds to its health department to be used to expand the Community-Based Adolescent Pregnancy Prevention (CBAPP) program, which targets 54 at-risk zip codes with high teenage pregnancy rates, for the purpose of reducing the rate of pregnancy among teenagers residing in those communities.[44] By 2002, this garnered the state a #2 ranking nationwide for largest decline between 1999 and 2002 with a decline of 2.36 percent of births to unmarried women 1999-2000 to 2001-2002, behind only Washington DC.[45] In East County, as with other counties in the state, CBAPP and other related state funding was awarded to nearly a dozen programs in a handful of community-based organizations to serve high-risk, pregnant, and parenting teens.[46] Collectively for East County, as with programs in other counties, CBAPP programs report over 95 percent meeting performance targets for prevented first and subsequent pregnancies, thus exceeding the statewide benchmarks that "at least 85 percent of those females who are not pregnant when enrolled in APPS will not become pregnant during their participation in APPS" and "at least 85 percent of those females who have at least one child when enrolled in APPS will not have a pregnancy during their participation in APPS."[47]

Since the majority of New York State's TANF-funded efforts to reduce reproduction among the poor are contracted out to community-based organizations with competitive bids, TANF caseworkers officially have little to do with reproduction. Though not delivered through the TANF office, however, these anti-natalist sensibilities are nevertheless present in the words and actions of caseworkers on the front lines. As evident in the following comment, not only have local caseworkers adopted the congressional perspective on children of poor women as public costs and drains on local tax dollars, but in this context the intake gauntlet emerges as an alternative to the family cap policy of discouraging childbirth that has been implemented in other states.

> When the federal time limit hits, the federal government gives less money to the state and so the state must make up the difference. That's our taxes! . . . They [other states] stopped giving more money for more kids . . . [But we] instead of just paying money to those who apply, people come through here and have to do all this stuff . . . [people get diverted or get jobs] so that's less they have to get paid by the state and the county.

The old system was seen as encouraging and even subsidizing women's reproduction, since having a child made one eligible for family aid and allowed them to stay out of the labor market to raise them. The intake gauntlet, however, has reversed this connection.

> [They are applying for] the same reasons, they don't want to work, they want the money, although now it's harder to get away with.

One of the main points of the work-first gauntlet's hassles is to encourage women to rethink the consequences of having children now that staying out of the labor market to raise them is no longer subsidized by welfare. As a caseworker explains, "We were going to give them reality."

The intake gauntlet is designed to avoid sheltering poor women from this "reality" of the challenges of balancing work and children. Not only does having children increase the "hassle factor" of work-first since alternative arrangements must be made for each child because they cannot accompany their parents through case processing, but as caseworkers point out, having children is the reason for, or cause of, the hassles in the first place.

> Job Coach: Some women just came in earlier complaining about all they have to go through in this system . . . "But we don't want to be in the system," they tell me. "But you applied!" "I need help," one says. "Why?" "My baby." "Why do you have the baby?"

Through such interactions, offering "If you don't want the hassles, don't have the kids," caseworkers frame the intake gauntlet as an exacted penance which can be avoided by not having children. Consistent with federal legislation, perhaps the most fundamental paradigm shift that caseworkers in East County urge since the 1996 reform is for clients to see having children when poor as problematic. In the reframing of the welfare contract through work-first, reproduction is no longer a right but a privilege—extended only to those who succeed in the market. It is a neoliberal approach in that it leaves the privilege of reproduction up to the market to sort out based on the merits of individuals. A job coach explains: "People are having children they can't afford. They should think first."

Caseworkers intend a message of deterrence, one that makes clear that the days of having children and counting on the government to financially help you raise them are over. It is part of a campaign to make an example of them and send the word out and get poor single mothers to "think first" before having children. Such efforts are consistent with Raspberry's approach, which argues against "coddling" single mothers. Instead, he advocates "shaming" them, making them visible reminders for the rest of the culture of the "poor choices" they have made and teaching other women that it is "morally wrong for unmarried women to bear children" and "cast[ing] single motherhood as a selfish and immature act."[48] Emphasizing this framing of reproduction when poor as selfish and immature, a caseworker attempts to make a client look and feel foolish for choosing to have a child. "Didn't you consider the costs before having the baby? Would you go out to a restaurant and order a meal that you can't pay for?" In an aside to colleagues, this caseworker explains, "It's like they don't think before doing things. They don't count the costs." Trying to get this message across, another caseworker confronts an applicant about costs.

> I asked her, "Do you know how much it costs to have a child?" and she said, "about $10,000," and I was pretty impressed with that. And I said, "Well who's going to pay for this, the hospital and all?"

The hassles caseworkers put clients through by scrutinizing their reproductive choices, and striving to remove incentives to have children by placing a gauntlet between eligibility and aid, are a microcosm of a broader political debate over how best to limit poor women's reproduction—what has been popularized as poor kids having kids. Though clients protest, as in the following case, caseworkers see it as part of their job to stand firm and uphold the integrity of the work-first gauntlet as a means to discouraging the "undeserving" from the privilege of reproduction:

> When she came in here she just threw her papers at me, [meaning tossed them on the desk to her], she just tossed them . . . She walked in and said, "Look, I don't know why you got me doing this. I'm pregnant, I ain't getting a job. You got me doing this, . . . I can't find a job."

Reiterating that she held her ground despite this challenge, the coach explained, "She already knew what she had to do, I didn't have anything new to tell her." From the work-first perspective, getting women to reconsider the new ramifications of becoming pregnant means not letting up on welfare compliance requirements even when they seem pro forma.

> TANF Interviewer: This woman is six weeks away from her due date and, because by the time she gets there she'll be done and won't have to go through it [work-first] (since it will be within the 30 days prior to due date that women are exempt) then she'll probably not have to finish, but I sent her anyway.

In addition to not being a good excuse not to work, caseworkers view pregnancy as even more reason to enforce work-first rules, even if only to get the message across that it is just not acceptable to have kids you can't afford.

> Caseworker: How can people just have kids without a way to provide for them? It's just not right, is it? I don't know how people can have the idea that they can just have kids and don't worry about who will pay for them. I can't imagine! . . . I don't understand it, like how can you think that way . . . Well, maybe if you're brought up that way.

Underlying this work-first perspective on reproduction are important assumptions that become overlooked as if natural and unremarkable. In the comments of these caseworkers as well as in national debates, childbirth and procreation among the poor have been framed as irresponsible, not as part of human nature. Procreation is not viewed as a human act that precedes any governing body, political climate, or economic status (such as being poor). Furthermore, as a job coach later explains, she sees childbirth as something that should only occur within marriage and among two parents who can afford a child. This, she asserts, would provide a solution satisfactory to both her and her employer, social services, which, as she explained, "doesn't want [their] case to open." In comments such as these, made at various levels of work-first processing, it is not the hassle factor of work-first intake and the low degree of success at navigating the work-first gauntlet that is problematic. Rather, it is the reproductive work of poor women that is questioned and placed on the defensive. Through the work-first lens, having children, or more specifically the reproductive work of poor mothers to reproduce society—the work of carrying a child to term, labor, childbirth, and the multitudes of care work that follow, for which many families receive income tax credits and tax exemptions—are cast in a light that is fundamentally pathological, as seen in the conversation sparked by the following comment.[49]

> TANF Interviewer: You know, I am wondering why so many young ethnic girls are pregnant, that's the reason most come through.

This one statement ignited a conversation that lasted for the duration of the paperwork processing that she and the other caseworkers in the room were doing, at least 30 minutes. Among the reasons and tangential topics broached were the following:

- Wanting somebody to love, a baby, because they don't experience enough love from their parents.
- It being due largely to the household, it's their family, it's what they've learned there.
- They, being kids, are selfish and they don't realize how hard it is to be a parent, so those school parent simulation programs with the mechanical doll should be expanded.

In such discussions caseworkers reconcile popularized understandings of a culture of poverty that frame poor families as a "tangle of pathology" with the work-first gauntlet approach to restructuring poor families in an effort to "fix" them.[50] Such understandings of "ethnic girls" also build on a racialized depiction of black and Latino "ethnic" families that frames as problematic their reproduction and the conditions under which it occurs in poverty. Cogently summarizing the broader discourse with which these caseworker assumptions coincide, Yeheskel Hasenfeld writes:

> The underlying premises of TANF about welfare recipients, their life circumstances, and why they rely on aid are driven more by stereotypic conceptions than by empirical research. The stereotype, of course, is of

the inner city black or Latino young woman who is sexually promiscuous, has babies in order to qualify for aid, refuses to work and take good care of her children, and squanders her welfare check on drugs. There is a pervasive assumption that poor single mothers are responsible for their predicament because they are lacking in work ethics and proper moral and family values, and that reliance on aid further corrodes their willingness to work, and reinforces intergenerational dependency on welfare. Therefore, the mothers must be weaned from aid as quickly as possible, and, if necessary, be coerced to work at any job so long as no great harm is done to their children. Moreover, it is assumed that once the mother works, even in a lousy job, surely her life circumstances will ultimately improve.[51]

Following from this narrative the efforts of work-first to prove a disincentive to poor (ethnic) reproduction, and in the process devalue its worth as labor, can be seen as an effort of the welfare state to solve the problem of the poor through limiting and/or eliminating the reproductive work of the poor.

Placed within a longer-term historical perspective, however, the devaluing of reproductive work within work-first is merely a recent iteration of attempts to regulate the reproduction of poor, ethnic, and predominantly black women. In the words of Dorothy Roberts:

> Considering this history—from slave masters' economic stake in bonded women's fertility to the racist strains of early birth control policy to sterilization abuse of Black women during the 1960s and 1970s to the current campaign to inject Norplant and Depo-Provera [injected temporary sterilization mechanisms] in the arms of Black teenagers and welfare mothers—paints a powerful picture of the link between race and reproductive freedom in America.[52]

Though East County did not implement forced birth control on poor mothers nor place a family cap which would refuse additional aid for children conceived while on welfare, the underlying concerns to which such policies are addressed are indeed present as organizers of caseworker sensibilities. It is important to note as well that these subagendas within the national welfare safety net are not merely part of an isolated strand of discourse. Rather, they are highly correlated with others that span the fields of health and law enforcement as well. As Roberts explains:

Plans to distribute Norplant in Black communities as a means of addressing their poverty, law enforcement practices that penalize Black women
for bearing a child, and welfare reform measures that cut off assistance
for children born to welfare mothers all proclaim the same message: The
key to solving America's social problems is to curtail Black women's birth
rates.[53]

From this perspective, the hassles of work-first and the disincentives to
reproduction effected by the intake gauntlet not only make sense; they are
a step in the right direction.

Childcare Work As Problematic

Beyond biologically reproductive work, the work-first lens frames ongoing childcare work as an equally problematic stumbling block for clients on their way to labor market integration. Though children are the
largest beneficiaries of TANF, comprising over three quarters of the total
caseload, from the perspective of work-first intake processing they just get
in the way. As one worker explains:

> Orientation Leader: The kids are a lot of work . . . I tell them to leave their
> kids at home or with someone. They have to prepare for employment.

Another caseworker explains:

> You can bring your child with you the first day . . . After that, you'll have to
> find somebody . . .
> Applicant: But at 8:45? School doesn't start until 8:45! [She urgently protests
> having to show up to work-first at the same time her children have to
> report to school.]
> One-on-One Interviewer: That's the only time. You'll have to make
> arrangements.

Within the work-first paradigm, the solution to childcare encumbrances
is to subcontract this work out to others.

> From day one we're asking them to start thinking about having a provider.
> Who is going to take care of your children . . . Once you start working,
> we will assist with childcare and transportation, although unfortunately,

during your job search [and approximately 30 days of intake] you have to take care of childcare and transportation yourself.

Entering into these arrangements requires beneficiaries to think of themselves as caregiving managers, rather than as direct providers. As part of inculcating this post-reform type of responsibility, clients are told they will need backup providers as well, for when their children get sick, if the sitter suddenly quits or becomes ill, and during summer and school vacations. The framework or script for this subcontracting relationship is institutionalized in childcare plans that TANF applicants must submit. It is also reinforced in interactions with caseworkers, such as the following exchange between client and job coach who emphasizes the critical nature of adequate care management plans and strategies.

> Coach: Well what if your cousin is watching him and he gets sick, what are you going to do?
> Client: I don't have anybody else; I'm all my son's got.
> Coach: Well you need to have a plan.

Within this framework the care work performed by parents for their children is not only a barrier to be overcome, it is also de-personalized and commodified; it is made equivalent to, and in actuality devalued in relation to the childcare work of any subcontracted employee since a subcontractor can be paid for this while a parent cannot.

Though endorsed as the new government-preferred solution to childcare encumbrances, the contracting-out framework does not render childcare work completely unproblematic to clients. They must still learn to "manage" childcare work by balancing these competing demands:

> Welfare Intake Worker: Like 50 to 70 percent of them [She is referring to the applicants that come through intake processing] have a management problem . . . Like they use excuses like, "I couldn't make it to welfare orientation because I had to put my kid on the bus." Like we all have to do things like that. You have to figure out how to manage those things. You could reschedule them but you don't want to get into that habit. Like if you allow them to have their own way too much. Like you don't want to get these people in the mind-set of rescheduling, so there, you don't accept that excuse.

Furthermore, subcontracting childcare work creates a new series of challenges since clients now must master the "masculine" skills of managing subcontracted providers.[54] Though caseworkers provide assistance in establishing these relationships, much of the responsibility for solidifying and maintaining them is purposefully left up to mothers themselves.

> [I] look for one [childcare provider] that is close to them. Then have them go to the provider and get some references from people who are already using the service. And then, if it sounds good, [I] have them go down and fill out all of the provider's paperwork. Then, if there is an opening, the provider will call us and let us know, "I'm going to take such and such beginning on May 10th, I have all the paperwork.". . . And I try to leave most of this stuff from here on out, between the provider and the client, up to the client. I mean we're already paying the bill [once they open their case]. So let them do the rest. They've got to take on the responsibility. We're asking them to be responsible for themselves. We're asking them to be more than responsible; we're asking them to take the jump.

Caseworkers also offer several options:

> Technical Assistant: Now we have three kinds of providers. One is the typical daycare. Then we have licensed childcare providers who have been trained and licensed and now their house has become the site of childcare giving. And we also have informal childcare such as your mother or sister or something taking care of the kid.

Though informal arrangements are allowed and often preferred by mothers, the flexibility with finding care does not transfer to a flexibility with outcomes. When it comes to childcare subcontracting, there is little margin for error. As with most of the work-first gauntlet the responsibility and culpability of inadequate arrangements rests with the applicant herself.

> Author: Suppose they don't [find a childcare provider] . . .
> Job Coach: Well they . . . [If] we made a conscious effort to help establish childcare for them and for whatever reason they don't show up the day that they're supposed to show up [assuming without children], their case will be closed and they'll have to start all over again.

Even when childcare has been found, applicants are not out of the woods. Simply finding reliable childcare is no guarantee that it will be extensive enough to render a mother unencumbered.

> Caseworker: I recognized her name and when I saw her coming up . . . She came in one day and it was very busy so the wait was real long and she had to leave and pick up her kids. She left and five minutes later they called her name. This is the third time, her third application for this. This is an ongoing problem this same eviction. This is her third application, . . . so she has to re-apply all over again.

For some mothers, finding adequate childcare is a challenge because of particularities with their children:

> Applicant: I'm all my son's got, I don't got . . . he was in daycare but he got kicked out of daycare, [explaining] he got a little rough, that's a problem.

For others, the problem is unreliable adults:

> The first day my kids' father watched the kids for me so that is why I was able to attend the meeting, but then that same day later on he got locked up in jail so I didn't have anyone to watch my children.

In another case, a relative quits:

> Legal Aid Attorney: Is she [sister] still minding your child?
> Client: No. She quit.

Still other times there are emergency situations, as a client explains following her failure to show up:

> My sister had to go to the emergency room with a broken wrist. I had no gas and no babysitter.

The gendered nature of these arrangements, aside from reference to mothers and sisters as potential caregivers, is further implicit in the fact that nationally, women comprise 98.5 percent of family childcare workers.[55] As Mary Touminen argues, this high concentration of women in the field of childcare giving is due to adherence to what Lise Vogel outlines as a "class-based ideology of the full-time, at-home mother" which has historically asserted that, among other things, "motherhood is morally and practically incompatible with labor force participation."[56] However, rather than adhere fully to this, the neoliberal work-first approach to families replaces such gendered breadwinner-homemaker ideologies with a gender neutral outlook that frees both women and men to participate in the low wage labor market. In the process, it also institutionalizes a disruption of the historical public and private sphere dichotomy.

> The emergence of child-care work as paid work increasingly challenges historical ideologies of liberal individualism, motherhood and care. When childcare becomes paid work, caring for children, perceived to occur in the "private" sphere of families and households, enters the market economy and becomes "public" work. Work believed to be performed for "love" is increasingly performed for money. Thus, paid child-care work challenges our dualistic understanding of not only ideologies of caregiving, but also conventional definitions of "work."[57]

Despite the 1996 legislation's preamble extolling marriage as foundational to society, frontline caseworkers in this research, as in the research of Sharon Hays, did not see regeneration of traditional family arrangements as part of their job description. Rather, their work was focused on shifting parenting responsibilities instead of solving parenting problems. As Sharon Hays writes, "In this light it appears that the social tension between the values of work and family have been resolved in favor of work. . . . what remains is the individualistic ethic of self-sufficiency and an image of the 'good society' as full of unfettered individuals busily pursuing their daily bread in the marketplace."[58] It is these imagined unfettered individuals that caseworkers seek to mold into ideal participants.

This is a reversal of previous efforts since Aid to Families with Dependent Children has traditionally been used as a means of strengthening the parent-child bonds of poor families—most notably by making it financially possible for mothers who choose to provide full-time care to do so. In fact, the initial plans for ADC, AFDC's predecessor, posited that "Freeing mothers from wage earning would help them 'rear [their children] into citizens capable of contributing to society.'"[59] Several years later in 1942, "government officials advocated more generous benefits free of work requirements precisely because they wanted to increase incentives for (presumably white) mothers to 'stay at home where they were needed.'"[60]

Consistent with these intentions, the 1946 Handbook of Public Assistance for the U.S. Department of Health, Education, and Welfare reflected these concerns by emphasizing "the social value of giving an impoverished mother the opportunity to choose to reject wage work in favor of 'staying at home to care for her children.'"[61] As Gordon explains, ADC was among the least controversial parts of the 1935 Social Security Act because it was literally equated with the presumed benefits of motherhood.[62]

Indeed, while various earlier welfare programs dating back to colonial days could be seen to even place pressure on women to approximate a middle-class paradigm in which women who could afford to do so felt obliged to stay home, this has changed in light of neoliberal sensibilities. Jill Weigt describes the new nexus of discourses that confound women's lives post–1996 reform: "If a mother can afford it, she is obligated to be at home with her children; if she lacks the resources to be at home, her task is to show her children how to work regardless of the conditions under which she must labor."[63] Noticeably absent from this equation is men.

Relationships with Men As Problematic

Through the lens of daily work-first processing, not only are reproductive work and childcare problematic, but so are relationships with men. In general, caseworkers tend to see their clients' relationships with men as at best ill conceived and tentative and at worst a trap that leads to pregnancy and long-term dependency.

> Caseworker: They see a revolving door of men in their mother's life and then they see a male and they're like, "Wow! He likes me!" and then they get caught up in it and before they know it—pregnant!"

Though such caseworker comments frame men as a large part of the problem, they are only a small part of the solution within the day-to-day framework of work-first—despite rhetoric suggesting that the punitive nature of welfare reform will make marriage (and resulting pooled income) look good in comparison as an alternative means to economic survival.

There has been much policy talk and much action in terms of making men responsible through enforcing paternity and getting stricter with child support. In fact, paternities established have risen from 676,000 to 1,555,000 nationally, and the collection of child support has increased from \$9.8 billion to \$17.9 billion between 1994 and 2000.[64] Nevertheless, the nucleus of the TANF unit, as with AFDC and ADC before it, remains women and children. Men, when they are present in the welfare office, are merely appendages or afterthoughts to the main case.

> Job Coach: I would say, of the people that come through we have mostly women with children coming through. Primarily, that's our number one population, and then next we have maybe two-parent families come in. Then after that I'd say we have men who are usually being added to the case, either to the mom's case or to the mother of their children's case, or the, however that works, they're usually being, like that gentleman who was here this afternoon, he's being added to someone's case. OK, so he has to come through and do the whole applicant process as well.

Since the same rules apply to men who are "added" to the case of a woman, having a man on one's case adds an additional layer of barriers to welfare aid since they must successfully navigate the same application gauntlet as women.

> TANF Caseworker: Basically, if he is in the household, he has to do the entire intake job search stuff etcetera, and if he doesn't they will deny the case. If the case is already open, they will sanction him and reduce the grant.

Though having men go through the same application process as women is intuitive, given the gender-blind stance of the legislation, caseworkers are not actually blind to gender. From their perspective, adding a man to the case—whether a husband, lover, or other—is generally seen as bad news from the point of view of compliance. Accordingly, when a caseworker sees that a man is involved, they will often recommend that the woman find a way to remove him from the case.

> Job Coach: Oh the guys, they don't come back or their job search is bogus or whatever and their, you know their significant others, um their case won't open up, so you know . . . .often enough we'll tell the girl at some point, you know what? You need to get him off your case because it's not going to open or he's not going to do what he's supposed to do, you know.

A caseworker presents a typical chain of events where men are involved:

Author: So you have to confront them sometimes; how does that happen?

Job Coach: No, just tell them it's a no-show, when there is a no-show you're going to have to go, re-apply and so then, you know, typically the girl's going to come in and he's not going to show up and you're going to say you need to get him off your case because he's going to prevent your case from opening up.

Author: So you wouldn't do that until that has already happened?

Job Coach: Well you could tell her on the phone, I mean depending on how that conversation's going.

Literature suggests that males often play an integral role in family life as a father figure and male companion to the mother, even when these males are not biologically related to the children they parent. When it comes to work-first, however, their most salient characteristic is that of an undependable liability. As another caseworker explains, where women are linked with their children for the long haul, and therefore are more willing to put up with the challenges and indignities of the intake gauntlet, men hold a much more tenuous position within poor families, especially since they are often not the father of the children involved.

Caseworker: I, my perception is that the guy is just on the girlfriend's case because it's convenient for him, especially if she has children from a previous relationship, which you can tell on the WMS from their last names and so forth. Um, my perception is this is just a guy who's going to be here temporarily, because she's used to guys who are temporary, and um we often tell um females, because we see it a lot, that they'll show up together the first time but then the girl comes and the guy won't come. And that prevents the case from opening up and that impacts on her children.

Not only are men seen as liabilities because they will potentially fail to perform, but when they do participate it can be at the expense of extra energy and effort on the part of the woman in their family. For instance, a caseworker explains:

Job Coach: We also get a lot of calls, "Well, my boyfriend is supposed to be there today but he's not." "Well, where is he?" "He's right here." "Well, we need to talk directly to him!"

Another recounts that this puts women in the awkward position of doing extra work to bring their man into compliance—work that is then vulnerable to being undermined by the attitudes, resentment, resistance, or other indiscretions of these men:

> Caseworker: You know like the girl will call up. Yesterday the girl called up because her boyfriend didn't show up for his appointment here. I put him as a no-show. She, [other coach] told them that, and she called me the next day and she identified herself by his name. I said, "You're not him." She said, "No he's right here." I said, "Well he's got to talk to me himself." So he calls me and talks to me and [I] said, "Well no we can't reschedule you. You should've been here yesterday." "Well you know I didn't feel like coming down." Oh OK, that's fine . . . but from our way of thinking, if you're too lazy to come get some free money [laugh] what do I care? If you don't care enough, why should I care?

Working with the presumption that men do not care, caseworkers often try to be proactive with women. Caseworkers sometimes explain this from the perspective that men often hold a "temporary" position within poor families, "so we know, we get a kind of feel for the guys who're just here for it's going to be some food and a place to hang out, hang my hat for the night you know, whatever."

However, they also stress that men are liabilities even if they have made a commitment to the family and are married.

> And you see that with married people [too], um often times the guy, not often times, but it has happened that the guy will let the wife do the job search for him and she'll bring back the job search and her job search will be identical to his job search and it'll all be in the same handwriting. [As a result they are both likely to be rejected for not completing an "independent" job search] . . . You can see that she does that because she wants her damn case to open up because she's got children and he don't want to do anything so she's fudging the process so that her case opens up.

As one caseworker explains, he senses that gender is active in such a way that men experience intense embarrassment about having to apply for assistance in a way that women don't, or are more willing to put up with. As Susan Traverso explains, welfare has traditionally been not only linked with women but considered unmanly and shameful for men to participate in since before the early 1900s.[65] Perhaps in part due to this stigma, there is a general feeling that men are liabilities because they "do not want to be bothered" by the harrowing process of the intake gauntlet.

> Author: It's just guys don't want to come in here or they don't want to do job search?
>
> Job Coach: Right, and then they yeah they don't want to be bothered, they just want . . . and so the girl is left to, you know, to fend for herself and her children which anybody would do. You know anybody's going to do what they have to do to feed their family, there's no mystery about that.

While it may seem clear-cut and without mystery to this job coach, as a prescreener in the welfare office explains, "Just get[ting] him off your case" is not a simple matter of paperwork. Being on a case is in general synonymous with being in the household:

> Author: When a woman is applying for TANF, whom does she have to include on her case?
>
> Frontline Screener: Everyone in the household must be included; she's got to include them. If he lives there she's got to put him on her application. Later the caseworker may decide if he is on the case.

As a caseworker clarifies:

> TANF Caseworker: A husband always has to apply, unless he is not living with her. He will also be on the case, unless perhaps exempted because of SSI. Now if a man lives in the household but is not married to her but is the father of her child, or at least one of her children, he also has to apply and he will be on the case. See, there is legal responsibility in both of these cases for the children. Now if the boyfriend is living in the household and she is just pregnant, then he doesn't have to apply until the baby is born, maybe he thinks he earns too much money or something. And if it is just a boyfriend or other man living with her and he is not the father of any of her children, then he does not have to apply, just verify how much money he contributes to the household.

Given these constraints, if a woman wants to get the father of her child or her husband off of her case, it is not as simple as leaving him out of the paperwork. A supervisor clarifies, "If he is in the household she has to list him, and if she doesn't, it's 'affirmative misrepresentation' and we will deny the application." Clarifying the situation, a caseworker explains:

> Caseworker: You can't just say I don't want him on there [my case]. . . When they say you need to get him off your case, what they are saying is you have to kick him out [of the home]. It's not ideal but if he's not participating it's detrimental to the children.

Kicking him out of the home involves a major restructuring of family life. It is also very difficult to fake.

> Caseworker: We have lots of people where the husband or boyfriend, they just don't want to do all of the required things like the job search and all. And then all of a sudden on the next application he is not there. So that looks suspicious to us, we send out an investigator. Now if it is investigated or if the landlord confirms that he is no longer living there, then we will take him off the case, like if she convinced him to move out. But if he leaves, then we will still go after him for child support.

These patterns would seem to place the blame solely on the shortcomings of men or on women for failing to screen their men for reliability and dependability. This interpretation, however, would overlook extensive research indicating a dearth of marriageable men with stable jobs that pay a living wage, and the massive societal upheavals of urban jobs that have left men of color disproportionately disadvantaged.[66] It also overlooks the centrality of a key demographic conundrum over which poor women, especially of color, in East County and nationwide have no control—a numerical lack of men.

Nationwide, a rise of female-headed single-parent families has been linked with an unbalanced sex ratio, one that in the major city in East County leads to four African-American men for every five African-American women between the ages of 20 and 59—and more to the point leaves approximately two African-American men for every three African-American women during the prime partnering and childbearing ages of 25-29.[67] Given these numbers, having every African-American woman settle down in a heterosexual, monogamous relationship with someone of her own ethnic/racial group is a numerical impossibility—nearly one-third of these women will not have a partner within their age group.[68]

Reflecting this reality, an African-American female explains:

It's hard because men have it easy. They have two to three women per man, so it's very easy for him to not stay committed. A woman like me is looking for commitment and will try almost anything just to keep that commitment going . . . I'm gonna accept this BS he's giving me because . . . without him . . . it's gonna be hard for me to find someone else to [be with] . . . seeing it as, "if I let him go, this [other] woman's gonna have him.". . . I don't want to be alone.[69]

Reflecting on the double-bind that this demographic situation presents to women, Lane and colleagues write:

Faced with an increasing proportion of single African-American mothers, social policy discourse has grown more strident in trying to create incentives that will lead these women to wed, as if their single status was a personal preference that could be changed by social policy bringing forth the right combination of carrots and sticks. Yet, the mathematical fact is that there are fewer African-American men than African-American women. Two factors account for the dearth of men of color: incarceration and death. By assuming single motherhood to be an idiosyncratic behavioral pattern and ignoring the disproportionate premature death and incarceration, contemporary marriage promotion policies obscure the pattern of racism constraining African-American women's reproductive choices.[70]

Reflecting this noted pattern of imprisonment, East County experiences a similar skewed demographic to that of other locations in that African Americans comprise a little over 9 percent of the population yet over 50 percent of the inmates incarcerated.[71] Reflecting on this situation, an African-American woman explains:

I feel that we don't have enough males around here . . . there [are] not too many boys around here because [they're] locking everyone up.[72]

These perceptions and attitudes, reflective of the demographic conundrum, have immediate implications for work-first, which pushes women to distance themselves from men just as they are struggling against an imbalanced marriage market/sex ratio to keep them. This also helps to explain why women are willing to take on the extra work of facilitating their men's job searches and putting up with undependability even when it jeopardizes their case from opening. As Guttentag and Secord argue, not only do female-dominated sex ratios increase female-headed families and decrease the proportion of women with committed male partners throughout their childbearing years, but they also reduce women's bargaining power within relationships and encourage women to make sacrifices and go out of their way to please and keep their male partner.[73]

Unfortunately, although rates of incarceration and premature death are staggeringly unequal between whites and African Americans, public policymakers, like the general public, fail to consider them relevant to the analysis of poverty and single motherhood.[74] As a result, caseworkers are left in the dark. One implores her colleagues for an explanation:

> Why would a woman have a child without being married to the guy? There are lots of people out there [motioning to outer room with clients] who have been together for 5 or 6 years, etc. and then all of a sudden decide to have a child, why would you do that?. . . Marriages have so many benefits for children. . . . Maybe I am just old-fashioned.

As with the plethora of recent marital policies foisted toward poor families, work-first "ignore[s] the unbalanced African-American sex ratio and assume[s] that the dramatic rise in African-American single motherhood is a capricious choice."[75] This not only fails to take into account how the doubling of single-parent, female-headed families between 1965 and 1990 is related to the co-occurring war on drugs that tripled the African-American prison population, but it also overlooks the alternative family and nurturance structures that poor families, often of color, have evolved in order to address these structural challenges to family life.[76]

While the men involved in poor families may be providers of fatherly support in nonfinancial ways that are beneficial to poor mothers and children, as the literature suggests, from the perspective of work-first they are primarily barriers to be overcome. Work-first thus creates and enforces a paradigm where men are expendable, judged so on the basis of their difficulties in navigating the same gauntlet women have trouble negotiating. As with women, no valuation is taken of their care work (i.e., spending time with children, taking them to the park, and contributing to household work) in service to the family or its importance in reproducing strong children. Rather, their roles as biological "fathers" who fail to provide financially are inspected while their role as care-giving and nurturing "daddies," biological and not, is overlooked and therefore expendable.[77] In the restructuring of poor families according to the incentive structure of work-first, fathering care work is devalued as is women's care work. Not surprisingly, then, emphasis on child support payments, such as seen below, reveals that men's involvement is accepted as a sometimes necessary casualty of getting through work-first intake.

> Applicant: What if child support is voluntary?
> Caseworker: We will take them to court and provide it through the agency. I know it may cause problems, especially if you have a good relationship with him, but unfortunately that's how we have to do it if you are applying for welfare for that child.[78]

While some women refuse to sign child support forms making them ineligible, or pretend not to know the identity of their child's father, others find that waiting for fathers to cooperate adds yet another barrier to work-first compliance.

> Applicant: I need $182 a week for childcare, the Department of Social Services said that in order to be eligible for them to pay childcare I have to be receiving child support. I need to go to school in the fall, how long till child support is active?
> Caseworker: A long time.
> Applicant: How long?
> Caseworker: It may take years if they [fathers] don't cooperate.

In these interactions then, as with other compliance requirements, men are viewed in terms of their ability to comply and provide financially. Their work as role models and caring "daddies," as well as the work women do to build families that include men, are subordinated to the work-first goals of creating unencumbered female workers.

The problematic nature of relationships with men within work-first is a new twist on an old tale. Men have historically been alien to welfare. At various points in U.S. history, families with men have been categorically ineligible for aid. At other points, discovering evidence that a woman had consorted with a man, or men, was grounds for sanctions or the termination of aid to a woman and her children. Such was the premise behind "man in the house rules" and unannounced "midnight raids" that searched for any evidence of a man, along with a list of other contraband.

Prior to the 1996 reform, welfare was much maligned for encouraging single-parent households by creating an incentive structure for women to live without men. Since government was providing the breadwinner role for these women, the argument went, there was no need for them to settle down with a man. In the new structure, however, men have not become endeared. Rather, they are pushed farther away as the informal caring and fathering work done by many biological and nonbiological "daddies" becomes a liability if these men are unwilling to subject themselves to the work-first gauntlet. Despite rhetoric about building families and encouraging "responsible fatherhood," day-to-day work-first interactions encourage women to distance themselves from men because of their potential to encumber case processing and thus make women and children less likely to successfully navigate the intake gauntlet. Day-to-day work-first interactions also encourage overlooking the racial dynamics that so significantly impact the interaction of poor family life with the labor market.

Poor Families in the New Economy

The logic of neoliberal labor market restructuring presents itself as one of empowerment. But as I argue here, the work-first approach also intervenes in the restructuring of poor families and devalues the significance of their race and gender identities. Their productive power is given clear priority over their reproductive functions to the extent that only those families achieve access to aid who are able to and learn to subordinate care work so that it does not conflict with labor market demands—whether by limiting reproduction, contracting out childcare, or tailoring relationships with men. According to work-first rhetoric, poor women, if they assume "personal responsibility," will be liberated from dependency, with the opportunity to reap the benefits of the free market once the government ceases its tradition of pampering the poor. However, as seen in the preceding analysis of this chapter, the welfare state does not so much remove itself from the equation as enter into a new mode of regulating the everyday lives of poor families. In the terms of Paul Smith, the government engages in a new project of subjectification, creating "subjects of value" that are "well suited to the demands and needs of late capitalism."[79] These subjects are reminiscent of what Joan Acker termed "disembodied workers," unencumbered by family obligations and ready to subsume all other concerns to the interests of their employer.[80] The result is a reordering of productive and reproductive family functions and a disregard for persisting inequalities of race in order to bring the poor into alignment with the labor market interests of the new economy.

Such a course of action, however unquestioned it may be in policy debates, is not unproblematic. It leaves the value of family needs to the discretion of the market and, as Irwin Garfinkel notes, "Capitalism respects no traditions, not racism, not the family . . . but it does undermine caring. If not restrained, it will undermine caring and the family."[81] This appears to be the case as the implementation of the reform according to principles of neoliberal capitalism focuses the lion's share of attention on the work ethic of adults and in the process overlooks the number one welfare constituency—children. As of 2005, children comprised 76 percent of the TANF caseload nationally. This is the highest proportion since 1966, but even at its lowest point in 1984, children made up 66 percent of the welfare caseload.

Catherine Kingfisher argues that "neoliberalism 'degenders' women by defining them primarily as productive citizens (i.e., workers), disarticulating their identities as mothers and caregivers from their identities as citizens."[82] At the same time, it disembodies them by rejecting their experience of race as meaningful. Along with fluctuations in the global labor market and racial undercurrents, the 1996 welfare reform, by virtue of its requirement that all mothers work, has advanced an unprecedented and controversial stand on the relationship between poor women, their families, and the labor market. In contrast to prior welfare legislation, it vigorously asserted a shift away from what Deborah Little terms a "Family Wage Welfare State" to a "Universal Breadwinner Welfare State."[83] As Hays similarly examines, welfare reform can be seen as representing a triumph of both classical liberal individualism and liberal feminism.[84] Women, no longer viewed as dependent on men or relegated to the sphere of the home, are expected to work in a gender- and race-neutral workforce, living up to a universal notion of personal responsibility. As Jane Collins notes, ironically "these reforms, which required poor women to work for their benefits rather than claiming them as mothers, placed new groups of women on the threshold of economic citizenship at the moment that the social contract around the benefits of work itself was changing."[85] It is an unfortunate coincidence, if coincidence at all, that poor women are being compelled to prioritize work over family just as work itself is undergoing transformations of reduced stability, compensation, and fringe benefits within a neoliberal new economy.

7

"Don't Blame Me, It Wasn't Up to Me!"

Policy Recommendations from Everyday Experience

Previous chapters have explored how neoliberal common sense guides work-first innovation, performance goals, technology, casework, and the transformation of family life to accommodate a new political economy. Though work-first common sense is indeed prevalent, not everyone buys into it; resistance appears in a variety of forms that reveal tensions at the welfare office. Work-first offices are places characterized by conflicts over social work philosophy and confrontations between clients and caseworkers. This chapter probes the ways in which both clients and other human service professionals express resistance to work-first as they experience it in their daily lives. I examine the ramifications of this experience for future policy reforms. Work-first hinges on caseworkers' efforts to change client *behavior* through selling work-first common sense to them. The behavior change that is the crux of work-first welfare reform, however, depends on the degree to which personal experiences and understandings can be socially ordered according to neoliberal values.

It is not surprising that people experience and understand things differently; it is consequential, however, when these different standpoints empower people to resist forms of extra-local social organization, such as work-first common sense, that otherwise tend to command accountability and to a large extent "override" the perspective of local individuals.[1] When such spaces of resistance are created, competing ways of framing the status quo become possible, and common sense loses some of its power. The dynamics of behavioral conditioning by work-first staff and resistance by clients and community members set the stage for a political battle over welfare.

In this account, local resistance emerges as a critical element of the on-going social construction of work-first common sense. Local resistance presents narratives that question the logic of work-first. These behaviors emerge as politically consequential for clients as well as for the field of social work. Work-first casework in East County is built on a neoliberal-style philosophy that competes with established and more progressive "social work" approaches. The older model of helping poor families by providing resources to address their immediate and long-term needs with ongoing government guidance and support had the effect of "decommodifying" them, or allowing them to survive without having to sell their labor as a commodity in the market. The TANF model involves coaxing them to change their behavior in accordance with neoliberal ideals that advocate self-sufficiency and personal responsibility to work in the labor market as the best way to address poverty.

In contrast with social work emphases on structural inequalities, work-first focuses on the individual, using a "tough love" approach to behavioral conditioning. Rather than ascribe high moral worth to clients, work-first endorses "raking them through the coals" to compel participation in the labor market.[2] Thus, the narrative of work-first casework is a tale of constructing new practices, and destroying old ones.

While some members of the social work community feel compelled to "broaden their horizons and view many domestic social justice issues within a global framework," work-first insists upon an individual responsibility approach.[3] Anti-oppressive social work theory asserts attention to global macro-level forces—seeking to empower clients "through partnership, client choice, and seeking changes in the agency and wider systems that adversely affect clients." In contrast, the work-first agenda insists that clients adapt to neoliberal strategies for globalization that are unresponsive to client needs.[4] Just as communities, regions, and nations must adapt to global restructuring or pay the price, neoliberal casework enforces this "survival of the fittest" mentality on clients.

At the heart of these differing casework perspectives are political and ideological assumptions. U.S. and European social workers increasingly begin their work with the poor from a global perspective of social exclusion. From this perspective both countries and classes of people "lose out in global competition." This results in the "marginalization of people or areas and the imposition of barriers that restrict them from access to opportunities to fully integrate with the larger society."[5] In contrast, work-first begins from a framework of the underclass. Rather than focus on the political realm by placing "the onus on people who are doing something to other people," as the social exclusion framework does, "the central tenet of the underclass or culture of poverty argument, in contrast, is that miserable conditions are self-induced—the poor do it to themselves."[6]

Work-first casework thus holds broader relevance as a political tool in the ongoing battle between competing neoliberal and progressive approaches to social work. In this struggle, work-first sets a precedent for future programming, and its nationwide prevalence provides the neoliberal approach an upper hand in future policy debate. As Katherine van Wormer notes:

> Policies and values are intertwined. As the tides of political change come and go, and as the public mood shifts, so do the social policies. And just as values play into the creation of policies, so do policies into values. Change the policies . . . and they soon become part of the status quo.[7]

In this sense both the discourses and the everyday practices of work-first casework are part of a power play that reversed decades of social work tradition. The 1996 welfare reform has established neoliberal work-first common sense as the incumbent way of thinking. In future policy debate, the ousted social work profession can reemerge only as the challenger.

The following pages first explore how TANF implementation emerges in the locally lived experience of caseworkers as a place of conflict and confrontation, rather than as a site where they are able to forge positive relationships with the clients they serve. I explore this frustrating experience of caseworkers as characteristic of a neoliberal approach to social work. I then use this disconnect between hoped for and actual relationships with clients as a starting point from which to explore the resistance of clients and other community human services workers to work-first. Rather than medicalize this resistance as "dependence" or "laziness," as the dominant work-first discourse does, I interpret these points of local and personal resistance as based in the expertise of these people's own lived experience. Attempting to create sociological knowledge *for*, rather than *about* these people, I then proceed to lay out the beginnings of policy recommendations that can be drawn from their experiences, given the context of the preceding chapters. Finally, I use the constructive nature of this exercise to examine work-first resistance not as recalcitrance but as the vanguard for what may be considered resistance to the neoliberal welfare approach, and as support for a new era of reform that is more solidly pro-worker and pro-family.

Work-First as a Place of Conflict and Confrontation

Under the banner of the new federalism, intergovernmental restructuring in the United States has shifted discretionary decision making from federal to local levels under the pretense of encouraging local control over welfare reform. This forces caseworkers to decide when and how to enforce personal responsibility while at the same time accommodating pressures to cut caseloads. Implementing work-first transforms the local office into a place of conflict and confrontation. These conflicts are dramatically reflected in caseworker comments.

Caseworkers who may see themselves as "just trying to help" become embroiled in frustrations and frictions that extend far beyond the welfare office. In the words of one caseworker:

> It can be very stressful. Particularly when you're really trying to help the client and they're giving you grief. . . . It makes you want to say, "Why am I bothering to try?" You know? That's probably the hardest part.

In the words of another caseworker, "We give bad news about half the time." As expressed in the following conversation, even veteran caseworkers can find this to be a challenge. Gretchen, a caseworker of ten years, who is herself wrestling with how best to treat clients, shares what has happened to some of her colleagues when clients became angry with staff attempts to enforce responsibility:

> Someone spit in Elena's face . . . I have a friend in [another] city that got hit with a stapler. [A client] threw it at her.

Vocalizing the underlying theme to these anecdotes, Valerie, an older caseworker who has also had trouble with clients who complained about her, says "[it] can be very confrontational, very stressful." Robert, who entered casework in the years since the reform, offers:

> Basically everyone responds the same way, they get angry. We try to disarm them, and we're supposed to have the skills to talk softly and let them vent first and then talk with them, . . . but ha, it's hard to do this.

Echoing these themes, another coach laments that caseworkers become the target of blame:

Job Coach: [Speaking emphatically he exclaims] They get mad! They curse us
out! They, you know, swear us out. They blame the fact that they are going
to get evicted or their children are hungry or their lights are going to get
shut off and all that information. We get blamed for all that.

One caseworker provides an example of this blame and how it affects her
emotions.

Job Coach: One lady this morning [was] doing it [she refers to a Job Contact
sheet] at the front desk, and the team leader saw it and told me that it can't
count. It's incomplete. She [the applicant] was very irate, and she's the one
who said to me, "So what are my four kids supposed to do, starve?" She
left here crying and I felt so bad for her, I wanted to say, "Don't blame me,
it wasn't up to me!"

A TANF intake worker explains, "I feel like a drill sergeant, I think they
see me that way as well. I don't think that they like me."

Other caseworkers routinely speak of similar distance from clients.
Another job coach remarks about a nightmare provoked by his encounter
with clients:

Job Coach: I've been having this re-occurring dream or nightmare lately. I'm
going to . . . a ball game or going to a play and somebody's going to recognize me and be like, "Hey! You're that guy from work-first who wouldn't
accept my job search at 12:30!" . . . And the stands will empty and I'll get a
beating . . . Or I'll be in a bar and some guy will be a bit gone and be like,
"You! [Indicating the man recognizes him.] How do you like me now!?"
[Using this slang, he laughs as he tells this, mock play-acting an applicant
punching him.]

This dream, warmly received and quickly joined by other caseworkers'
personal anecdotes (both actual and dreamed) about encountering clients
in public, provides some insight into the emotions involved in confronting applicants.

When asked how they deal with these tensions, one caseworker explained,
"Phh, well we try to just take it in stride." "Taking it in stride," however, requires work. Caseworkers are forced to reconcile their desire to be liked
with the work that their job demands of them. This obliges them to adapt
their self-image as well. A caseworker rationalizes his coping mechanism.

Job Coach: Well, you know. I tell my children, I tell my oldest boy I'm a professional asshole . . . [He lets out a small laugh.] 'Cause I'm a landlord, I'm
a referee, I work for this job, and I'm a stepfather. So . . . you know there's
days that everybody I see is pissed off. . . . They're not usually mad at me.
They're just mad at what I have to tell them today, or . . . the situation they
put themselves in. . . . I just happen to be the person [to confront them]
and I understand that. . . . They're angry whatever, and most of the times,
I think you have to understand that they're really not mad at you, they're
mad at the situation they find themselves in and you happen to be the
person for that moment; you're public assistance to them. They yell at you
because you're the system.

This "system," however, is not the same one that existed before the 1996 reform. It is much more confrontational and paternalistic. In the words of a
former client, "caseworkers are rude, obnoxious, condescending, and they
treat people like they are less than them because of their need. . . . You
shouldn't have to tuck your tail between your legs to get aid and that's how
they make us feel." Accordingly, a welfare support group leader reports,
"We have mothers who call in tears because of how they were treated . . .
they don't want to get aid they are eligible for because they don't want to
deal with it." This is a far cry from the ideals often espoused by those who
consider social work historically to be the premiere "helping profession."
It is a new approach to social work based on neoliberal values.

A Neoliberal Approach to Social Work

Since the 1960s, a change in thinking about the appropriate approach to
take with the poor occurred—not because of academic research on poverty, and in large part in spite of it. "[T]he conservative approach to [wel-
fare] reform came to dominate, in part because of the turning of national
politics to the right."[8] Lawrence Mead, one of the 1996 welfare reform's
most widely recognized proponents, explains that most poverty researchers tended to hold a more liberal perspective than newly elected legisla-
tors. The politicians were disinclined to give weight to the research because of the different ideology behind it.[9] In essence, Mead describes a
conflict over goals:

Reformers blamed poverty mostly on low work levels and other lifestyle
problems that seemed to make families poor. Most academics, in contrast,

wanted reform to focus on the economic well-being of the poor, and they looked to government for solutions.[10]

What work-first offered, then, was an alternative to the established social work practice, which began to be viewed as too socially liberal.

The work-first approach to human services has been several decades in the making and has distanced itself from the ideological foundation and professional organization of the social work establishment to such a degree that professionally accredited social workers today might not consider work-first to be social work at all. The genealogy of today's work-first casework dates to the late 1960s and early 1970s when social service reforms split welfare casework from a comprehensive approach implemented by one social worker into two separate and specialized tasks: social workers would provide services and eligibility workers would assess need.[11] Though done under the auspices of protecting clients from the arbitrary and capricious discretion of social workers and keeping a tight handle on fiscal expenditures, this division can also be seen as an effort to begin dismantling or at least weakening the social work profession by diluting its power and restraining its access to government funds.

Placed in this historical context, work-first's additional division of eligibility work between means-tested eligibility workers and work-readiness-tested job coaches further dilutes the authority of human service caseworkers with respect to awarding state aid to the poor. PRWORA's work-first approach moreover shuns human capital investment and intensive social work supports in favor of immediate employment. This is consistent with two decades of reductions in aid for social work functions (federally as well as in New York State) which have served to marginalize the role of social work within welfare.[12]

Not only does work-first compete with social work practice, but as some social workers have argued, it is in direct conflict with it. Noted social work scholar Yeheskel Hasenfeld argues that, "under the provisions of PRWORA, which attempts to transform welfare departments into employment and social service agencies, the social service orientation becomes compromised and corrupted."[13] Chief among his concerns is that TANF breaks from the three factors central to all social work values and practice principles—"(a) a belief system that ascribes high moral worth to the clients; (b) a service technology that is individualized, tailoring the services to the specific needs and attributes of the clients; and (c) staff-client relations that are based on mutual trust."[14] Since TANF subscribes to a paradigm whereby compliance is achieved through mechanisms of reward and punishment that are not necessarily aimed at the long-term well-being of the client, Hasenfeld argues that TANF undermines both the possibility for "a sustained trusting relationship with clients" and the integrity of the entire social work enterprise.[15]

Mimi Abramovitz, a social welfare researcher, asserts that "welfare reform's policies and practices have hindered the ability of social service providers to help the indigent move out of poverty and into lives of greater economic independence and social security."[16] Sharon Hays, who has studied welfare reform from inside the welfare office and inside the lives of welfare mothers, similarly reports that, though work-first caseworkers may "want clients to recognize them as (family like) mentors who can support and guide them through hard times," this image "not only conflicts with the bureaucratic structure of welfare, it also bears little relation to the explicit goals of welfare reform."[17] These critiques assert that the work-first approach is counter to social work values, practice, and principles, and yet it employs the connotation of the social service orientation as a cover to "endorse and legitimate a flawed policy."[18] In the words of Hasenfeld, under TANF "there are few rewards for time spent counseling clients or for helping them obtain needed services. Indeed, clients with problems become problem clients."[19]

In the pages that follow, I offer suggestions stemming from local experience about how to improve what is problematic about the current state of affairs. These policy recommendations grow out of critiques that originate from disjunctures between ideology and lived experience with work-first in East County. They are not critiques of the people who staff the welfare office. They are reactions to the incongruity between their local experience and the common-sense assumptions of the work-first approach.

Policy Recommendations

The majority of policy research on welfare reform offers technocratic tactics for tweaking childcare, job training, or transportation protocols. In contrast, the policy recommendations offered below involve paradigmatic shifts in the ways we think about serving these families and the end goals we wish to accomplish with welfare programs. In other words, they involve reconsidering some fundamental assumptions of current practice.[20] This does not mean that these recommendations will be relegated to the abstract and general. Quite the contrary, the analysis of the preceding chapters affords us a background to engage with the details of the present policy in order to advocate specific "reforms."

Furthermore, the following recommendations assume the current political and social dominance of the neoliberal paradigm, and accordingly take the current institution as a starting point rather than wistfully wishing for a different reality. The emerging neoliberal welfare state, like previous ones, is not monolithic, despite the power of its ideological leverage over local jurisdictions.[21] Cross-scalar tensions and contradictions exist which could create new opportunities for re-conceiving and re-envisioning welfare as pro-labor and pro-family, as well as pro-work. As suggested by the theoretical work of Jamie Peck, reconstructing the welfare state according to progressive visions may even be facilitated by the infrastructure that the 1996 reform has created.[22] Given the familiarity with the work-first infrastructure that I offer in the previous chapters, it is possible to imagine recalibrating the "extra/interlocal channels" of performance measure monitoring. New performance measures could accommodate a redefinition of work that includes balancing parenting and paid work and a renewed valuation of the need for workers' and clients' rights and so on. Furthermore, these channels could be tweaked to encourage inroads on the local level into overcoming labor market inequalities and discrimination that the current work-first approach glosses over. These reforms, however, necessarily begin with and remain accountable to the lived experiences of local families and human service providers. It is with this in mind that I offer the following strategies in each of the following areas: (1) education, research, and monitoring; (2) legal remedies; (3) legislative policy action; and (4) social protest and grassroots organization (see table 7.1).[23]

Innovation and Common Sense

Gaps in the logic of work-first common sense appear in the words of resistance voiced by clients and human service caseworkers, often away from the welfare office. Though work-first has garnered unprecedented buy-in among the public in general, upon closer inspection clients and human service professionals in East County provide considerable evidence that work-first is not all it is held up to be. These "disjunctures" contribute to the formation of a counter-narrative to the work-first discourse that assumes all who resist processing and low wage work are lazy and irresponsible. Instead, this narrative provides a way to see such resistance as political. Though these critiques emerge within the context of

TABLE 7.1

Chapter	Education, Research, and Monitoring	Legal	Legislative Policy	Organizing, Social Protest, Grass Roots
Innovation and Work-First	Track ideological bias & innovative opportunities	Vigilance on workplace standards	International focus from pro-profit to pro-labor	Seek to balance ideological lobbies
Performance Measures, Rights, and Common Sense	Monitoring long-term well-being	Monitoring & emphasis on fair hearings	Track education, career, & justice performance	Seek check & balance on worker & client rights
New Technology and New Customers	Redirecting technology to serve the poor	Emphasize right to privacy & labor market leverage	Independent client/employer departments	Advocate technology to empower workers
Buying into Work-First	Document continuing poverty despite work	Guard low-wage worker labor protections	Anti-behavior to anti-poverty & community input	Collective worker identity centered on living wage
Work-First & Families -Gender	Explore innovative family-centered policy options	Defending reproductive liberty	Child-based performance measures	Recentering children; validate "other parents"
-and Race	Study continuing significance of race	Class-action civil rights vigilance	Inequity-sensitive performance measures	Broaden beyond identity politics

clients' experience of work, it is not necessarily work itself clients object to; rather, it is a specific type of low wage work that does not raise working mothers and their families out of poverty.

> Client: Work is a good thing. But working and still poor, then something is wrong with the system. . . . The problem is that work-first is expecting people to go out and get jobs below living wage.

Another client corroborates:

> East County's welfare reform is expecting people to go out into society and obtain employment that's not paying them a living wage and, in that aspect, people aren't still able to meet their basic needs such as rent, utilities, food, and other household needs.

The voicing of such concerns by various clients and former clients, and their meeting and sharing of ideas at a support group sponsored by a local charity, gives these complaints a communal feel. It furthermore suggests that, as with labor issues internationally, low wage work sponsored by work-first can be considered a collective problem, rather than an individual one.[24] In this instance, a member of the support group gives voice to her grievances as a member of a newly created "workforce of slave laborers."

> You're told to work and take whatever you get regardless of whether you have a preference, like you prefer to work with old people or something . . . It's creating a workforce of slave laborers.

These sentiments, however, are not limited to work-first clients. Perhaps not surprisingly, there are a considerable number of human service workers in East County who share similar sentiments about the low wage labor market and similar desire for change. A social service professional who now works with a major local philanthropy explains that, from his perspective work-first does not result in self-sufficiency:

> It's funny though self-sufficiency [in the case of TANF]. . . more and more we are seeing a phenomenon, research showed—we enlisted a professional firm to do some research—and um one of the things that it pointed to was that in this community right now, in the county, we have a lot of people, and I'm trying very carefully to not call them the "working poor," okay, but that population of people who are working, but needing additional public services that continues to rise. . . . And it's becoming a real, real challenge in this community right now that TANF doesn't address.

Recognizing that all is not well in the community and that there is an increase in the "working poor" has led this community worker to question the assumptions of work-first self-sufficiency and to challenge welfare reform's purported "success." A former client voices a similar contention that, contrary to popular acclaim, welfare reform is not a success.

> They say, "look it's working" and I say, "who's it working for?"I mean you will have a few token success stories but, for the majority I don't think it's working . . . I think the program needs to be looked at in terms of reality and nonreality in terms of how are they affecting people in taking them off welfare and putting them to work and people still can't afford to buy Pampers.

This critique points to a central empirical question of this book—who is served by work-first?

As explored in chapter 2, closely examining "who it's really working for" reveals that work-first casework is not a neutral apolitical enterprise. Rather, it involves caseworker complicity, whether conscious or not, with using state authority and power—determined by capital investors in favor of a highly motivated low wage workforce—to impose an agenda of workforce integration on poor mothers. In addition to enforcing behavioral compliance, the work-first institution seeks to win the hearts and minds of clients so that they "buy in" to the ideological values of a "low road" human capital investment approach to economic prosperity. The preceding chapters collectively laid out a foundation for understanding these connections as they link powerful capital lobbyists with frontline case practices and the conversion and socialization of clients. Yet a good deal more *education, research, and monitoring* is needed to examine exactly how this relationship has changed since the reform and how it continues to affect specific work-first implementation decisions and policy adjustments. This is part of a larger project that Marchevsky and Theoharis discuss in terms of revealing the ideologically biased assumptions taken for granted in the vast majority of contemporary welfare and poverty research.[25] As Catherine Kingfisher asserts, "the symbolic pollution of relief recipients tends to complement the rational concerns of capitalist elites for the maximization of wealth and power and the systemic imperatives of capital accumulation."[26] Though the present analysis reveals the relationship to be one of potentially exploitative class power dynamics, the wide popularity of welfare reform and its purported success at reducing caseloads is indicative of the broad purchase which the elite lobbying effort of neoliberal interests has garnered in the general populace.

The interests of lobbyists have become ubiquitous not only in the general population, but also among the "working poor." Despite structural decentralization, the 1996 reform is characterized by an almost militant reassertion of ideological centralization.[27] Rhetoric of responsibility to self-sufficiency through work dominates local sites of welfare administration.[28] Barbara Cruikshank describes this approach to case management as part of a neoliberal attempt to govern that relies on the consent and participation of poor people in their own reform and regulation.[29] Marchevsky and Theoharis further assert that within this approach "the role of government is now to discipline the poor in governing themselves."[30] Through profaning poor families, as Piven and Cloward argue, "relief practices are not merely a reflection of market ideology; they are an agent in nurturing and reinforcing that ideology."[31] The profanation of the "dependent poor" legitimates a reduction of governmental protections for labor:

> Relief recipients tend to accept, internalize, and endorse their symbolic profanation. Such stigmatization discourages demands for social rights because clients see themselves as unworthy of greater assistance and perhaps undeserving of the assistance they already receive. Moreover, degradation of relief recipients has an equally powerful effect on those who remain in the labor market. Fear of the profaned and stigmatized status associated with those detached from the labor market deters workers from making claims on the state for assistance, security, or protection even in times of economic hardship.[32]

As the preceding chapters have highlighted, welfare politics have been reframed in terms of a moralistic duality between deserving and nondeserving poor families. All who refuse to participate in the low wage labor market are stigmatized. Placed in historical context, this is a crucial complicity of government in what Bluestone and Harrison describe as management's contemporary effort to secure "a docile work force that would swallow wage concessions without a major fight."[33] This strategy's social welfare component is cogently conveyed in the words of Piven and Cloward: "The ritual degradation of a pariah class . . . serves to mark the boundary between the appropriately motivated and the inappropriately motivated, between the virtuous and the defective."[34] In other words, "to demean and punish those who do not work is to exalt by contrast even the meanest labor at the meanest wages."[35] In this context, *legal advocacy* is needed to push for greater protection of the dignity of work and the continued promotion of dignified workplace standards for work-first participants and other low-wage workers.

Neoliberal attempts at welfare reorganization should not be understood apart from wider discourses of neoliberal globalization faced by displaced professionals and dying communities. In such scenarios, globalization is portrayed as the natural, inevitable, or implicit source of economic rules. The global is seen as the optimal scale or level on which market forces should act (as opposed to bodily, household, community, and national levels). In relation to the global, the national scale, or level, shrinks in insignificance out of deference to the global, in order to accommodate global pressures. Yet, the local is the level at which the lives of everyday people must cope and adapt to global market forces.[36] Not only local states, counties, towns, and communities, but also local workers and poor welfare families must do their best, not to shield against globalization, but to maximize their potential in it and to accept the lot they receive as what they rightfully deserve under the rule of the global economy.[37] In this sense, welfare reform is simply a re-scaling of responsibility for surviving in the global economy—the local and individual must take on responsibilities that the national level assumed during and since the Great Depression.[38] In this sense, the narrative of personal responsibility "performs the important ideological function of harnessing welfare 'reform' to the national interest, imagining that the integration of former welfare recipients into the workforce will promote self-sufficiency and material well-being for all."[39]

In the rise of the neoliberal world order there has been a clear emergence of a predator in the form of globally mobile capital. Global economic reconfiguration has allowed firms to play both ends against the middle, holding sovereign states captive by threatening to move jobs overseas while at the same time squeezing previously unfathomable concessions out of workers, often despite and even with the aid of historically entrenched and rigid unions. A new paradigm for welfare policy must address more holistically the "welfare" of the nation, and potentially groups of allied nations, by reinvigorating collaboration between the state and organized labor, and pushing for strengthening and the eventual equalization of labor standards worldwide.[40] In this way, legislative policy action can take an active rather than a passive role in structuring the dynamic international economy to be pro-labor as well as pro-profit. From the perspective of *social protest and grassroots organization* this would likely entail attempts to fund a lobbying and information-disseminating counterbalance to the neoliberal right that has grown into the vast apparatus described in chapter 2.

As Yeheskel Hasenfeld argues, "What the majority of the poor need is not welfare reform, but a reform of low wage work."[41] Deploying leverage over international governing bodies that are highly influenced by U.S. policy and politics is one means to furthering international labor laws. Reforming policy from a pro-profit to a pro-labor program can become a mechanism for a positive transformation of the low wage labor market. This transformation is needed in terms of inequalities as well as of greater stability, readiness to accommodate work-family balances and opportunities for health care. Since the low wage labor market in contemporary form is being reproduced through new logics of neoliberalism and global economy at an exponential rate, it is necessary to break from advocating a simple retreat to welfare statism. Instead, we should work toward a new policy configuration that responds to and takes into account "the political economic developments that have brought about its [the welfare safety net's] demise in the first place."[42] Such policy, enacted through *legislative policy action*, can also include attempts to duplicate for the urban poor the programs that created the suburban hegemonic white American middle class (SHWAM). Already under way across the nation is an emphasis on revitalizing urban centers.[43] Replicating the college loans, home loans, and investments in infrastructure that fostered the rise of the SHWAM would go a long way to creating an urban renaissance.

Finally, chapter 2 also explored how the TANF structure systematically taps into the entrepreneurial creativity of community leaders in local government and business. In doing so it links welfare restructuring with a creative spirit that has been the hallmark of U.S. growth and prosperity. This innovative cadre of leadership has the potential to remain one of welfare's greatest assets for future reforms. Though presently employed to orchestrate a neoliberal shift in policy, these creative synergies are not beholden to economic liberalism. Rather, the loyalties and aspirations of those who have taken a leadership role seem to reside above all in trying to make life better for the people in the communities they serve. Currently a wellspring of interest in social entrepreneurship has inspired the public's imagination and a growing body of literature has emerged. Nevertheless, a good deal more *education, research, and monitoring* is needed to examine how best to incorporate this growth within welfare policy and to encourage local administrators to interact with and engage this trend in ongoing fashion.

Measuring Work-First Performance

As detailed in chapter 3, the work-first performance measure infrastructure hyperfocuses on compliance and cutting costs and in some ways misses out on the larger picture of climbing out of poverty. It increases individual accountability to work but fails to support human capital investment such as education and summer jobs. It also contributes to neglecting worker rights, and in the process erodes worker protections for both clients and caseworkers.

A story shared with me by a program leader of a summer jobs program was one of several representing a theme of work-first missing out on the bigger picture.

> If it's done the right way, training programs can work. But there are so many rules that the work-first folks put on. We had young people—we could take young people up to 21 years old in a summer jobs program. So we had young moms who were on welfare and they were getting, let's round it up to 1,000 bucks to 1,200 bucks a week from summer work. Work-first would call them in and reduce their welfare grants that amount—or whatever formula they had to follow. So these were modest summer jobs that might lead to at least something they could put on a resume, or a job application, likely not a full-time job. But in work-first's minds they needed to reduce their welfare grant because that's what it cost them, this county and state, money and grant money which made no sense at all. So we were particularly frustrated with that. So in terms of allowing people the opportunity, enabling people to be self-sufficient, we are our own worst enemy in the case of this system and it's real difficult.

A former client shares a similar story:

> My niece went to work like they wanted her to. She got two paychecks and was cut off of welfare just like that! She had no budgeting training or career training or anything. The reality is, if you are stuck without specific training in nursing or whatever field you want to be or a degree, you're stuck. It's creating this workforce of slave laborers. If the reality is they want people independent of the system, people need a livable wage to take care of your family. . . . We as Americans should have a roof over our heads; we're entitled to it. . . . I want time spent going to work or college counting [in performance measures] as a "work experience." They don't even have to pay for it, just count it! That's going to guarantee a higher than minimum wage . . . but folks are not willing to complain because they are scared their caseworker will retaliate and they think they are the judge and the jury.

In stories such as these, a recurring theme emerges of work-first being "our own worst enemy." Rules that mandate work seem to contradict the goals of long-term gainful employment and financial solvency. At the same time, clients and concerned community members feel they have no effective mechanism for appealing to work-first for changes and exceptions. This situation, however, can be changed with targeted policy reforms.

With respect to *education, research, and monitoring,* considerable research is needed to document exactly what types of worker protections and appeals processes are noticeably lacking among both clients and caseworkers. As far as clients are concerned, this is particularly difficult since performance measure accounting has seemingly squeezed out reporting on rights violations and conciliations, making work-first implementers considerably less accountable to protecting the rights and long-term prospects of clients. To force counties and states to once again prioritize collecting and reporting these data may require a new series of *legal remedies* not unlike those employed during the 1960s and 1970s to establish and ensure fair hearings in the first place. As Evelyn Brodkin claims, "Arguably the shortest and clearest route to improving accountability is to give welfare clients the capacity to protect themselves as service consumers, rejecting participation in programs that do no more than put them through the hoops under the guise of teaching responsibility." As she further asserts, "The ability of welfare recipients to enforce ambiguous state obligations to provide assistance will be suboptimal in the context in which rights are uncertain, voice is risky and exit means forgoing basic income support."[44] Most immediately, there is a need for increased legal aid. In New York State, for instance, currently less than 10 percent of appellants have legal aid assistance.[45]

Increased legal aid is needed not only in welfare offices but also for issues arising in the broader labor market. The U.S. Commission on Civil Rights reports that, "Unlike other employees, welfare workers who experience discrimination often do not have recourse options. The cost for filing a discrimination complaint is much higher for welfare-dependent and other low wage workers because of the fear that if they file a complaint, they will lose employment and subsequently other benefits."[46] Paired with legal aid, welfare offices could offer regular town/neighborhood meetings to provide technical assistance to people navigating the welfare system and to let the public know what services are available, particularly targeted toward immigrant families. They could also encourage a climate of looking out for and upholding worker rights in the broader labor market by partnering with community organizations to publicly emphasize clients' and workers' rights in addition to what is legally owed to them as part of the new welfare contract.[47] This would also encourage a place in the welfare institution for fostering *social protest and grassroots organization*, since, in addition to legal aid, this is a major form of checks and balances on worker and client rights. Whereas companies that do not receive the tax breaks they demand (corporate welfare) have the leverage to relocate in protest, lower wage workers must resort to such collective and localized responses. In keeping with a new emphasis on worker and client rights, union-organizing work could also be counted toward required work-related activity hours. This would make labor organizing also beneficial for local administrators who are worried about participation rates. Allowing work-first caseworkers to join unions would be a logical extension of this approach.

Shifting welfare office behavior to emphasize worker and client rights, however, will require more than legal and grassroots efforts. It will require *legislative policy action*, and particularly the introduction of new performance measures for fair hearings. These could include new reporting requirements for reasons for appeals, types of violations, and other factors that will allow targeted responses to emergent patterns of rights violations. In conjunction with fair hearings, new performance measures or at least reporting mechanisms could be introduced to assess the extent to which fully complying with work-first guarantees living wage employment. Such performance measure and reporting changes, however, would also require considerable restructuring of the ways in which technology is deployed in welfare offices. While federal reauthorization retains participation rates as the primary measure of success in TANF, work-first agencies would need to be encouraged, if not forced, to look beyond this kind of short-sighted process measure and concentrate on measuring outcomes meaningful to workers and employers, including educational attainment, career advancement, wage gains, and job retention.[48] This would go a long way toward re-establishing clients as customers to be served.

New Technology and New Customers

As explored in chapter 4, the new technology of work-first not only links a multitude of service collaborators but also establishes the state as an adversary of poor families and an ally of employers. Through a multitude of surveillance functions, this new alliance prioritizes employers as customers over poor clients. It also erodes the labor market bargaining power of clients, leaving little potential for the state to assume an advocacy role for the poor as they enter the labor force. As the bowling analogy goes, "it's like trying to bowl two balls at once."

The head of a major local philanthropy, while providing an overview of what technology means for the broader service provision network, explained that one important piece of missing data is where TANF clients go once they leave the welfare rolls.

> Caseloads dropped. Where did the people go? And what are they doing now? . . . All of those people that are going through the [70 or 80] food pantries [in this county] on a regular basis, . . . how many were in some sort of a TANF situation or are in this work-first because they may very well be working at this kind of a [low wage] job but they can't make it through the month without some sort of food system. . . . I just spoke to a food pantry director and what she said to me was that it was not an emergency service; it is a sort of safety net now, as much as this is becoming a service for a chronic problem now and that's a huge issue in this community. . . . Well there's more request for food programs, there's more need for this kind of an operation. Numbers are increasing, and it appears that it's because people who are working $7, $8, $9 an hour jobs, whatever the wage, is their expenses are just more than their income is for the month. And they need these kinds of services in order to get through. . . . I think that it is related to wages that some people are getting after leaving TANF.

Despite this noticeable problem with low wage jobs, work-first clients have limited flexibility and leverage to negotiate for higher salaries. As one client explains, they are under heavy surveillance to take any job they are offered and to keep it. "Work-first scrutinizes every move we make." In addition, it promises to work with employers to improve retention and actively punishes clients who quit. As another client explains, "Take the abuse [from employers] because if you don't they will kick you off of public assistance."

More *education, research, and monitoring* are needed to address two questions: (1) how the broad diversity of emerging work-first information technology directs caseworker discretion in local communities; and (2) how this technology can be transformed from simple surveillance to a role of advocacy for the poor. John Gilliom has suggested *legal remedies* in the form of strategies to redefine and protect the right to privacy. It may also be possible to mount a strategy based on the right not to have one's labor market bargaining power undermined by state intervention.[49] This strategy provides a foundation for new directions in *legislative policy action* that seek to shelter clients from the surveillance functions of the welfare office.

Given the adversarial nature of present welfare office—client relations, there is good reason to examine the feasibility of separating into two distinct entities the pro-business surveillance and the client advocacy functions of the welfare office. Yeheskel Hasenfeld argues that successful alternative programs that show promise of enabling the poor in becoming gainfully employed tend to have three characteristics in common: "They are voluntary, they are available to all poor people, and they exist outside of the domain of the welfare department."[50] He gives examples in the Center for Employment Training (CET) in San Jose, California and the New Hope Project in Milwaukee. Another model offered by Vanessa Tait is that of workers' centers. Over 100 workers' centers nationwide have emerged to support the needs of low-income workers. These centers focus on empowering workers through combining labor market participation and the political consciousness that develops via participatory learning. To such ends, workers' centers have often involved classes on labor history, legal rights, the environment, gender relations, as well as more welfare-population-oriented themes such as workers' rights in the contingent economy, unions and organizing, environmental racism, and welfare reform.[51] Though part of ongoing workforce investment and development will necessarily incorporate employers, workers and employers have differing agendas. Attempting to serve both within the same organization is vulnerable to a conflict of interests in which the priorities of one constituency must be placed above the other.

As part of a strategy of separation of client-serving and employer-serving functions into distinct and autonomous departments, the priority of welfare technology itself could be shifted from a focus on client surveillance to client service. The U.S. Commission on Civil Rights has argued that "customer service concerns are often linked with civil rights" and that "states should be required to develop an individualized approach to training, so that appropriate 'curricula' can be developed for each recipient based on her or his needs."[52] There is also a more fundamental issue at hand for work-first technology. The majority of this technology is deployed to monitor and regulate clients rather than assist them. It can and perhaps should be refocused to maintain records and report on labor market inequities that directly affect clients on a daily basis: good and bad employers (i.e., which ones offer the most generous benefits and treat their workers with dignity and consideration of encumbrances), slum landlords, predatory lenders, local crime and neighborhood watch information. As one community member explains, there are many out there who capitalize on the vulnerability of the poor: "People need financial services. They are getting ripped off. They go to [tax preparer] and get their tax return and they charge 30 percent fees!" Caseworkers are well positioned to participate in collecting and collating these data by utilizing interview techniques with clients that are similar to those currently being used to scrutinize their backgrounds. Engaging in such information collection and reporting would not only foster more positive client-caseworker relations, since clients would be empowered as both informants and beneficiaries of publicized data analysis, but it would firmly cement the institution that carries it out as an ally of the poor with whom longterm career support and advocacy is a feasible next step.

Such an approach would also reposition government as an ally to welfare-related *social protest and grassroots organization.* The welfare rights movement in the 1960s was orchestrated under the goal of providing a governmental shelter from employers for the poor. As presently configured, however, welfare is cast as a team effort on the part of government and employers to enforce participation in the contingent workforce. Caseworkers relate to clients as adversaries rather than advocates. What welfare could mean in the age of a global economy is government teamed with clients in support of stronger, more equitable bargaining and negotiating power between poor workers and their employers. Such a paradigm shift would break out of the welfare rights versus welfare responsibilities binary and the individual versus structural conundrum. It would address all of these aspects of the welfare/poverty dilemma in a holistic capacity and become a source of advocacy for non-welfare participating poor families as well. In effect this would broaden the focus of organizing, and the constituency base, from welfare recipients to the labor market in general. Seen in the case of poor workers' unions, poor working parents and welfare clients can and will assume roles of labor leadership if enabled with appropriate resources.[53]

Buying into Work-First

Under work-first, "it is assumed that once the mother works, even in a lousy job, surely her life circumstances will ultimately improve."[54] However, this is not necessarily the case. A vast literature identifies a "dual" or "split" labor market such that there are two types of jobs—good and bad. Good or primary jobs offer steady work, predictable hours, generous salaries, sick pay, vacation, family-friendly policies, health and retirement benefits, and career advancement. Bad or secondary jobs are characterized by the opposite. Though the turbulence of the new economy has stirred and muddied the waters quite a bit, introducing a host of middle ground possibilities between the poles of primary and secondary jobs, such a distinction not only still exists but uncertainty over the distinctive characteristics of primary and secondary jobs frame a critical debate over the merits and efficacy of work-first policy.[55]

Neoliberal thinking emphasizes the ultimate role and responsibility of the individual in attaining self-sufficiency. In contrast, students of the divided labor market argue that the stepping stone model of career advancement, where each job leads to a better one, is appropriate for those entering the primary labor market but is misguided in the case of welfare clients who tend to enter the secondary labor market. Several years of steady work in food service, janitorial services, housekeeping, or secretary assistance seldom make a person more marketable to move up the career ladder as it were—at least not without an infrastructure that allows them to advance their education and training and diversify their professional skills. Without such an infrastructure, low wage workers tend to be "trapped" in a series of low wage jobs, vulnerable to undependable and constantly shifting work schedules and ineligible for even basic family benefits and career advancement opportunity.[56] Even if "better" jobs exist, without an infrastructure to connect and prepare these low wage workers, this line of argument asserts, a spatial and/or skills mismatch is likely to remain, leaving poor workers in poor paying jobs, keeping wages down, and leaving better jobs unfilled.[57]

This debate is central to understanding the political economy that surrounds work-first in East County, where the average hourly wage of welfare clients who find jobs is $6.07 and the average weekly hours for the job is 31. This leaves the average family who finds work through work-first with a $9,347 annual income after 50 weeks of work (this is below the poverty level of $9,827 even for one person with no children).[58] This is not unique to East County. National research suggests that former welfare recipients are filling increasingly temporary and contingent positions, often in low-end manufacturing and service sectors.[59] In fact, one estimate suggests that only 10-20 percent of welfare recipients have attained "relatively permanent, above poverty stability" despite nearly 60 percent leaving the welfare rolls.[60]

In her widely acclaimed work on welfare reform, Sharon Hays argues, "The work rules of reform might be interpreted as aimed at creating a vast population of disciplined, and obedient workers who are hungry enough (and worried about their children enough) to take any temporary, part time, minimum wage job that comes their way, no matter what the costs to themselves or their family." She further asserts, "It is very unlikely that the majority of welfare mothers will have a chance to climb permanently out of poverty."[61] The Workforce Alliance similarly argues that, now that the 1996 welfare reform is in place, the central problem is poverty despite work. Approximately 75 percent of adults who receive TANF supports have worked more than half their adult years, and families with one or more workers now comprise approximately 70 percent of families with incomes below the poverty line.[62] Despite a rise in median income for families receiving welfare benefits, from $7,196 in 1997 to $11,820 in 2002, 69 percent of these working families lived in poverty as of 2002.[63]

Providing a local example of being caught in a cycle of poverty, a director of a community agency exclaims, "All this talk about work-first, but where are the jobs? Work-first doesn't do much good." Another expands upon his similar critique of work-first.

> With welfare reform, TANF is just huge right now because you got people, they have to work 30 hours a week in some mindless thing that they're not really getting trained to do anything to better their lives to become more self-sufficient. . . . One of our biggest challenges has been to try to confront the work-first people who we had shared clients with. We wanted to put our clients in training so that they could have a clear career path and their whole thing with clients was: we must make them work in order for them to get their welfare grant. It was a real conflict. I, as the executive director, would come in and try to convince the people on the other side to free up this person to get training so that they're not working a job forever at $8 an hour. They're never going to be self-sufficient with that. But under their rules that's what they had to be doing and they could then provide them with food stamps or day care, some transportation or whatever else as long as they kind of stayed working. I call it warehousing people, and that's it, basically that's a warehouse for a person.

Reinforcing this idea of warehousing, a former city employee shares an anecdote about how the work-first system misses out on opportunities to help people climb out of poverty and into self-sufficiency:

I wish I would remember the lady's name, Noramara, or whatever her name was. She was a person who was doing ironing, you know how you take your clothes to the dry cleaner they have these huge irons that they use? That's what she was doing. It's like $8 an hour. She wanted to be in nurse training. She was going to start with LPN and eventually I remember, nursing, even at that time in the early 2000s and late '90s was a field that had a shortage of workers and if you're on our end now, you can make a ton of dough, and talking about being self-sufficient, you can almost name your hours with such a shortage. Work-first wouldn't let her get started as an LPN in order to kind of work her way up because she had to be in this mindless job. And we were going to pay for the training! The training dollars, education dollars weren't the issue, the issue was that they would not let her out of her service to TANF or welfare-to-work service. It was just a terrible. I remember it was an awfully tense time because this woman had all the, she tested well, she just had every possibility that she was going to be successful, but they wouldn't let her go, and I remember she became a real cause for us.

Though work-first is built upon a stepping stone model, the state assumes no responsibility in confirming, let alone guaranteeing, that the stepping stones are in place.[64] The 1996 PRWORA limited educational components of "welfare-to-work activities" to training programs that directly prepare individuals for a job that exceed no more than 12 months. This policy remains in place despite evidence from post-reform research that "having a high school diploma or GED certificate was the single most important factor in determining whether these women found work and the conditions of the work they found."[65] In 2000, less than 1 percent of TANF federal funds were spent on education and training and only 5 percent of TANF recipients participated in them.[66]

Not only must this low road approach to labor market prosperity be scrutinized in future *research* for its potentially detrimental long-term effects on national productivity and the well-being of poor families, but research suggests that the concept of welfare dependency that justified an un-generous low road approach must be scrutinized for its inaccuracies. Economist Trudi Renwick argues that "welfare dependency"—the problem that TANF was originally set up to address—is largely a thing of the past, if it ever existed at all as described in popular anti-welfare discourse.

By comparison, fewer than 20 percent of parents with incomes below the poverty line receive TANF income supplements, and many of these parents are working or in between jobs. In fact, some four out of every five adults who receive TANF income supplements have worked more than half their adult years. Today's problem is poverty despite work. TANF needs to be reformed to make it work as part of a larger wage subsidy and career advancement system designed to tackle this economic problem. Under such a system, cash assistance should be thought of as a "work support" for parents with unstable, low wage jobs, and also as a supplemental form of "financial aid" for low-income parents who are trying to better themselves through education and training.[67]

Such assessments of the reform give credence to the argument that while "much attention has been given to the personal responsibility portion [of the 1996 Personal Responsibility and Work Opportunity Reconciliation Act]. . . [t]he work opportunity language deserves similar attention, especially for racial and ethnic minority groups who have historically competed, and are presently competing, in a discriminatory labor market."[68]

There exists a disconnect between the publicly defined problem of "welfare dependency" and the material experience of "poverty despite work." Future *legislative policy action* that truly seeks to make the stepping stone model of labor market career advancement realistic for welfare clients needs to shift focus from anti-behavior to anti-poverty. The current focus is on conditioning behavior change that is consistent with an assumed stepping stone trajectory. Work-first conditioning forces clients to disregard behaviors that, while dysfunctional within a stepping stone paradigm, may actually be quite functional if a stepping stone path is indeed a myth as some researchers suggest.[69] One way to address this is to continue offering services to the working poor with no time limits since most leavers from public assistance are in jobs that pay below poverty wages and have unstable and erratic work hours. Thus, any week spent working any hours (since full-time work is so elusive in this sector of the market) will not count toward the five-year limit. This will ensure that needed supplementary aid will stay in place for those who are working, and as this change trickles down to the front lines of intake work, it will reduce pressure to weed out all who are not able to work full time and emulate an unencumbered worker. It will also ensure that, as with the mantra "any job is a good job," any job will be an adequate job since the government will ensure a living wage by making up the difference. In addition, education grants such as free tuition to community colleges should be made available automatically to any client who consistently works for a given period of time. As one former client exclaims:

> Bring back more school aid. If you are stuck without a specific training, it's slave labor. If you want people to be independent of the system, they need a livable wage, need an education. Count education as a work activity!

Schooling that is paid for by clients should also count toward work participation. In addition, feedback from the community is an important check on caseworker behavior and it provides a necessary pulse from the community on how well welfare is meeting community needs. Such feedback should be formalized in terms of regularly scheduled community "town meetings" on welfare and a welfare advisory/oversight board that include a considerable number of the client constituencies served. Also of potential use is incorporating a performance measure based on routine client and even employer satisfaction surveys. This can be paired with *legal vigilance* to ensure that those families laboring in the contingent and low-income labor market receive all of the low wage labor protections afforded under the law.

Such efforts to reach out to clients as stakeholders in welfare would also provide a formalized and legitimated forum for *social protest and grassroots organization.* The U.S. government has a long history of anti-labor policies, but this stance has intensified since the 1980s.[70] In the current process of liberalizing U.S. and overseas markets with neoliberalism that diminishes government regulation of capital, we need to maintain a balance by also diminishing controls over labor. Supporting clients in labor organization could be one effective way of doing this. Chad Alan Goldberg discusses how welfare/workfare participants have used rallies and threats of work slowdown to improve their working conditions and pressure cities to give them permanent jobs.[71] Furthermore, there is precedent for such labor organization to take shape in what has emerged in recent years as poor workers' unions. As Vanessa Tait describes, these unions are founded in geographical/community (not shop-floor) relationships; they not only include a politics of place that counters the abstraction of global labor markets, but they are also given to incorporating shared concerns that are broader than work alone.[72] Concerns ranging across work, jobs, welfare, utility rates, neighborhood preservation, redlining, education, housing, etc., converge to provide a broader base for both solidarity and action. They also hold potential for redefining low wage workers, welfare recipients, and other stereotyped groups by crossing borders and bridging conceptual boundaries between people (workers, welfare recipients, and workfare participants) and principles (civil rights, workers' rights, and welfare rights). In Tait's observation, as trade unions join forces with workfare organizing, they move toward a broader understanding of who "workers" are.[73] Recent statistics suggest that there is considerable potential for solidarity between welfare recipients and non-welfare recipients. Research using longitudinal national data estimates that nearly 59 percent of all American adults will spend a year or more of their adult life below the poverty line by the time they turn 79, that over one-third will resort to means-tested cash programs, and that two-thirds will resort to some form of welfare programs for assistance by the time they are 65 years of age (i.e., before tapping into retirement safety nets).[74] Given this harsh reality, poor workers' unions thus can build broad-based solidarity, including on the same continuum not only parenting and caregiving work, but also workfare, advocacy for clients, and workers' rights.

Work-First Gender, Race, and Families

Chapter 6 explored the interrelated dynamics of gender and race within the work-first approach to welfare. In the policy recommendations that follow, however, I separate gender and race for purposes of clarity.

GENDER

As examined in chapter 6, the work-first approach systematically emphasizes the productive role of poor welfare families in the economy and de-emphasizes and discourages their reproductive and caregiving role. In so doing, work-first assumes a myopic and present-centered stance on labor market productivity by focusing on what limited paid employment parents can do now, without further training, rather than the long-term view of how to make their children as productive as possible for both society and the economy. In the process of reinforcing a work ethic among adults, children are overlooked, yet they currently make up over three-quarters of the TANF population. The current day-to-day institutional efforts of work-first staff focus the lion's share of their efforts on the one-quarter of the population who are adults. They thereby emphasize the

FIGURE 7.1

Percent of AFDC/TANF Caseloads that are Children By Calendar Year

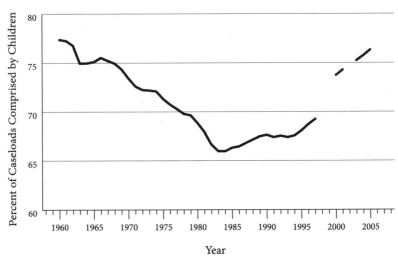

Source: http://www.acf.hhs.gov//programs/ofa/caseload/caseloadindex.htm#afdc

weak economic potential of the 9.6 million low-skilled parents and other adult family members instead of targeting their investment of time and resources on the educational, emotional, and career potential of the 30.8 million children (see figure 7.1).[75]

Furthermore, these efforts are largely aimed at forcing low-income families to fit into an employment-family balance, in which all parents are employed, that has worked for middle- and upper-class families primarily because they can hire workers from lower-class families as maids and childcare providers.[76] Throughout this book it has become apparent that adults are the primary focus of welfare intake processing and that arrangements for children are secondary.

As women, clients feel that they are unfairly discharged from the system because they have familial obligations. As one welfare support group member explained:

> There needs to be something in place to, instead of seeing people as being noncompliant, to find out what the barrier is, you know to help that person do the job search or whatever.

Often these reasons for "noncompliance" have to do with gender-role responsibilities such as caring for family members in need, a job that is stereotypically left to the women in a family. The member continues:

> I know this woman who is going through TANF and she is not able to feed her children. They depend on her. Something's wrong. She's in school, trying to get her GED. She doesn't drink or smoke. She's got some issues, but she needs to feed her kids. I end up feeding them. They eat at my house!

These gender responsibilities, however, are only the tip of the iceberg. They are complicated by a variety of other factors as well.

> People are dealing with family emergencies and at that time work-first is not a priority on your agenda. You're dealing with your emergency situation at that time, so other things become secondary until that crisis is handled.

Providing an example of this, the support group member recounts the story of a woman who lived in the building next door to hers.

> Work-first kept denying her. So I took her to a food pantry food giveaway. On the way back she said, "I'm facing addiction, I have no food, and I'll be damned if I have time to jump through their hoops." The bottom line is that her immediate concern was taking care of herself and her family, not work-first.

Our current system of incentives and sanctions is preoccupied with changing the behavior of the one-quarter of the welfare caseloads who are adult mothers and hoping that by changing their behavior, children and society will be better off. In the immediacy of family need, this means that children are most likely to receive aid only as long as their parents comply with an institutional work ethic. In fact, as this research reveals, work-first attends to children by trying to make them invisible; caseworkers focus on preventing children from getting in the way of efforts to coax, cajole, and motivate their mothers into the low wage labor force.

What began as a system for supporting widows with children has been transformed by recent reforms into an institution that ensures that single mothers work full time and place their children in the care of low-paid childcare providers. There are a myriad of options between full-time parenting and full-time work with childcare. The lack of client ability to choose from among these options is an important caveat to the welfare system. It denies clients the right to choose from among parenting options and in this respect is problematic from the standpoint of day-to-day experiences of parenting.

Welfare does not have to be this way. *Legislative policy action* could refashion welfare as the centerpiece for developing work-family policy that is feasible for all social classes, policy that encourages all American families, mothers and fathers, to optimize their simultaneous contributions to their families and the new economy. Since the early 1990s, welfare policy has assumed a role of local experimentation aimed at improving implementation through experience. Most of the attention has been concentrated on the relationship between parents and work. Welfare policy, recentered on the vast majority of its constituents—the children—could become a vanguard for catalyzing, implementing, and testing the advantages and disadvantages of policies such as flextime, telecommuting, innovative childcare arrangements, new home tutoring programs, and job sharing. At a minimum, policy that encourages balancing work and family could involve extending the time limit, such that if a parent (male or female) is working part time (to enable part-time caregiving), they would effectively receive ten years of assistance to supplement their earnings rather than five while not working. If a client is working and is still in need of assistance, it should not count at all toward the time limit. This would mean a mixture of part-time and care work would be acceptable work activities for TANF eligibility. Furthermore, TANF performance measures can be expanded to include factors of family enrichment, such as educational attainment of children and parenting benchmarks set by clients themselves.

This agenda would be poised to serve primarily the needs of poor working families; yet, there could be a spinoff for long-term national economic policy, which could only stand to benefit from a higher quality of training and socialization for future workers. These suggestions alone set forth a tall agenda for future *education, research, and monitoring.*

Also implied in this agenda are *legal remedies* that take the right to parent seriously. As Dorothy Roberts writes:

> Reproductive liberty must encompass more than the protection of an individual woman's choice. . . . It must encompass the full range of procreative activities, including the ability to bear a child, and it must

acknowledge that we make reproductive decisions within a social context, including inequalities of wealth and power. Reproductive freedom is a matter of social justice, not individual choice.[77]

This critique is eminently relevant to the work-first infrastructure to the extent that poor women, often of color, are discouraged from reproducing because of the added hassles it involves within the welfare system. Public rhetoric also villainizes poor women's reproduction as the cause of poverty. Legal protections for reproductive liberties promise to be a complex but important area of reform for poor families.

Social protest and grassroots organization can have a meaningful role to play in shifting the focus for work-first from exclusively the relationship between parents and work to include the relationship between parents and children. As Jill Berrick suggests, "Efforts on behalf of children would garner great public support, would ensure long-term benefits to society at large and would reflect public policy at its best."[78] Further, grassroots efforts can advocate broadening the scope of welfare toward greater recognition and awareness of nonbiological caregivers as well, such as "other mothers" and "other fathers" who have not yet been fully incorporated into policy.[79] Efforts can be made to encourage government to incorporate consideration of these family networks into policy assumptions. In total, these recommendations would move toward a model that values parenting responsibility as much as workforce accountability.

RACE

In addition to gender, chapter 6 examined how matters of race complicate work-first policy. In East County and elsewhere, ignoring the relevance of race though color-blind approaches is problematic. As Susan Gooden writes, "Much research focuses on individual factors contributing to long-term welfare dependency such as teen pregnancy, intergenerational welfare dependency, family formation, and the lack of minority business development, but the role of institutional racial barriers does not receive similar consideration."[80] In addition, a growing body of literature identifies race as consequential in work-first administration.

Research on the 1996 reform has noted that public sentiment favoring welfare reform with punitive work requirements solidified just as the percentage of the welfare rolls constituted by blacks and the percentage of blacks receiving welfare peaked.[81] The U.S. Commission on Civil Rights reports that "numerous studies prove that welfare reform has done little to eliminate historical discrimination in public assistance. People of color encounter insults and disrespect as they attempt to navigate the welfare system."[82] Additionally, studies of interstate variation in welfare provisions have found that states with higher concentrations of black welfare clients have been associated with more punitive and less generous work policies.[83] Particularly, "states with higher percentages of Hispanic and black recipients at the time of welfare reform were more likely to adopt shorter time limits, family caps on benefits, and stronger sanctions than states with lower percentages of minority recipients."[84]

In addition to state-level patterns, local variations in race have occurred. According to the U.S. Commission on Civil Rights:

> Numerous studies have found that white recipients are more likely to be encouraged to pursue an education, are less likely to be sanctioned, and are more likely to receive childcare subsidies than other groups. Other studies have found that welfare agencies are least helpful to blacks in providing job-readiness skills and more helpful to whites, Hispanics, and Asian Pacific Americans. They are also least likely to provide basic academic skills, enrichment, or tutoring services to black recipients.[85]

The National Urban League Institute for Opportunity and Equality found that work supports including childcare, transportation assistance, and college degree assistance were more generously provided to white than to minority working mothers.[86]

Though work-first is officially a color-blind policy, and though caseworkers insist race is immaterial to processing, not all clients agree. Some see race as very meaningful and notice patterns that are reflective of the analyses noted above. As one client explains:

> The [White] welfare worker said in a condescending way, "You can get work if you really try." [The client offers her translation] People like you, black, are lazy.

Offering an explanation, she adds:

> You feel race is a factor, especially when you're being talked down to. They could be just having a bad day, but it seems racial.

In addition to interactions with caseworkers, clients see race as making a difference when interacting with employers in the low wage labor market. Though it is hard to know for sure, race is in the back of some of their minds.

> Again, you can't put your finger on it, but there's this gut feeling. Is this really because they don't see me as qualified or [because of] . . . race?

Following up on this theme, a client shared a story about a member of her family who was also black and a welfare beneficiary, as she encountered what seemed like racial dynamics when working on a work-first-related job site.

> She got a job at one of those expensive stores at the mall and there was a problem where it looked like [racial] discrimination. They weren't pleased with the way she wasn't able to afford and dress the way clientele of the store do and they looked down upon her, made her miserable there and she just couldn't take it anymore. . . . Well of course the [welfare] worker told her to let them know about it next time before she just walked out and of course she had been telling us what was going on for weeks. And so here she was, damned if you do, damned if you don't. Take the abuse because if you don't, public assistance will kick you off because you quit the job. It's called a voluntary quit.

Despite caseworker insistence that gender and race are not of concern in the labor market, gender and race make notable differences in wages even in the low end of the unskilled labor market as reflected in the data for East County given in table 7.2.[87]

Overall, among those who found work though work-first in East County, women earned an average of $6.06 per hour for every $6.66 that men received (approximately 90 cents on the dollar). In 11 out of the 14 occupational categories recorded, men earned higher average wages than women, and in the highly male-dominated occupations such as construction, women earned as little as 87 cents on the dollar compared with men. On the opposite side of the spectrum, in female-dominated fields such as education, women earn as little as 75 cents on the dollar compared with men.

The average hourly wage overall for welfare clients who found work in East County also differed by race, with whites earning approximately

TABLE 7.2

Summary of Types of Jobs Obtained by Welfare Clients by Gender
Between January 1, 1995 and November 30, 2000 (n=5978)

Occupational Category	Percent of Those Obtaining These Jobs That Are Women	Female: Average Hourly Wage	Male: Average Hourly Wage	Female: Average Annual Salary Based on 50 Weeks Worked	Male: Average Annual Salary Based on 50 Weeks Worked	Average Difference Female- Male
Clerical	95	6.81	6.55	$10,908	$10,496	$412
Construction	11	6.25	7.15	$11,510	$13,165	$(1,655)
Critical Care Tech.	0	-------	8.11	-------	$9,124	-------
Education	90	5.99	7.97	$9,090	$12,095	$(3,005)
Food Service	80	5.55	5.60	$7,777	$7,842	$(64)
General Laborer	47	5.89	6.20	$9,591	$10,099	$(507)
Health	100	5.15	-------	$9,013	-------	-------
Healthcare	94	7.27	6.31	$11,187	$9,708	$1,480
Laborer	100	5.15	-------	$10,300	-------	-------
Maintenance	73	5.66	5.99	$8,515	$9,023	$(508)
Managerial	72	7.24	6.98	$12,012	$11,587	$426
Manufacturing	67	5.97	6.42	$11,261	$12,100	$(838)
Misc.	60	5.87	6.25	$9,167	$9,766	$(600)
Retail	88	5.55	5.67	$7,583	$7,751	$(167)
Security	48	5.52	5.55	$9,036	$9,087	$(52)
Services	81	5.81	5.99	$8,527	$8,789	$(262)
Technical	51	7.37	8.30	$13,020	$14,658	$(1,638)
Woodworkers	0	-------	7.56	-------	$15,120	-------
Grand Total	76	6.06	6.66	$9,858	$10,828	$(971)

Source: Agency records compiled by the author.

$6.12 as compared to $6.02 for blacks and $5.98 for Hispanics (see table 7.3). When averaging the mean wages of occupational categories by race, the difference grows to a mean wage of $6.64 per hour for whites as opposed to $6.08 for blacks. This is not entirely surprising given that research on welfare leavers has found as much as a 35 percent difference between blacks and whites after leaving welfare ($10,403 mean income for whites as compared to $6,736 for blacks).[88]

Counting the bold and italicized average hourly wages for each occupational category, we find that whites only experienced below average mean hourly wages in 3 occupational fields as opposed to 11 for blacks, 10 for Hispanics, 9 for Asians, and 6 for those labeled 'other.' Not only do they receive lower pay in the same fields, but, as Holzer and Stoll report based on their study of four urban cities, "relative to their white counterparts, black and Hispanic welfare recipients are less likely to be

TABLE 7.3

*Summary of Average Wages by Race and Types of Jobs Obtained by Welfare Clients
Between January 1, 1995 and November 30, 2000 (n=5978)*

Occupational Category	White (n=3049)	Black (n=2279)	Hispanic (n=386)	Asian (n=151)	Other (n=112)	Overall Average
Clerical	6.85	**6.71**	**6.74**	**6.79**	6.79	6.79
Construction	7.33	**6.54**	**6.28**	**6.00**	**0.00**	7.05
Critical Care Tech.	8.11	**0.00**	**0.00**	**0.00**	**0.00**	8.11
Education	6.40	**6.06**	**5.70**	**6.00**	**0.00**	6.19
Food Service	**5.48**	5.68	5.62	6.68	**5.33**	5.56
General Laborer	6.19	**5.89**	**6.01**	6.28	**5.74**	6.05
Health	**0.00**	5.15	**0.00**	**0.00**	**0.00**	5.15
Healthcare	7.59	**6.96**	**7.20**	7.62	·**6.66**	7.22
Laborer	**0.00**	5.15	**0.00**	**0.00**	**0.00**	5.15
Maintenance	5.82	**5.68**	**5.74**	5.54	5.97	5.75
Managerial	7.47	**6.65**	**5.74**	7.00	**0.00**	7.16
Manufacturing	6.42	**5.91**	**5.95**	5.88	5.93	6.12
Misc.	**6.00**	6.07	6.31	5.43	**5.55**	6.02
Retail	**5.55**	**5.54**	5.63	6.16	5.64	5.56
Security	5.64	**5.45**	**5.55**	4.25	**0.00**	5.53
Services	5.86	**5.83**	**5.69**	6.17	6.08	5.85
Technical	7.93	7.96	**7.24**	7.5	**7.00**	7.83
Woodworkers	7.56	**0.00**	**0.00**	**0.00**	**0.00**	7.56
Grand Total	6.12	6.02	5.98	6.03	5.90	6.07

Note: Averages by race below overall average are boldface.
Source: Agency records compiled by the author.

hired in suburban and/or smaller establishments, and for blacks, in the retail trade industries."[89] Such data give weight to the thoughts and concerns about race and gender that are voiced by some work-first clients in East County. However, this does not mean that caseworkers come to see gender and race as structural issues from the perspective of case processing.

As a general rule, caseworkers are proud that there is no special protocol that varies by the race of clients; as far as they are concerned, they treat everyone the same. This is a microcosm of the larger welfare institution in which structural factors are subsumed to individual responsibilities, and matters such as racial inequalities are evaded. In the course of enforcing the personal responsibility imperative of work-first and striving toward reduced caseloads and increased employment, caseworkers— black and white—tend to conform to work-first's color-blind approach by assigning the significance of race to the realm of the individual. Though they do not deny the existence of racism, they insist that race is simply a distraction from work-first goals.

[Black Caseworker]: Racism is a cop-out. You can tell if an employer looks
at you and doesn't want to hire you when you walk in because you're
black. Then when that employer calls, don't call them back! Go to another
employer!

For this caseworker, as with many of his colleagues, race is not a factor,
or at least not something deserving of being addressed publicly.[90] He
does not deny it exists, he just denies it is any of the government's business as far as his program is concerned. Accordingly, he constructs it as
a personal or private matter, the implications of which could be managed
through more persistence on the part of the individuals themselves, pri-
vately—he apparently overlooks the fact that refusing a job is grounds for
TANF ineligibility.

Though a multitude of research identifies patterns of racial inequality
in a series of case studies, there is no uniform national standard for such
data collection.[91] As a result, much more *education, research, and monitoring* are needed not only to identify where and how racism and discrimination exist, but also to understand more comprehensively how shared
experiences of inequality can form the basis for collective action on the
part of welfare mothers. At the least, the U.S. Commission on Civil Rights
argues:

The Administration for Children and Families within HHS should collect
and disseminate standardized data by race/ethnicity on welfare recipients,
those denied benefits, those sanctioned, and those exempted from work
requirements. Data should also be disaggregated by subpopulations, particularly with respect to immigrant welfare recipients, so that state and
local agencies can assess usage patterns and better determine the unique
needs of various communities. The data should be produced in a uniform and easily accessible format and made available to researchers and
practitioners.[92]

Such changes in data collection and reporting would allow analyses of issues of race in conjunction with analyses of the tomes of data already collected and made publicly available. It would also allow future researchers to
break free of what has been described as "a post-civil rights model for welfare research" that simply does not pay attention to race in favor of scrutinizing individual client characteristics as the root of the problem.[93] Making
such data available would also allow further research, such as the present

study that "treats poverty as a political, economic, and ideological effect of capitalist processes and state activity" rather than "imagining the poor as invisible, passive, pathological, or in need of charity or moral reform."[94]

Legal remedies that also address issues of race within their structural context can join these research efforts. To date, "civil rights enforcement efforts are hampered by the fact that relatively little data have been collected on the distribution of benefits, sanctions, and access to services by race and ethnicity, and there is no uniform national standard for such data collection."[95] While simply collecting these data will not enforce civil rights, it will provide clues as to where to focus legal strategies such as class action lawsuits. For instance, they may reveal a utility for legal team–based anti-discrimination testers who could visit welfare offices under the guise of clients to ensure that guidelines are followed.[96] Also relevant may be legal training. The U.S. Department of Health and Human Services has published anti-discrimination guidelines that include specific examples of welfare policies and practices that constitute racist actions. Such information can be made available to organizations of clients concerned about welfare rights.[97] In addition, Congress can be pressured to allocate funding for stronger enforcement of civil rights laws, improved training of caseworkers, and outreach to employers of welfare recipients. They could potentially give the Office for Civil Rights at the Department of Health and Human Services the resources necessary to investigate allegations of discrimination and monitor the activities of state welfare offices to ensure adherence to federal civil rights statutes.[98] Such shifts in *legislative policy action* are crucial if we are to proactively address issues of race in the labor market. As the U.S. Commission on Civil Rights asserts:

> Without civil rights protections in the legislation, welfare reform cannot lift *all* [emphasis in original] Americans out of poverty. Based on its own review and numerous studies, the Commission encourages Congress to promote policies that will alleviate the disparities and advance the objectives of reform. The Commission's recommendations are offered in three categories: (1) those that will facilitate the enforcement of civil rights laws, (2) those that will safeguard against discriminatory treatment, and (3) those that will prevent future disparate impact.[99]

Racial disparities have been noted in caseload declines, case management services, and employment outcomes, yet there persists a "lack of national attention to the role of case management and labor market

TABLE 7.4

Each Standard Applied to Existing Local Racial/Ethnic Groups Separately Rather Than to Heterogeneous Caseload as a Whole		Minumum Level	Bonus Level
Employment	% of welfare clients that obtained a job	35%	40%
Wages	% of clients earning $8.50/hour or over	20%	25%
Health Insurance	% of clients with health insurance available through employer	30%	40%
Job Retention	% still employed after 30 days	75%	85%
	% still employed after 90 days	50%	60%
Educational Activities	% of clients without high school diploma in educational activities	75%	85%
Educational Advancement	% of clients without high school diploma that complete GED	20%	30%

Source: Standards adapted from Goodin 2003.

discrimination in explaining differences in employment outcomes among recipients."[100] Though PRWORA is covered under Civil Rights legislation, and PRWORA Section VIIB makes clear that work-first cannot legally discriminate, PRWORA evaluation standards do not require evaluation of racial disparities or bias.[101] Written guidelines give consideration to some structural labor market factors such as unemployment rates, yet at the same time ignore others such as institutional racism, in favor of focusing on individual client factors.[102] One way to rectify this is to take affirmative action, or what Gooden calls "concerted attention," by integrating race fairness into performance measures.[103] For instance, new legislation could set race-specific benchmarks and require that separate versions of the following chart be produced for each ethnic group separately, as well as in aggregate (see table 7.4).

Applying each of TANF's performance standards to each relevant racial/ethnic group separately will ensure that caseworkers and administrators will focus on creating positive outcomes for all clients. Under the current system, work-first agencies can meet their performance goals by focusing on white clients, while leaving disadvantaged minorities unattended to. Such a structural change to the work-first approach would force the apparatus of the state to address patterns that appear on a structural level along racial lines, rather than to simply ignore them and insist that the root causes are individual-based. Shifting from an individualistic view of poverty to incorporate structural dynamics will also provide a basis for social protest and grassroots organization that will encourage groups of clients to act collectively to address not only issues of race, but also broader labor market inequalities. Reporting data by race on the local and national levels would highlight the inequalities that suppress the careers of chronically low wage workers and make work-first more accountable to ameliorating them.

Resisting the Neoliberal Welfare State

Though caseworkers and clients largely buy into the work-first approach, there is also evidence of doubt and skepticism. Caseworkers at times admit that they are frustrated and that clients "really can't make it" in the low wage economy. Some clients and human service workers in the community, whom I interviewed, also offer extended critiques that call into question the broader class relations of welfare. In the present political climate, however, few "government workers" are inclined to associate themselves or their union with what have been publicly portrayed as unskilled, black, single, and lazy clients.[104] Barbara Cruikshank argues that what is needed is a conceptual reframing of resistance, suggesting that "what we take for 'real' political issues has bound us to forms of resistance that are not effective."[105] The efforts of the past, though dated, nevertheless provided us with a foundation for thinking and a sense of evolving circumstances.

In Nancy Fraser's critique of late-capitalist political culture she identifies four forms of "client resistance" to welfare state power—individual resistance, establishment of informal "survival networks," client insistence on the primacy of their own subjective narratives over institutional "therapeutic" narratives, and the "political" formal organization of clients to challenge administrative interpretations of their needs.[106] This consideration of "political" resistance is based in traditional Marxian and materialist approaches that note the development of a shared, "expressly political identity" or "shared consciousness" based in clients' similar socioeconomic situatedness in relation to the welfare state. Though Fraser only considers formally organized groups of clients to be "political," Piven and Cloward have for some time conceptualized political resistance in broader terms. They contest that "requiring that protests have a leader, a constitution, a legislative program, or at least a banner before they are recognized as such—is to divert attention from the many forms of political unrest and to consign them by definitions to the more shadowy realms of social problems and deviant behavior."[107] Within this context, as Ewick and Silbey argue, "to dismiss everyday forms of resistance on the grounds that they are individualistic, unprincipled, and temporary is to foreclose crucial questions about the relationship between power and resistance."[108] Furthermore, it overlooks the potential that James C. Scott attributes to unspoken "hidden transcripts" that accompany the "public transcripts" of everyday interactions between the more and less powerful.[109] Though they often remain unspoken thoughts (except among equals), these transcripts contain poignant passive resistance strategies, and form the foundation of "potential acts, intentions as yet blocked, and possible futures that a shift in the balance of power or a crisis might bring to view."[110]

Whereas Fraser's conceptualization assumes a foundation in the fact that welfare clients are brought together in welfare waiting rooms and, as a result of their common participation as clients they come to articulate collective grievances, other variations of political mobilization in opposition to the welfare state also exist.[111] For instance, both Alice Burton and Catherine Kingfisher discuss potential labor solidarity between welfare clients and their caseworkers based on their common material base in reliance on the state.[112] However, like Fraser and Piven, Burton and Kingfisher are limited by their alignment of "the terms of resistance with the terms of welfare."[113] As the preceding chapters of this book explicate, the relations of the welfare institution are much wider than the official components of the state. The political mobilization of those negatively impacted can be similarly widened. Currently, solidarity between stigmatized clients, caseworkers, and the general public is marginal.[114] Few are supportive of a platform of clients' rights as existed in the 1960s. When the platform is expanded to address the broader neoliberal restructuring, however, new possibilities emerge. Client resistance is no longer recalcitrance but also, potentially, a personal and political stand in opposition to:

- imposition of the Standard North American Family and suburban hegemonic subjectivities
- tension between mothering discourses and work expectations
- the neoliberal worker construct as gender-, race-, and class-blind
- the influence of capitalist elites on the policy agenda and spending of public funds
- the perceived fallacy of the stepping stone philosophy
- erosion of worker rights
- removal of a national safety net entitlement

- undermining of fair hearing protocols
- the abandonment of equality as a public policy goal within the neoliberal agenda
- disproportional state support for employers as opposed to workers in adapting to the emergent global economy

Recognizing client resistance as confronting broader neoliberal meta-discourses offers new potential for broad-based solidarity. What were formerly "welfare issues" specific to welfare constituencies become visible as one of many connected fronts that implicate and link workers of all sorts who are concretely impacted by the rising dominance of neoliberal common sense. Welfare is a labor issue as much as a poverty issue.

The roots to this approach can be seen in emergent critical scholarship. Barbara Cruikshank argues that critical attempts to theorize state power have been "limited in their potential to imagine new forms of resistance because they fail to account for political power beyond the state."[115] In other words, a broader foundation from which to respond to emergent problematic aspects of neoliberal restructuring is needed. Fraser acknowledges sites of power in welfare as shaped by both political power of the state and the terms of discourse employed. Similarly, for Cruikshank the borders of state action and political economy are not traversed by random or "runaway discourses" but rather by broadly coordinated "strategies and relations of rule."[116] These understandings implicate the role of work-first common sense in both social organization and resistance.

Despite the power of its ideological leverage over local jurisdictions, the emerging neoliberal welfare state, as with previous ones, is not monolithic.[117] Cross-scalar tensions and contradictions exist which, if recognized, create new opportunities for re-conceiving and re-envisioning welfare as pro-labor and pro-family, as well as pro-work. The entrepreneurial nature of welfare reform creates such a window. As suggested by the theoretical work of Peck, reconstructing the welfare state according to progressive visions may even be facilitated by the infrastructure that the 1996 reform has created.

In the process [of developing alternatives to workfarist approaches to welfare] some of the same extra/interlocal channels that are currently being used to great effect in the diffusion of workfare may be appropriated for contrary ends—for example, by discrediting the discursively constructed models upon which the workfare policy process is dependent, pulling apart reform generics and the stylized knowledges upon which they are based and bending and stretching rule systems to make space for the development and validation of nonworkfarist alternatives.[118]

Given the familiarity with work-first infrastructure conveyed in this book, it is not impossible to imagine recalibrating the "extra/interlocal channels" of performance measure monitoring to accommodate a redefinition of work that includes balancing parenting and paid work and a renewed valuation of the need for workers' and clients' rights. These channels could quite conceivably be tweaked to encourage inroads on the local agency level into overcoming labor market inequalities and discrimination that the current work-first approach glosses over.

By furthering a neoliberal project of individual responsibility within the state, work-first discretion corresponds with and epitomizes what Collins calls the "power-evasive era" in which power is maintained by denying its existence.[119] In this paradigm, power dynamics and inequalities that exist along lines of class, gender, and race are evaded by espousing the assumption that the market is a neutral entity. Besides being a contested assumption, a micro-personal approach to poverty is problematic. It is cloaked in terms of the gifting of individual empowerment, but it serves to undermine broader-based efforts of empowerment through collective action.[120] For Bourdieu, the threat that neoliberalism poses to collective action is evident in contemporary attempts toward "atomization" of "workers, collectives for the defense of the rights of workers, unions, associations, cooperatives; even the family."[121] New efforts to resist neoliberal common sense have their work cut out for them; to be effective they must counter these trends.

8

Conclusion

Envisioning "a New Common Sense"

In the common sense that dominates work-first, the welfare state is a victim of changing times. Due to globalization, international competition, and rising public budgets, welfare states have become obsolete as protectors of the populace. Welfare is facing an identity crisis. The old models have become antiquated and must now become leaner and meaner to adapt to global market forces that do not guarantee job stability and do not tolerate the inefficiencies of social protections for families and workers that do not offer labor productivity in return. Neoliberal strategy is seen as the best, if not the only, means to reordering the provisions of the state for citizen well-being.[1] State and federal policymakers must reacclimate in the face of changing and expanding economies. From this vantage point it is easy to see how the actions of reducing welfare caseloads and telling people they must become self-sufficient rather than rely on the government have replaced the policy goals of reducing poverty and ensuring child well-being.

I began, however, from the assumption that labor markets do not simply emerge as natural. Rather, they are created.[2] In the preceding chapters, I examined how the U.S. welfare state, through work-first policy, and specifically the work of frontline caseworkers, takes an active role in creating the low wage, unstable, and highly expendable workforce that it claims a global labor market demands. It is an expressly neoliberal approach that enlists the state itself in minimizing the role of government in global economic affairs. Though this is to some extent an international phenomenon, as many welfare states have entered a phase of retrenchment in recent decades, the importance of locating such research within the United States is magnified because of its role as leader of the pack. It not only has the least generous welfare policies, but it also seems to be cutting services the most. In the words of Jill Quadagno,

"The U.S. appears to be on the verge of becoming a welfare-state leader in undoing the core programs of the New Deal."[3] The case study of a single county in New York State that I have presented is a microcosm of a broader picture that involves the range of welfare provisions (including health insurance and social security) in a renegotiation of the terms of the state's social contract with the American people. In each of these negotiations, the neoliberal approach claims an overriding accountability to the global economy.

As I explained in the introduction, this study began with the everyday experience of clients and caseworkers who engage the work-first welfare system. This experience became the point of entry through which I examined the day-to-day function of the welfare office. Throughout, my intention was to discover what aspects of current policy need to be tweaked in order to make it responsive to the needs and interests of these individuals. Furthermore, how can these needs and interests be articulated when they contradict the dominant ways of thinking fostered by neoliberalism? The result is a map that traces routine everyday work-first practices outward from the local toward the extra-local where the ways of thinking and organizing local work originate. In the process I paid particular attention to the political and economic nature of these organizing patterns, noticing the distributional consequences of state actions for power and material resources. Most notably, my empirical findings revealed an abdication of the state's role as a check and balance on the reach of economic interests, an abandonment of its role as an agent of civic equality, a weakening of its role as protector of families, and its emergence as an eroding force rather than advocate of universal/international labor standards. My analysis of these shifting roles revealed that work-first more than acquiesces to the will of global capital holders; it originates from their worldview. Their interests are its driving force and their ability to steer discourse is the vehicle by which their extra-local interests enter into local sites like East County. Work-first ideology and conceptual currencies of personal responsibility, tough love, self-sufficiency, and work readiness are the medium by which the standpoint of elites becomes dominant among non-elite government functionaries and poor families at today's welfare office. What emerges is a work-first agenda for dealing *with* poor families, not an agenda *for* these poor families. This policy agenda is taken for granted as "an objective knowledge that, appearing to view the world from no place, in fact operates from the standpoint of the patriarchal [and class-hegemonic] relations of ruling."[4]

What would a sociological analysis of work-first welfare from the standpoint of poor mothers and caseworkers whose interactions are mediated by TANF look like? This is what I have tried to create in the preceding chapters. The analysis I presented in this book is an institutional ethnography. It involves a detailed study of the institution of welfare, and is also devoted to making explicit the relations of ruling that are currently in place (and making them accountable to the everyday life experiences of the people who interact in today's welfare offices). Beginning from this point of entry, larger macrodynamics and literature were traced, as is standard practice in the social sciences, but with the caveat that they are traced and framed as they become relevant to understanding the daily experiences of welfare caseworkers and clients. This is an intentional break from standard practices that instead seek to fit local experiences into existing literature and policy agendas. In the mind of Dorothy E. Smith, the pioneering architect of the Institutional Ethnography approach, such conscious selection of the standpoint of people rather than the institution amounts to a sociology *for* people, rather than *about* people.[5]

Combining these methods makes a micro-level analysis possible from the standpoint of caseworkers and clients on the ground. Attention to a bird's eye view, however, also enables a critique of broader patterns that are not possible from the vantage point of the welfare office proper. On the ground, the only policy critiques that seem feasible are generic recommendations about how better to implement work-first goals. Indeed, this is what the majority of post-reform research produces. To social work scholar Sanford Schram's lament, it seems:

> The social science of poverty is impoverished in its ability to provide structural or even poststructural critique of the current state of affairs. . . . [It] is conducted in ways that largely constrain its ability to be a source of alternative policy approaches. The net result is that existing welfare policy, with all its limitations, is affirmed in general even as it is challenged in specific.[6]

It is precisely this phenomenon of institutional capture that the Institutional Ethnography approach is designed to avoid. From the perspective of this completed analysis, issues of moral deservingness and compliance with program requirements that consume vast amounts of research attention in other cases, fade into the backdrop of grander themes of welfare state adaptation to the global economy and changing relations of class, gender, and race. This does not mean that local voices are not heard; just the opposite. Local experiences form the empirical foundation for this analysis and the point of genesis for new possibilities for the state in an international age precisely because they, rather than dominant policy agendas, own the standpoint from which this analysis departs and to which it returns. It is from this standpoint rooted in local experience then that the identity crisis of the welfare state and ideas for future policy directions emerge.

Welfare Identity Crisis in an Era of Globalization

Globalization has presented nation-states throughout the world with an identity crisis. How will they handle the changing demands of the economy, and what guarantees and protections will they offer to their citizens? At the center of this dilemma is the changing face of the welfare state and its role within governmental strategy. Though the 1996 welfare reform was reauthorized in 2006, the monumental shift in welfare policy that it brought about is far from a closed case. This book has been about the frontline entrepreneurs who are continually revising and refining the standards of the state, but beyond this, I have also intended the analysis of this work to provide a portal into how patterns of globalization, labor relations, and race, class, and gender intersect in the contemporary welfare office. In the process, I have attempted to highlight the blending of welfare state adaptation to globalization and the neoliberal strategy that it almost takes for granted.

By acknowledging the broader political economy of neoliberalism, I have endeavored to move the debate about welfare away from a shouting match between bleeding heart liberals and heartless conservatives. Instead, I have focused on the neoliberal character of current welfare policy so that it becomes possible to recognize its ideological influence on the mainstream of policy. At the same time, this approach makes it conceivable to de-couple globalization and neoliberalization.

This aim is consistent with what institutional ethnography approaches to social research describe as explicating contemporary relations of ruling in order to reveal them for what they are—ways of ordering and managing social life that are more political than natural, and that furthermore can be changed to improve people's everyday lives only once they are explicitly recognized. Recognizing that economy and politics have historically not been as separate as neoliberal economic rhetoric leads us to believe, it also becomes evident that this is not the first time that we have been faced with an identity crisis at the nexus of economy and politics.

Stemming from the seminal work of Karl Polanyi and later the work of Mark Blyth, we see that the creation and sustenance of the free market system involves an ongoing dissonance between cultural efforts toward liberal markets, on one hand, and protectionism, on the other.[7] Social history has been the result of an awkward, unnerving, and politically contentious "double movement," in Karl Polanyi's terms.[8] The movement toward market orientation is kept from destroying society by a balancing movement consisting of "a network of measures and policies . . . integrated into powerful institutions designed to check the action of the market relative to labor, land, and money."[9] In the present, as in the past, when economic interests have forged ahead, placing concern for advancement over social stability, "society [has] protected itself against the perils inherent in a self-regulating market system."[10]

By recognizing how neoliberal policy strategies have filled the void left by globalization's identity crisis of the state, we see a cautionary tale of what can occur when economic interests of capital holders become entwined in social policy. We also gain empirical knowledge of the extent to which each of the two components of a Polanyian double movement has taken effect and how much farther each may go to achieve balance. In the preceding chapters, I argued by way of example and localized documentation that, despite seemingly uncritical praise in the mainstream media, work-first welfare is capable of being critically examined. The underlying assumptions of caseworkers reveal fundamental problems in implementation practices and in the overarching conceptualization of what welfare should be. Dominant discourse and frontline assumptions in the years since the reform have framed the issue of poverty as a matter of individual responsibility and shortcoming, portraying casework as a politically neutral response to these "pathologies." I have sought to reframe welfare practices as indeed very political and rooted in neoliberal sensibilities that in the long run serve to redistribute power and agency away from both workers and the poor. The result is a welfare package that, while pro-work, fails to be pro-worker or pro-family (see table 8.1).

Throughout work-first intake processing, clients are disempowered as workers. Starting with the intake gauntlet described in chapter 2, work-first represents a casework strategy that has redefined program success as diverting clients rather than providing a safe haven from a potentially exploitative labor market. I show how these processes are aligned with

a corporate-lobby-sponsored ideological approach that emphasizes entrepreneurial approaches to work responsibility yet offers no pro-labor
component to preparing mothers for the labor market. The discourse of
neoliberalism is both politically motivated and counter to social protectionist aims. Following from it, caseworkers use a cookie cutter format of
intake socialization to routinely refuse to validate client excuses, explanations, and requests for noncompliance. This approach, when paired with
an increased emphasis on individual accountability yet a neglect of client
rights (chapter 3), further diminishes the ability of poor mothers to advocate for themselves and the individualized needs of their families within
the labor market. With the eroding guarantee of a social safety net, clients
find themselves more vulnerable to the need to please employers since
they cannot trust that they can rely on government support if their efforts
in the labor market are thwarted.

This increased dependence on and vulnerability to employers is further
enhanced, as explored in chapter 4, by case management technology's re-
shuffling of welfare priorities. Caseworkers come to view poor mothers
less as their primary clients than as the derelict individuals whom they are
to whip into shape so that they better serve the needs of employers and
taxpayers in general. In chapter 5 I explored the processes by which ideological buy-in to work-first is socialized among administrators, caseworkers, and clients. This results in an internalized worldview that is pro-work
but not pro-worker. In chapter 6, I explored how the neoliberal values of
work-first apply to the family life of the poor. This is characterized by a
shifting of priorities; family productivity in the labor market has risen in
value, while its reproductive work is devalued.

In addition to being disempowered as workers, poor families are disembodied and separated from the concrete circumstances of their life.
Instead, as I explored in chapter 2, they are viewed as commodities that
work-first seeks to regulate in accordance with corporate-centered welfare
goals.[11] In addition, accountability structures for caseworkers and a reduction of protections for clients work together to discourage family commit-
ments and to push families to accept job insecurity and a lack of guaranteed safety net (chapter 3). Furthermore, the de-skilling of caseworkers
renders them less capable of assisting families in need. Corresponding
with this restructuring of casework, the surveillance case management
technology discussed in chapter 4 serves to obscure both family needs
and the fact that children are TANF's top constituency. Instead, the lion's
share of caseworker attention is directed to work-first case processing

TABLE 8.1

Chapter	2 Innovation and Common Sense	3 Work-First Performance Measures	4 New Technology and New Stakeholders	5 Work-First and Ideological Buy-In	6 Work-First and Families
Work-first disempowers people because it:	crowds out social and labor protectionism with its neoliberal discourse	enforces working responsibilities but not work or safety net rights	shifts leverage so state and employers are allied against clients	socializes agenda of neoliberalism: pro-work but not pro-labor	diverts families to labor market rather than protecting them from its vagaries
Work-first disembodies people because:	poor families are commodified and regulated to serve corporate-centered interests	it acclimates families to job insecurity and lack of guaranteed safety net	recordkeeping obscures encumbrances from institutional record	priority is given to ideological concepts over material experiences	women must subsume reproduction, childcare, and relationships to accommodate market demands

goals of monitoring the labor force behavior of mothers. Also obscuring the lived experiences of poor families, chapter 5 examined how the underlying ideology of work-first is predicated upon a buy-in among caseworkers and clients. This buy-in is maintained at the expense of emotional work that serves to keep outward behavior consistent with institutional expectations. Finally, as examined in chapter 6, obscuring family and care responsibility disembodies clients. Client efforts to nurture and care for their families are constrained by work-first policy as implemented on a daily basis. Mothers who wish to successfully navigate the intake gauntlet to secure aid for their families learn that reproduction, childcare, and relationships with men all emerge more as liabilities than resources in the world of work-first. As families attempt to manage these liabilities, they are forced to restructure reproduction and caregiving relations to accommodate market demands that play out along racial lines.

On the whole then, the 1996 welfare reform, for all of its pro-work and pro-family rhetoric, serves to undermine the long-term empowerment of poor workers and their families by reinforcing their commodification in a global market. In this context, client resistance, construed as due to laziness and personal weakness, finds new meaning as refusal to participate in a process that ultimately serves to disempower clients in the labor market and disembody them by separating them from their socio-material realities. It will require more than technical suggestions to address these problems. As Jamie Peck asserts, when it comes to ameliorating neoliberalism's problematic contradictions, "appropriate responses will have to be political rather than managerial."[12]

Re-reforming welfare so that it offers a long-term solution to poverty would require a wholesale evaluation of neoliberal economic policy and a comprehensive strategy for ensuring the well-being of both poor families and poor workers. This is not the task of one person; it is a collaborative task to which the scholarly, policy, and constituency communities must contribute. I have included a set of specific policy ideas for work-first in the preceding chapter, but here I offer broad themes for consideration in developing strategy for future policy reform, given the present ascendancy of neoliberalism and the context of globalization.

The Role of the State in the Global Economy

Though neoliberalism arose to prominence in the 1980s, neoliberal strategy is far from a monolith. It is now a dominant way of thinking about and solving problems that is not static—as seen in the work of welfare entrepreneurs. Neoliberalism takes many different forms and is constantly re-tooled in the face of its own contradictions, as proponents and detractors negotiate a complex political field.[13] In this sense, the actual form that neoliberalism takes and the extent of its influence on public policy is still being debated and various strands stand to gain and lose sway. Globalization itself is not the problem; how we approach it is. At the center of debate is the role that the state should play in balancing the global economy. As James Midgley argues:

> Controlling the processes of globalization does not involve the domestication of some abstract construct but will require that the myriad actions of individuals, organizations, corporations and governments that directly affect human well-being at the international level be shaped through purposeful policy intervention. This point has obvious relevance for any analysis of the relationship between globalization, social welfare and social justice.[14]

With the 1996 reform we have seen a move toward greater economic liberalization in the face of global markets. What remains to be seen is the extent and nature of a Polanyian double movement in which liberal market capitalism creates conditions so unacceptable to local people's daily lives that it catalyzes a spontaneous counter-demand for economic protection.[15] Below I offer three areas for consideration implied in the analysis of the preceding chapters. These considerations involve discerning the appropriate roles of the state: as a check and balance on economic power, as an agent of civic equality (beginning with the protection of children and their life chances), and as advocate for international labor standards.

A Check and Balance on Economic Power

What the vast majority of post-welfare reform scholarship fails to note is the extent to which neoliberalization of welfare policy incorporates a pro-capital bias. By sidelining this broader dynamic of political economy in favor of technocratic analyses of program implementation and outcomes, scholars overlook the centrality of power dynamics to the genesis and status quo of work-first policy. This book contends that avoiding this issue serves to reify rather than challenge contemporary dynamics of poverty. Where chapter 2 traces the pathways of influence that capital-holding elites have used to steer welfare policy toward serving their interests, the following chapters illustrate how these interests extend to frontline practice. Work-first has been widely touted as a pro-market solution to poverty. The present analysis makes plain that once the market is further divided into employers and employees, it is the employers who are favored. Recent scholarship suggests that successful adaptation of the workforce to globalization requires policy that focuses on strengthening both the supply and the demand sides of the labor market.[16] Given the uncertainty of future employment and market relations, it is imperative that both workers and employers meet approaching challenges in a resilient, strong, and empowered stance. In the case of work-first, however, we see a plan that tends to sell labor short in seeking to meet the demands of employers.

Perhaps the most notable contribution this analysis offers for the role of the state in an era of globalization is to make the case that the precedent set by work-first for future welfare policy has serious flaws (or lack of Polanyian balance). It involves critical points in which clients would benefit if we changed direction. One glaring aspect from the standpoint of poor families would be a new emphasis on the state living up to its potential as a check and balance on economic forces. To be sure, asserting a strong role for the state would break from current neoliberal practice. It would entail conflict with certain captains of the economy rather than advocating collusion with profit accumulation. Neoliberal visions of the state minimize its necessity and purpose in its own right, choosing instead to cast the ideal role of the state as supplier of infrastructure, a conveyor belt, for the facilitation of international economic activity. As seen here, however, this approach leaves the state open to and even willing to submit to manipulation by those who have capital and seek further accumulation through favorable policies. Under this mode of operation the state can too easily shift from serving the needs of un-capitaled citizens to the needs of those with resources.[17] These conditions are counter to what scholars of modern democracy have come to refer to as civic equality.

An Agent of Civic Equality

Much policy research has focused on the effectiveness of TANF in bringing about personal responsibility among poor women. Few, however, have examined how this concept serves as a social organizer of behavior that obscures and reinforces a vast inequality of citizenship. This book addresses the work-first approach to personal responsibility as one that reinforces neoliberal conceptions of a society in which one's well-being is up to the individual, while obscuring a reality in which individuals do not have the same rights. The modus operandi of culling mothers who cannot balance work and family from the aid rolls represents a landmark shift away from universal attempts to protect all young families from the vagaries of the market. The dependence of the marriage market on the labor market reveals that under TANF there is no guaranteed right to reproduction. By this same dynamic, the inequalities of U.S. citizens at birth become magnified in the years immediately following, during which childcare, schooling, and healthcare are also dependent on the labor market prospects of their parents. Furthermore, the interpretive lens of personal responsibility leads poor parents to assume full responsibility for remedying the disadvantage their children face. Not only is the birthright of young citizens subject to great variability, but so is the prerogative of citizens to enlist the aid of the government in counteracting inequities of race and class. These conditions perpetuate inequalities of citizenship that begin even before birth and which set the stage for a multiple-tiered citizenry over the life course. Concern for remedying this tiered citizenship finds one possible remedy in civic equality.

Recent scholarship on civic equality has emerged out of concern that democracy itself is threatened when wealth inequality becomes so large that the very wealthy can insulate themselves from the "common" everyday lives of others.[18] In this perspective, the global mobility of wealth—that seeks to expand itself by offering below living wage pay, insisting on unstable work schedules and no benefits and threatening to relocate to an un-unionized and less demanding country—is an example of a broader "loss of respect . . . for honest manual labor."[19] It is symptomatic of a way of thinking about and valuing work based on the level of salary earned, such that professionalized, abstracted, "thinking" careers in offices take higher priority and receive more dignity than those involving the production of food, shelter, and other necessities. Civic equality represents a corrective to this loss of solidarity. It is also, however, an alternative to socially liberal criticisms that have recommended a return to AFDC's attempts at redistribution of wealth. AFDC enacted a form of "money liberalism" by writing checks to poor families. In contrast, civic equality advocates "civic liberalism." Michael Walzer talks of civic equality in terms of a sphere of life in which money and vast inequalities of wealth, that tend to so dominate life today, are devalued.[20] Similarly, Mickey Kaus defines civic equality in terms of restricting the spheres of life in which money matters.[21]

Christopher Lasch goes even further, arguing that vast inequality is inherently "incompatible with democratic ideals" for the simple reason that its influence beyond the realms of commerce (in the civic realm of politics for instance) is so difficult to limit: "When money talks, everybody else is condemned to listen. For that reason a democratic society cannot allow unlimited accumulation. Social and civic equality presupposes at least a rough approximation of economic equality."[22]

Following from these critiques, proponents of civic equality, such as Kaus, advocate investing in and expanding the public spheres and institutions in which all citizens can and do meet as equals: universal day-care facilities, a national health plan, and an investment in public schools to the extent that they are so good that even the wealthy want to send their children there. Beyond this, however, civic equality would also encompass comprehensive campaign finance reform and a reinvestment of federal monies from subsidizing suburban sprawl to rebuilding urban centers. Such an effort would go a long way toward creating what Ray Oldenberg touts as participatory democracy's critical "third spaces" such as taverns, coffee houses, local bars, and eateries, in which people meet as equals to discuss and mull over civic happenings of the day.[23]

The analytical lenses of unequal globalization, divergent labor markets, and inequalities of gender, race, and class suggest that, in addition to civic equality, there is value in a role for the state in fostering meritocracy within generational cohorts. The narrative of work-first asserts the theme of upward mobility through its stepping stone philosophy. In particular, work-first efforts psychologize, individualize, and stigmatize those who are in poverty because they assume the existence of a stepping stone in the labor market and thereby interpret a lack of upward mobility as due to deficient or lazy mentality. Though the preceding chapters draw on dual labor market literature to call into question how realistic this assumption is (namely how feasible it is to expect poor workers to climb a career ladder that increasingly starts and ends in unstable below living wage jobs), the challenge they present is not to the underlying idea of upward mobility. Rather, the analysis provided in this book demonstrates how a high road infrastructure of upward mobility is thwarted in favor of a low road approach to labor market discipline that obscures the fact that class is most strongly tied to the wealth of parents.

In the Unites States, the intergenerational transmission of wealth explains a large proportion of the resource inequality and why it persists—over four-tenths of relative difference in parental incomes is transmitted, on average, to the children.[24] The likelihood of inheriting one's parent's economic class is greater in the extremes. For instance, the probability of a son being in the same earnings quintile as his father is .422 for those in the first (lowest) quintile and .360 for those in the fifth (highest) as compared with probabilities hovering between .25 and .28 for the middle quintiles.[25] Overall, income inequality is considerably higher and inter-generational economic mobility considerably lower in the United States than in other OECD countries.[26] According to Bowles and Gintis, wealth accounts for more than 30 percent of the intergenerational income corre-lation in the United States, while IQ inheritance contributes very little (1-2 percent) to intergenerational income transmission.[27] Combined, vastly expanding wealth inequality and the intergenerational transmission of wealth make for a nation that lacks civic equality as well as the ability to function as a meritocracy. Whereas Kaus advocates limiting the scope of money, concern for meritocracy recommends doing so across generations. Rather than foster upward mobility and give poor families equal footing in the labor force, the work-first approach exacerbates these conditions. Re-asserting a role for government in limiting the intergenerational trans-mission of wealth could take the form of greatly enhanced estate taxes and restructuring college and other costs so that they are borne by adults in later life (such as a proportion of future income rather than upfront college fees for which parents must co-sign).

A civic equality approach makes sense within the broader paradigm of adaptation to a global economy when paired with recent scholarship in this area. For instance, Holzer and Nightingale argue that, in the face of trends of global offshoring and retiring baby boomers, the United States will have a critical need for improved levels of math and science education throughout the workforce.[28] A globalized U.S. workforce will need to be an overall well-educated and well-trained workforce. Though concerted efforts to make higher education available to citizens of all social classes will require such targeted programs as means-tested and/ or universal merit-based scholarship, a more immediate need is equal-izing academic preparation and achievement in the pre-K and K-12 years.[29] As Robert Lerman warns, a civic equality approach need not pursue a "college for all" philosophy since this will likely do little to diminish high school dropout rates.[30] Rather, nationally coordinated efforts at "career and technical education," such as career academies, tech-prep programs, and apprenticeships, can offer a realm of human capital development as part of a comprehensive and inclusive national economic plan—as a supplement to merit-based efforts to increase low-income student access to higher education.[31]

Though a civic equality approach to education fosters a high road approach to global economy adaptation, it is not a comprehensive approach in itself. Given the impending effects of retirements, offshoring, immigration, and other factors including technology, economy is likely to develop unevenly and to some degree unpredictably across the nation in years to come. Policy will need to produce mobile workers much as it has fostered mobile capital. Workers will need both a skill base and support infrastructure for income security and upward mobility in a fast-paced and changing labor market. Key considerations will require de-linking health coverage from employer provision and offering some form of earnings insurance for between job transitions and continued accumulation of savings and retirement. Removing employers from the healthcare equation would allow worker mobility and transition to occur without loss of benefits. Though a universal or single payer healthcare system faces tremendous political hurdles, experiments such as that in the state of Massachusetts that mandates individual coverage show that new strategies are possible.[32] In addition to health, earnings insurance plans such as that proposed by Gary Burtless offer stability for workers in a time of economic uncertainty. Under such a plan, involuntarily displaced workers would be insured for losses in wages or earnings (for several years) between jobs or during in-between jobs. Such a proposal would encourage quick searches for a new job and help ease the burden of lost wages due to involuntary job loss and prolonged job searches.[33]

Finally, as alluded to in our discussion of the challenges work-first presents to parents, a civic equality approach would seek to expand work-family policies so that families of all classes could benefit. While there is clear evidence that family-friendly work practices such as parental leave, sick leave, flexible work schedules, and early childhood development programs benefit the health and well-being of children and parents, low-income families are currently least able to access these benefits.[34] Work-first as currently implemented exacerbates this by forcing poor women to act as if their families do not exist rather than accommodating their needs. Recent proposals to finance childcare and expanded coverage of parental leave through unemployment insurance payroll taxes, as recently done in California, offer some possibilities. Jane Waldfogel, for instance, draws attention to a system in the United Kingdom that requires employers to consider employee requests for flexible work schedules.[35] Though it is no guarantee that all requests will be granted, such policies force parenting considerations into the center of decision making in public life, rather than relegate them to the private sphere, and it succeeds at putting un-family-friendly policies on the defensive. In work-first, parents have to defend their caregiving needs to employers who expect unencumbered workers.

Overall, these strategies have one thing in common. They seek to equalize opportunity for children and workers of all social backgrounds. Fostering within-generation meritocracy would provide a more level playing field for all U.S. citizens, while at the same time allowing them to distinguish themselves within the realm of our capitalist economy.

Advocate for International Labor Standards

As one of the primary boundary institutions of society, the welfare state also performs the role of setting labor expectations for both employers and employees. My analysis shows that work-first contributes to a broader neoliberal agenda of eroding workers' rights. Interestingly, at the same time as social service protections are being eroded, new social service workers are recruited to enforce a reduction of rights on the worse situated welfare clients. This is a microcosm of a broader mentality of individualism that isolates workers as individuals, undermines unionization, and pits local labor groups against one another in competition for employers. A need to counteract this trend, yet remain competitive in the global labor market, presents a third role for the state within the global economy—advocating for international labor standards. While the neoliberal policy agenda of recent decades has encouraged trade standards and agreements, it has shied away from labor standards and agreements. A change in this stance would offer one means of moving from pro-work to pro-worker.

This is a particularly pressing concern since, despite predicted shortages of labor when baby boomers retire, increased competition from workers overseas—India, China, and Eastern Europe in particular—may very well lead to slack labor markets in the United States with declining wages.[36] The underlying lesson of this concern is that U.S. labor policy cannot go it alone. If U.S. citizens want basic labor standards, their best chance of securing them, without simply scaring mobile capital into flight or off-shore, is to strive to make these standards universal. This way job creation will be based on goodness of fit with workforce training rather than margin of profit from wage exploitation. Such changes, however, cannot be achieved alone. Foreign policy should be consistent with domestic needs and seek to partner with other economic allies to guarantee basic standards of living and make it easier for workers to engage in collective bargaining so that their interests are represented in global labor adjustment strategy.

Cosmopolitan approaches to globalization complement this emphasis on human well-being rather than capital accumulation. At its core is "the belief that the forces of globalization can be domesticated to serve human interests."[37]

> Cosmopolitanism is today widely linked to the idea that the world's nation-states can cooperate through multilateral institutions, international law and human rights conventions to promote human well-being and social justice.[38]

The struggle between the interests of capital and labor as seen in the domestic spotlight of work-first welfare is a microcosm of a broader neoliberal trend. The United States has been a leader in the neoliberal shift, as it was with the original Bretton Woods agreements. By this same token it can take the lead in a more cosmopolitan approach to globalization that would revisit and rekindle its leadership role. Not only does this approach encourage a re-emphasis on the United Nations and other international bodies, but the role of certain international organizations such as the International Monetary Fund and the World Bank need to be reformed "so that they do not function as the agents of international capitalism but fulfill their original purpose of promoting the economic welfare of the world's nation-states and their citizens."[39]

Welfare and the American Dream

"Workism" has been an uncontested aspect of most welfare reform research.[40] As Paul Harrington notes, "Americans define themselves by their work. Many of our most important values, such as competition and self-reliance, are forged through the discipline of the labor market. Employment with a steady paycheck and a chance to move up fulfills the promise of opportunity in America."[41] However, "work cannot be understood outside of a broader perspective on social reproduction and the global political-economic processes that produce poverty, racial and gender inequality, and the massive income polarization that has intensified in the past two decades."[42] New policy must re-focus on work but place workers themselves at its center. Importantly, capital and employers should not be conceived as enemies but rather partners in renewed governmental zeal to invest in its workers. What is fundamentally different about this approach is that the interests of workers, rather than the upward accumulation of wealth, are the paramount policy focus.

Reframing policy from the perspective of U.S. workers rather than global capital lobbyists can be the cornerstone of a collectivistic approach to shifting welfare from pro-work to pro-worker and pro-family. This requires us to radically restructure how we presently think about the social services of the state and to revisit an early debate of social work that pitted individualistic versus structural approaches to helping the poor. The individualistic carried the day then, but that was a different time and a different economic situation. Researcher Sharon Hays reports a nearly steady 60/40 split between employed and unemployed former welfare recipients between 1998 and 2002, suggesting that every time someone in the unemployed category finds a job, someone in the working category loses one.[43] It is not surprising then that Mark Rank discusses the contemporary economic outlook for the poor in terms of musical chairs, with millions of poor mothers moving in and out of low wage jobs—the government may focus on getting someone a job but someone else is always left out.[44] He argues that, as a result, we need to focus not just on getting people jobs but on changing the structure of the economy. To think strategically as a nation requires thinking about structure, not just about individuals. As we saw in the preceding chapters, looking only at individuals serves mainly to disempower them. We need to redefine "welfare" not as a government handout but as economic justice, as Vanessa Tait argues. Instead of allowing workers to be exploited at the hands of employers, we need to defend the right to a decent job at a livable wage. In place of lip service for the work of caregiving, we need genuine state support.[45] Rather than the "Contract with America" of the 1994 Republican Congress led by Newt Gingrich, that brought about our current punitive and anti-labor welfare reform, Beth Shulman argues for "a compact with working Americans." In this she argues that:

> Americans who work should be assured: sufficient income to meet a family's basic needs, affordable health care, flexibility and support to properly care for one's family, opportunities to gain new skills, affordable and safe housing, a safe and healthy work environment, security in time of

economic adversity and retirement, the right to organize and collective bargain, [and] fair trade and immigration policies.[46]

There are likely few who would disagree with such a proposal; the problem is how to get there.[47] If we are to actualize such a compact, all government policies, especially welfare, must be aligned with its intent. The performance of welfare reform must be judged not on caseload declines but on the benchmarks of clients obtaining jobs, retaining them long term, and gaining promotions and wage increases that enable them to live the American Dream in a family structure of their choice.

Where Do We Go from Here?

How does a platform such as the one recommended by Shulman become enacted? Would it cost more? Wouldn't it make the U.S. economy less efficient? Perhaps not. Comparing U.S. spending on welfare with universal Scandinavian approaches that more closely approximate Shulman's ideal by de-commodifying labor and family life reveals more a shift in priorities than an actual increase in spending. If only social spending (excluding education) is examined, the United States spends approximately 17.1 percent of its annual Gross Domestic Product on social welfare, as compared with 36.4 percent for Sweden, 30.1 percent for the Netherlands, and 37.6 percent for Denmark. However, this does not account for the vast "shadow welfare state" in the United States that offers private entitlements to many with higher incomes—such as publicly subsidized private pensions and retirement accounts, mortgage tax deductions, and other benefits based on a person's location within private market relations rather than on legal or universal citizenship rights. When these "shadow" welfare benefits are considered, current U.S. spending approaches 24.5 percent of GDP as compared with 27 percent for Sweden, 25 percent for the Netherlands, and 24.4 percent for Denmark.[48] Though total spending differs little among these countries, the priorities to which these resources are devoted are in stark contrast. Unlike public welfare benefits which are open to public scrutiny, social spending on private benefits is far more utilized in the United States (over twice as much as in the United Kingdom and the Netherlands and over five times the amount of Sweden and Denmark).[49] Yet these benefits tend to be hidden in tax codes, riders to legislation, and court rulings, and they tend to be regressive in that they disproportionately serve the more well-off.

In the United States' liberal model of welfare, the state relegates aid to the needy on what Richard Titmuss has described as a residual or marginal basis, stepping in only when the market is seen as failing. In this paradigm, the emphasis is on making markets flow smoothly by emphasizing the commodification of all things, including labor.[50] In the more social democratic tradition of the Scandinavian nations and in the corporate conservative nations (such as Germany, Italy, and France), a greater emphasis has been placed on the de-commodification of humans. As Gøsta Esping-Andersen notes, "A hallmark of conservative ideology is its view that the commodification of individuals is morally degrading, socially corrupting, atomizing, and anomic."[51] Though much of the emphasis associated with these three welfare state models has been placed on their level of generosity (liberal, corporate conservative, and social democratic, ranging from least to most generous respectively), the relevance of welfare state priorities for the present analysis rests on their varying potentials for supporting worker coalitions in a global economy.[52]

Historically, worker unity, solidarity, and ability to form broad and functional coalitions is associated with the degree to which their labor is de-commodified.[53] First, de-commodification provides workers with leverage when bargaining with employers because they can afford to withdraw from the labor force when working conditions are not satisfactory. Second, broad de-commodification fosters a sense of social citizenship that has historically overcome even divisions between skilled guild members and less skilled laborers and the unemployed.[54] This is instructive in the case of U.S. welfare because de-commodification not only runs counter to the anti-labor trend dominant since the 1947 Taft-Hartley Act, but also because it points out that TANF has not succeeded in making the middle class its constituency, as have other welfare states. Broad coalitions of workers have historically been critical to sustaining job stability, healthcare benefits, and living wages in other nations. The incorporation of middle-class interests and "benefits tailored to the tastes and expectations of the middle classes," as done in Scandinavian nations, has incorporated the middle class as a powerful and central part of the pro-welfare state electorate.[55]

The middle class is critical to establishing "a comprehensive, universalistic, 'de-commodifying', full-employment welfare state" not only because the poor are a quite small and ineffective political lobby, but also because calibrating a welfare state to middle-class standards protects it from the kind of backlash that was seen in the United States in the wake of the

Great Society initiative.[56] This shift of standards need not emanate from a sense of benevolence for the poor. It is in the middle class's own self-interest to be involved in setting the welfare state agenda. The strength of labor resides in tight labor markets, which a full-employment, de-commodified labor approach fosters.[57] Furthermore, far from merely emerging as a passive byproduct of economic development, there is much evidence to suggest that welfare state institutions are themselves powerful mechanisms that shape future economic prosperity.[58] As Esping-Andersen argues, different welfare state approaches produce different post-industrial trajectories such that, judging from case study comparison, social democratic policy seems to produce more professional (good) jobs and less secondary (bad) jobs than the liberal model currently employed in the United States.[59] The difference between welfare regimes seems to lie not so much in specific policy mechanisms and expenditures but the degree to which they are calibrated to encourage de-commodification.[60]

Though comparing different welfare states has for some time been considered subjective because different states embrace different goals (social democratic regimes emphasize social equality and social justice, while corporate conservative regimes emphasize social integration, and liberal regimes emphasize economic efficiency and reducing poverty), recent data offer a possibility of comparative evaluation. In a study by Goodin, Headey, Muffels, and Dirven using data from 1984-1994, the authors argue that it is possible that "one welfare regime beats another at its own game" and hence provides "the best possible choice regardless of what you want it to do."[61] In their analysis, they found that the social democratic case outperformed or equaled the corporatist and liberal regimes across a ten-year period with regard to minimizing inequality, reducing poverty, promoting stability and social integration, and promoting various aspects of autonomy. In addition, the social democratic paradigm was surprisingly as good at sustaining economic growth and productivity as the liberal regime and better at distributing that wealth to middle-class earners. They report:

> The social democratic welfare regime is at least as good as (and usually better than) either of the other welfare regimes in respect to all *social* objectives we traditionally set for our welfare regimes. Furthermore, the social democratic welfare regime is at least as good as any other on *economic* objectives as well—at least if we assess economic objectives in terms of "bottom line" economic growth rates rather than in terms of the

various things that economists assert (without warrant in our evidence) to be causally connected to them.[62]

While such findings can not conclusively determine what the best course of action is for the future, the high performance of social democratic policy in comparison to liberal ones at the very least casts serious doubts on the infallibility of neoliberal economic doctrine. Social and economic objectives such as equity and efficiency need not be competing objectives that require a trade-off. If indeed the performance of social democratic policies is this good, a vast direction change in U.S. welfare and foreign policy may be the most fruitful course of action for the United States and the world.[63]

Changing the neoliberal course of U.S. welfare will take more than creating new policy. It will require revisiting the common sense that has been developed around the needs and responsibilities of the poor. It will also require recognition that work-first common sense is a political approach to poverty that fosters corporate-centered values. The premise of this book is that the common sense that holds institutions together is a social construction. The previous chapters demonstrate how the efforts of lobbyists, the work of local innovators, performance measures, and new technology all coalesce around the neoliberal values at the heart of the 1996 welfare reform. Caseworkers and poor families who buy into the work-first ideals are also implicated in upholding work-first common sense in daily interactions. As impressive as it may be in its scope and coherence, however, the institutional change seen in the reform also has its weaknesses. Families and workers are caught in the bind. Their local experiences are devalued in comparison with extra-local ideas that dominate the terrain of common sense. From the front lines of welfare today, the politics of common sense are invisible. It seems that work-first is the only logical/sensible way to handle the poor. Very little else can be conceived. This chapter, however, has explored what else is possible. Welfare is a political and economic tool as much as it is a national act of compassion. If used correctly, it can also become a tool of solidarity and civic equality.

Appendix: Collection of Data

I collected the data for this institutional ethnography on the TANF program through combined methods of participant observation, interviews, and textual analysis. As Dorothy E. Smith and others outline, the purpose of an institutional ethnography is to allow people to explore the social relations that structure their everyday lives by empirically tracing how local routines and practices are synchronized with broader ideas and political economy.[1] In order to do this I began with daily experiences of caseworkers and administrators and then connected their experiences to each other and to other material evidence found in government documents, reports, and other media of textual communication. Throughout this piecing together of information and tracing of connections between people, I was guided by the objective of elucidating the relevance of local experience within different layers or scales of society (i.e., interpersonal, city, state, nation etc.).

Between October 1999 and November 2002, I attended each stage of processing conducted by welfare related employees in East County, and compiled the majority of my field notes from there.[2] I conducted follow-up interviews and explored related sites of processing such as fair hearings through 2007. During this initial period I was generally on-site one day a week (the actual days varied to increase representativeness) for between one and eight hours. These hours included sitting in the welfare office waiting room, observing front-desk interactions, attending welfare orientation sessions and welfare-to-work orientation sessions, and observing supervised applicant job searches. Throughout this period, I formally and/or informally interviewed 42 professional caseworkers with regard to the work that they do as part of intake processing. In addition to taped and transcribed interviews, I heavily employed informal interviews in the sense described by other Institutional Ethnography (IE) researchers as being less planned and more of a continuous "talking to people" about their work and about texts and work processes as I explored them.[3] In this fashion, I was able to combine numerous intermittent questions about the intricacies of daily work actions concurrent with participant observation. In addition to this type of "on the spot" interviewing, I also accumulated questions to ask workers during their free time.

The use of participant observation and interviewing enabled me to identify a multitude of documents and forms that caseworkers activated in daily work. To gain greater insight into their use, I arranged to have several caseworkers in each stage of processing instruct me on how to utilize the paper files, forms, computerized databases, and reference materials that I observed in each location. In this way, I was able to "pause" their explanations to clarify fine points as well as develop follow-up questions to ask after observing caseworkers use these texts during future interactions with clients.

In addition to these interviews, and step-by-step instruction in "paperwork" processing, I observed (and took field notes) as caseworkers in each of these intake stages processed applicants (several hundred in total) for public assistance. While numerous questions arose from these interactions and caseworkers often used specific cases to explain their work, no names or identifying features were recorded with regard to applicants.[4] Additionally, applicants were informed that my interests were in observing caseworkers' behavior, not that of applicants.

Data on fair hearings were similarly gathered through observations of fair hearings proceedings for 36 clients in six counties in New York State and by interviewing caseworkers and other staff members. Since fair hearings are held with greater infrequency than daily processing, only being scheduled when appeals are filed, I adopted a broader institutional approach by including hearings in five neighboring counties that are on the same circuit as East County. Examining hearings in all six counties (including East County) provided me with a sustained contact with fair hearing officers and administrative law judges that worked the circuit, and it also gave me the opportunity to observe how the institutional relations I observed in East County were also reproduced in other counties. While interviews with welfare-to-work caseworkers in other counties confirmed the similarities of the reform's manifestation in various sites, with local variation of course, I do not include those data in this book other than to triangulate my analysis in East County. In total, of the hearings I observed, approximately 50 percent pertained to TANF aid and 65 percent involved Medicaid (these percentages include overlapping cases).

I interviewed and/or observed 22 different county representatives and 6 different administrative judges, most on multiple occasions.

In addition, throughout this period I volunteered in other community organizations, often ones that had been mentioned in discussions at the welfare office, and immersed myself in learning about how each organization worked. I continued to do this, seeking new opportunities to get involved in soup kitchens, work training programs, and community action groups alike. Through these contacts I added 17 additional interviews with welfare clients, members of welfare support groups, and staff at other related agencies, seeking their input on the work and processes produced in the reformed welfare system.

Notes

1. *New York Times* 1976:51; *New York Times* 1976b:42. As McCormack 2004:358 reports, this story was later shown to be a fabrication.

2. See the work of Frank Knight discussed in Blyth 2002.

3. For welfare mothers, see Edin and Lein 1997; Monroe and Tiller 2001; Woodward 2008. For caseworkers, see Beckerman and Fontana 2001; Seccombe 2007; Ridzi 2004.

4. U.S. Department of Health and Human Services 2003.

5. East County and all local names are pseudonyms.

6. U.S. Department of Health and Human Services, Office of Family Assistance 2002:1.

7. Peck 2001:16.

8. See for instance Peck 2001:8, 15.

9. BBC News 2005; Peck 2001:5.

10. See Peck and Theodore 2000:126; Shulman 2005.

11. Mead 2005:401–421.

12. For a discussion of the social construction of reality, see Berger and Luckmann 1966.

13. Havemann 1997:30, emphasis in original.

14. For instance, the Center on Budget and Policy Priorities reports that TANF outlays were $18.7 billion in fiscal year 2002, an increase of $166 million over outlays in fiscal year 2001, according to the Treasury data (Neuberger 2002). In comparison, Egan (2003:108) reports that annual spending on corporate welfare ranges from $65 billion by libertarian standards to $167 billion by liberal standards.

15. McCluskey 2003:n. 31.

16. For a critical discussion of this, see Marchevsky and Theoharis 2006, concluding chapter. See also Polanyi 1944.

17. McCluskey 2003:783.

18. Albo 2001; also as cited in Peck 2002b:209.

19. See Polanyi 1944:83–84, who asserts that the consciousness we have inherited was formed in the mold of liberalism.

20. Pence 1997:60.

21. Burstein 1991; Downs 1998:100–112.

22. Kingdon 1984:88–94; see also Burstein 1991.

23. Kingdon 1984:165.

24. Ibid., 205.

25. Goode and Maskovsky 2001:12.

26. Ruben 2001:439.

27. Ibid., 442.

28. Ruben 2001:440

29. Lind 1995, cited in Ruben 2001:441; see also Wilson 1987.

30. Ruben 2001:442.

31. Ibid., 441.

32. Smith 1999:172, 159, 159–160; Luken and Vaughan 2006.

33. Ruben 2001:443, emphasis in original.

34. Ellwood 1988. See also Ridzi 2004 for discussion of previous failed reforms.

35. Ellwood 1988:16.

36. See Mullings 2001:39; Wilson 1987.

37. Wilson 1987.

38. Morgen and Weigt 2001.

39. Goode and Maskovsky 2001:12.

40. Katz 1989:223.

41. Orloff 2001:152.

42. Mike Davis 1986, cited in Goode and Maskovsky 2001:7; Morgen and Weigt 2001:152.

43. Orloff 2001:148.

44. Ibid., 154.

45. Ibid.

46. Brown 2003:47.

47. Ibid.

48. Lieberman 2003:45.

49. Frankenberg 1993.

50. Lieberman 2003:31.

51. Though the United Kingdom would not necessarily be considered overly generous today, in its early days under the Beveridge model that was launched post–World War II, it ranked among the most de-commodified, due in part to the strength of the Labour Party. In the years since, however, it has not kept pace, setting it closer to the United States and Canada in comparison to the trajectory of the more generous and more pro-de-commodification Scandinavian nations. See Esping-Andersen 1990:53–54.

52. Lieberman 2003:31.

53. See for instance Amenta et al. 2001.

54. Lieberman 2003:36.

55. Ibid., 31.

56. Ibid.

57. Ibid., 36.

58. Ibid., 35.

59. Ibid., 32–33.

60. Gilens 2003:101–102.

61. Piven 2003:333; Avery and Peffley 2003.

62. Gilens 2003:125; see also Avery and Peffley 2003.

63. Gilens 2003:101–130.

64. Ibid., 129, note 19.

65. Ibid., 127.

66. Lieberman 2003:45.

67. U.S. Census 2004.

68. See Orloff 2001:137, 142–143.

69. See V. Smith 2002.

70. See Midgley 2007:31–32.

71. Ibid., 20.

72. Ibid., 23.

73. Polanyi 1944:133–134.

74. Blyth 2002:9.

75. Polanyi 1944:211.

76. Cohen 2002:87.

77. Ibid., 90.

78. This is not entirely unlike what Polanyi (1944:10) identified as haute finance.

79. See Polanyi 1944:10, 207.

80. See Midgley 2007:19.

81. For a discussion of the cosmopolitan perspective, see Midgley 2007.

82. Ruben 2001:436.

83. See for instance Midgley 2007.

84. Peck 2002b:188–189. See also Harrison and Bluestone 1988.

85. Peck 2002b:187.

86. Harrison and Bluestone 1988:33, cited in Peck 2002b:189.

87. Cited in Harrison and Bluestone 1988:25; see Peck 2002b:180.

88. Luken and Vaughan 2006.

CHAPTER 2

1. New York State Department of Labor 2000. Peck and Theodore 2000. Also see Marchevsky and Theoharis 2006 for an in-depth study of California's GAIN program as a "work first" model.

2.   Amy Brown 1997; Michael Brown 2003:51 argues that TANF's fiscal incentives have driven states to adopt a "work-first model."

3.   Evans 1995: 75, cited in Peck and Theodore 2000:136.

4.   State Policy Documentation Project 1999.

5.   TANF is called Family Assistance in New York State.

6.   U.S. Supreme Court *Goldberg v. Kelly* 1970.

7.   Office of the State Comptroller 1998; U.S. Supreme Court *Goldberg v. Kelly* 1970.

8.   Brown 1997; Meyers and Lurie 2005.

9.   Besharov 2003; Brock et al. 2002; Nathan and Gais 1999; Brown 1997; Ridzi and London 2006.

10.   Urban Institute 2006.

11.   Schram 2000b:45.

12.   This percentage is adjusted from 18 percent to account for repeated case openings among certain applicants. This was done by tallying all March 2000 applicants with case openings over the following 13 months and then subtracting all second (or third) case openings recorded for an individual applicant.

13.   Ruben 2001:436.

14.   Peck and Theodore 2000:124.

15.   Eikenberry and Kluver 2004.

16.   See for instance Swedberg 2000:13.

17.   Swedberg 2000:27; Weber 1988:1904–1905.

18.   Hwang and Powell 2005:180; see also Alexander 1992 for a description of uncritical adulation.

19.   Eikenberry and Kluver 2004.

20.   Swedberg 2000:26.

21.   Holm 1995:398–422.

22.   Ibid., 399.

23.   Ibid., 401.

24.   Ibid., 402.

25.   Phillips, Lawrence, and Hardy 2004:648.

26.   D. Smith 2005:217.

27.   Ibid.

28.   Bourdieu 1998. "Utopia Of Endless Exploitation." *Le Monde Diplomatique.* http://mondediplo.com/1998/12/08bourdieu.

29.   D. Smith 1999:174.

30.   Messer-Davidow 1993; Lapham 2004; Reese 2005.

31.   Messer-Davidow 1993:52; Lapham 2004:4.

32.   Lapham 2004.

33.   Messer-Davidow 1993:51.

34.   Ibid.

35.   Ibid., 55.

36. Ibid., 63–64.
37. See Reese 2005.
38. Messer-Davidow 1993:51.
39. D. Smith 2005:217.
40. Reese 2005; Messer-Davidow 1993; Lapham 2004.
41. D. Smith 1999:178.
42. Messer-Davidow 2002:222.
43. Reese 2005:153; see also Goode and Maskovsky 2001:12.
44. D. Smith 1999:79.
45. Polanyi 1944:130. Special thanks to Cory Blad for insights into the relevance of the "double movement" for this project.
46. D. Smith 1999:78.
47. Ibid.
48. Marx and Engels 1963:39.
49. Smith 1961, II:236 cited in Esping-Andersen 1990:33 and 1989:31.
50. Polanyi 1944:133.
51. O'Connor 1973:6. Special thanks to Cory Blad for insights into the relevance of the "double movement" for this project.
52. Polanyi 1944:105.
53. Polanyi 1944.
54. Peck 2002b:188–189; see also Harrison and Bluestone 1988.
55. Harrison and Bluestone 1988:25, see also Peck 2002b:180.
56. See Harvey 1989 in Morgen and Maskovsky 2003:320–321.
57. Esping-Andersen 1990:37.
58. Goodin, Headey, Muffels and Dirven 1999.
59. Esping-Andersen 1990.
60. Goodin, Headey, Muffels and Dirven 1999:41.
61. Esping-Andersen 1990:36.
62. Orloff 2001:152.
63. Cruikshank 1999:117.
64. Goode and Maskovsky 2001:8, italics in original. The authors also note that this is "in contradiction to other brands of right-wing conservatism such as that of Gingrich and, arguably, Reagan."
65. Hasenfeld 2000a:330.
66. Goodin 1988. See also Boleyn-Fitzgerald 1999:12.
67. Hasenfeld 2000a:330.
68. Handler 1996:116; also see Lukes 1974.
69. Handler 1996:117; also see Bachrach and Baratz 1962.
70. Handler 1996:117, italics in original. Also see Gramsci 1971; and Edelman 1971.
71. Handler 1996:117.
72. Lukes 1974:23.
73. Peck 2001:175.

74. As Lindblom and others have argued, commodification of labor "is a freedom behind prison walls" (Esping-Andersen 1990:37).

75. Ibid., 36.

76. As Foucault has assessed, power is fundamentally productive, of knowledge, truths, realms of practice etc.; here we see it in the act of producing a neoliberal mind-set among clients. See Morgen and Maskovsky 2003:330.

77. See Kingfisher 2001:288.

78. Piven 2001:142, 143.

79. Goode and Maskovsky 2001:8; see also Abramovitz 1988.

80. Goode and Maskovsky 2001:8.

81. Weigt 2006:343.

82. Ibid.

83. Ruben 2001:436.

84. Gonzalez 2007:201.

85. Hargadon and Douglas 2001 cite: Granovetter 1985; Dacin 1997; Dacin, Ventresca, and Beal 1999; Lounsbury and Glynn 2000; Ventresca et al. 2000.

86. Alexander 1992:10; 1993.

87. Hargadon and Douglas 2001:476.

88. Powell and DiMaggio 1991:9.

89. Ibid.

90. See Hargadon and Douglas 2001; Alexander 1992:9.

91. Hargadon and Douglas 2001:476.

92. Herbert A. Simon 1981:55, cited in Hargadon and Douglas 2001:479.

93. See for instance the discussion by Hargadon and Douglas 2001:478.

94. DiMaggio 1997:269.

95. Smith 2005:217.

96. Hargadon and Douglas 2001:476–478.

97. Alexander 1992:9.

CHAPTER 3

1. See Ridzi 2007.

2. Center on Urban and Metropolitan Policy 1999; Center for Budget and Policy Priorities 1999; Steuerle and Mermin 1997; Loprest 1999a, 1999b; Jencks 1997; Harris 1996.

3. See Brodkin 1997; and Naples 1997 for discussion of the new contract of welfare reform.

4. McKenna 1998.

5. Papandrea 1998.

6. Nathan and Gais 1999.

7. Ibid.

8. See Handler 1973; Walkowitz 1999; Leidner 1993; Attewell 1987.

9. See Ridzi 2007.

10. NYS Welfare Reform Act 1997:206.

11. NYS Welfare Reform Act S128 1997:159.

12. O'Connell, Betz, and Shepard 1990:262.

13. Hamilton and Scrivener 1999:15.

14. U.S. GAO 2001:12; Hamilton and Scrivener 1999:15.

15. Besharov and Germanis 2002.

16. Weekly family participation requirements remain 20 hours for single parents of children under age 6; 30 for other single parents; and 35 to 55 hours for two-parent families.

17. Renwick 2006:1.

18. Hasenfeld 2000b:186.

19. Renwick 2006:4.

20. Hamilton and Scrivener 1999:19.

21. Ibid., 20.

22. NYS Welfare Reform Act 1997:153 2. A. p. 107.

23. The actual report for TANF is recorded monthly, but rates must be met for the federal fiscal year based on an average of monthly rates (1300.8 8–20 (A3) NYS Instruction manual).

24. Hasenfeld 2000b:190.

25. Silver and Farrell 1998.

26. Peck and Theodore 2000:121.

27. Brown 2003:50.

28. Brodkin 1997; Handler 1973; Lipsky 1980.

29. Levy 1992:221.

30. Ibid., 225.

31. Brodkin 1997; Relave 2000.

32. London 2003; Ridzi and London 2006.

33. See Naples 1997; also Brodkin 1997.

34. Brodkin 1997; Naples 1997.

35. Lens 2006:255–284.

36. McClenny 1996.

37. Pataki 2000. In addition, the state experienced a decline of 52 percent in welfare caseloads since 1995—which is similar to the 53 percent decline nationwide (Statistical Abstracts of the Untied States 2000). East County (the location of the present study) has consistently met or exceeded its participation rates and has reported an estimated caseload decline of over 42 percent (according to county budget caseload figures) between 1995 and 2000.

38. In their analysis of MDRC's Urban Change project, Marchevsky and Theoharis (2006:225) found evidence to suggest that "welfare reform had produced a sharp increase in disentitlement and discrimination inside the system." See also pp. 228, 230.

39. Joint Legislative Audit Committee 2001; State of New York Office of the State Comptroller 1998. This audit considers client wins to be not only official reversals but also instances where counties withdraw or change their actions once a client appeals.

40. Lens 2005:13–54.

41. State of New York Office of the State Comptroller 2001.

42. Hays 2003 notes similar violations of policy in Wisconsin's W-2 program. Marchevsky and Theoharis 2006:167, 228 note it in Miami Dade County and California's Riverside GAIN program, describing caseworker mentality with the goal "to reduce the rolls by any means possible" (167).

43. Marchevsky and Theoharis 2006:127 similarly discuss that in California's GAIN program, despite lip service to "rights and responsibilities" the emphasis is placed on responsibilities and actual rights in terms of concrete assistance are "never spelled out."

44. Anderson 2002:162–170.

45. See Parrott and Wu 2003; and Matthews and Ewen 2005.

46. Marchevsky and Theoharis 2006:164 in their research with clients of California's GAIN program report that for many of their informants, "the most frightening aspect of welfare reform was its unpredictability, particularly the lack of consistent rules and information."

47. See Lipsky 1980; Reich 1988; Bovens and Zouridis 2002; Vinzant and Cothers 1998; Wilson 1987.

48. See also Gilliom 2001.

49. Sarat 1990:317.

50. Dehner 2002:3.

51. Marchevsky and Theoharis 2006:231.

52. Barley and Kunda 2004.

53. See Peck 2002a:343; Quadagno 1998.

CHAPTER 4

1. Nathan and Gais 1999: chapter 9.

2. Hercik 1998; Relave 2001.

3. George Bush 2004;, Quadagno 1998; Brookings Institute 2002.

4. Jamie Peck 2001: 6. See also Jane Collins 2006, 4.

5. Jodi Sandfort 2003:605,606.

6. Sandfort 2003; Jodi Sandfort 1999:314–339.

7. Relave 2001.

8. Sandfort 2003:626.

9. Ibid. 627.

10. Emphasis mine. U.S. Chamber of Commerce 2006.

11. Ibid.

12. Robert Pear 2002:A18, cited in Reese 2005:168.

13. See Marchevsky and Theoharis 2006:124.

14. Loprest 1999, 2003.

15. Lerman and Ratcliffe 2001.

16. Bartik 2001:72.

17. Piven 2001:145.

18. Ibid.

19. Ibid.

20. Marchevsky and Theoharis 2006:243.

21. Piven 2001:146.

22. Relave 2001; National Association of Social Workers 1992.

23. Marchevsky and Theoharis 2006:133.

24. Ibid., 132.

25. Ibid., 152; note "verbal abuse, disrespect from employers, and unstable employment" in California's GAIN program.

26. Ibid., 133.

27. Sandfort 2003:627.

28. Peck and Theodore 2000:126; Marchevsky and Theoharis 2006:138, 173.

29. Korteweg 2003:454.

30. Ibid.

31. Peck and Theodore 2000.

32. Bartik 2001:72.

33. Peck and Theodore 2000.

34. Tilly 1996, cited in Piven 2001:142. Piven 2001:135–151.

35. Tilly 1988:451–458; Peck and Theodore 2000.

36. See page 184 in Holloway Sparks 2003:171–195, cited in Reese 2005:151.

37. Joseph 1995:1706–1708, cited in Reese 2005:150–151.

38. Reese 2005: 151.

39. Ibid., 153; see also Goode and Maskovsky 2001:12.

40. Reese 2005:166.

41. See Piven 2001:142.

42. Reese 2005:168.

43. Peck and Theodore 1999:6, cited in Reese 2005:167.

44. McCoy 1998:415.

45. Morgen and Maskovsky 2003:328.

CHAPTER 5

1. For welfare mothers see Edin and Lein 1997; Monroe and Tiller 2001; Woodward 2008. For caseworkers see Beckerman and Fontana 2001; Seccombe 2007; Ridzi 2004.

2. Marchevsky and Theoharis 2006:125 discuss similar use of former recipients as motivational speakers in California's GAIN program.

3. Orloff 2001:136.
4. Ibid., 154, emphasis in original.
5. Ibid., 148.
6. Ibid., 137.
7. Ibid.
8. Boleyn-Fitzgerald 1999.
9. Murray 1997:126; see also Boleyn-Fitzgerald 1999.
10. Gingrich 1995:71; see also Boleyn-Fitzgerald 1999.
11. Mica 1995, cited in Boleyn-Fitzgerald 1999.
12. Seccombe 2007:11–12.
13. Clinton 1996:2216, cited in Boleyn-Fitzgerald 1999.
14. Schmidtz and Goodin 1998:5, cited in Boleyn-Fitzgerald 1999.
15. Close Up Foundation 1998.
16. Kincaid 1990:139–152.
17. See Ellwood 1998 in Cho, Chung-Lae, and Wright 2004:447–468.
18. Béland and de Chantal 2004:241–264.
19. Orloff 2001:154.
20. Ibid., 152.
21. Adair 2002:462.
22. Morgen and Weigt 2001:152.
23. See Ridzi 2004.
24. Hays 2003:38.
25. Mead 2005:412.
26. See Fraser 1989:154.
27. Schram 2000a.
28. Marchevsky and Theoharis 2006:125.
29. Ibid., 126.
30. See Raspberry 1995:A19 in Adair 2002:463.
31. Marchevsky and Theoharis 2006:126.
32. Ibid., 116; Adair 2002:455.
33. Hochschild 1983:7.
34. Ibid.
35. Bourdieu 1988:291, endnote 31.
36. Ibid., 100–101.
37. Ibid., 167.
38. Ibid., italics in original.
39. Naples 1998.
40. Bourdieu 1988:166.
41. Korteweg 2003:451–452.

CHAPTER 6

1. Ridzi and London 2006.
2. See Cherlin 2001.
3. Mullings 2001:45.
4. Collins 2000:78.
5. See Peck 2002b:195.
6. Romero 1992.
7. See Ehrenreich and Hoschild 2002.
8. Mullings 2001:38.
9. Ginsburg and Rapp 1995:3 cited in Mullings 2001:37.
10. Fraser 1989:144, 149.
11. Ibid., 144.
12. Overall, 90 percent of adult TANF recipients are women. U.S. Department of Health and Human Services 2004.
13. Ibid.
14. U.S. Census 2000a.
15. See Holzer 1996; also U.S. Department of Health and Human Services 2004.
16. For data on national caseloads, see Lower-Basch 2003.
17. Data for 2002 from U.S. Department of Health and Human Services 2004.
18. U.S. Census 2003; U.S. Census 2000b, 2000c.
19. U.S. Census 2004.
20. See for instance Segal and Kilty 2003
21. Fraser and Gordon 1994.
22. See Katz 1989.
23. Cruikshank 1999:108.
24. Griffith and Smith 1990:4.
25. Moynihan 1973: 17.
26. Fraser 1989:148.
27. Piven 2002 cited in Weigt 2006:337.
28. Weigt 2006:339.
29. Marchevsky and Theoharis 2006:141.
30. Marchevsky and Theoharis 2006:189 similarly notes mothers choosing to care for their children over work-first requirements in California's GAIN program.
31. PRWORA Section 101.
32. Ibid.
33. Ibid.
34. Goode and Maskovsky 2001:12.
35. Raspberry 1995:A19, cited in Adair 2002:463.

36. PRWORA Section 401(a,1).
37. Berrick 2005:138.
38. Ibid., 139.
39. Roberts 1997:209.
40. Ibid., 210.
41. Crouse 1999.
42. Gibbs 1994:24, cited in Roberts 1997:210.
43. The Lewin Group 2003.
44. Donovan 1999.
45. Office of Family Assistance 2007. Though it should be noted that New York did not receive a bonus in 1999, 2000, or 2001 since it was ranked 35th, 7th, and 4th respectively in each of these years but did not experience a decline.
46. NYS Office of Children and Family Services 2006.
47. Ibid., 17.
48. Raspberry 1995:A19 in Adair 2002:463.
49. See Roberts 1997:213 for discussion of tax credits and exemptions.
50. African-American families were first characterized as a "tangle of pathologies" in the Moynihan Report and this characterization has taken root in ongoing congressional debates since. See Haney and March 2003:466.
51. Hasenfeld 2000b:187.
52. Roberts 1997:4.
53. Ibid., 7.
54. See Fraser and Gordon 1994; Fraser 1989:144–148.
55. Touminen 2000:112–135.
56. Vogel 1993:40, cited in Touminen 2000:115.
57. Touminen 2000:117.
58. Hays 2003:84.
59. Alan and Chisman 1985 in McCluskey 2003.
60. Solinger 2001 supra note 60, at 148 in McCluskey 2003:801, note 116.
61. Ibid.
62. Gordon 1994 supra note 27, at 253–255, 293–303 in McCluskey, 2003 note 61.
63. Weigt 2006:347.
64. U.S. Department of Health and Human Services cited in Brookings Institute 2002.
65. Traverso 2003.
66. Edin 2000:112–133. See also Wilson 1987:83 for a discussion of the "male marriageability pool index."
67. See U.S. Census 2000b; also see Lane et al. 2004:405–428.
68. Importantly, this off-balance ratio does not appear until age 20, offering support to the argument that it is due in large part to disproportionate incarceration and early death rates among African-American males. See Lane et al. 2004:424.

69. For a fuller discussion of this citation see Lane et al. 2004:406.

70. Ibid.

71. This provides indirect evidence that the unbalanced sex ratio is due to disproportionate incarceration. Rosenthal 2001; Lane et al. 2004.

72. For a fuller discussion of this citation see Lane et al. 2004:413.

73. Guttentag and Secord 1983. See also Lane et al. 2004.

74. This is also asserted by Lane et al. 2004.

75. Lane et al. 2004:423.

76. Ibid.

77. Haney and March 2003.

78. Lane et al. 2004:417.

79. Smith 1997:222 cited in Goode and Maskovsky 2001:9.

80. Acker 1990.

81. Garfinkel 2002.

82. Kingfisher 2002 in Morgen and Maskovsky 2003:329.

83. Little 2002.

84. Hays 2003.

85. Collins 2006:8.

CHAPTER 7

1. Luken and Vaughan 2006:301.

2. See Hasenfeld 2000b.

3. van Wormer 2005:2, see also p. 4. See also Polack 2004:281–290.

4. van Wormer 2005:4. See also Payne 1997; Dominelli 2002.

5. van Wormer 2005:5 and Barker 2003:403, cited in van Wormer 2005:5.

6. van Wormer 2005:5; see also Byrne 1999.

7. van Wormer 2005:1–10.

8. Mead 2005:402.

9. Ibid., 401.

10. Ibid., 406.

11. Burton 1991.

12. Abramovitz 2002; Hasenfeld 2000b:185.

13. Hasenfeld 2000b:185–186.

14. Ibid., 185.

15. Ibid., 191.

16. Abramovitz 2002:16.

17. Hays 2003:64.

18. Hasenfeld 2000b:186.

19. Ibid., 190.

20. For a critical discussion of mainstream welfare reform research see Marchevsky and Theoharis 2006:202.

21. Haney 1996.
22. Peck 2002a:353. See also Evans 1995:75 in Peck and Theodore 2000:124. Jamie Peck examines work-first approaches as philosophically "workfarist" because they require activities designed to increase employment prospects as a precondition of aid.
23. Cazanave and Neubeck 2001.
24. Sharone 2007.
25. Marchevsky and Theoharis 2006, concluding chapter.
26. Kingfisher 1996; Morgen and Maskovsky 2003:328; Goldberg 2001:194.
27. Béland and de Chantal 2004:241–264.
28. Goldberg 2001; Korteweg 2003; Ridzi 2004.
29. Cruikshank 1999; see also Marchevsky and Theoharis 2006:272 note 13.
30. Marchevsky and Theoharis 2006:118.
31. Piven and Cloward [1971] 1993:149 cited in Goldberg 2001:193–194.
32. Goldberg 2001:194–195.
33. Harrison and Bluestone 1988:14, cited in Peck 2002b:189.
34. Piven and Cloward [1971] 1993:149 cited in Goldberg 2001:195.
35. Piven and Cloward [1971] 1993:3–4 cited in Goldberg 2001:195.
36. For a discussion of (G)local see Beukema and Carrillo 2004:5.
37. See Peck 2002a and 2002b for a detailed presentation of this perspective.
38. Peck 2000:357.
39. Morgen and Maskovsky 2003:323.
40. See for instance Bluestone and Harrison 200:238 in Peck 2002b:203.
41. Hasenfeld 2000b:198.
42. Morgen and Maskovsky 2003:329.
43. Brookings Institute 2008; Katz 2007.
44. Brodkin 1997:25.
45. Dehner 2002:3.
46. U.S. Commission on Civil Rights 2002.
47. Ibid.
48. Renwick 2006:8.
49. Gilliom 2001.
50. Hasenfeld 2000b:196.
51. Tait 2005:145–147, 154.
52. U.S. Commission on Civil Rights 2002.
53. Tait 2005.
54. Hasenfeld 2000b:187.
55. See Barley and Kunda 2004 for new combinations of jobs in the contingent work force.
56. See Peck and Theodore 2000:126; Shulman 2005.
57. Holzer 1996.

58. U.S. Census Bureau 2004.
59. See Heinrich 2005; Boushey 2001; Loprest 1999a and 1999b, 2003.
60. Hays 2003:59.
61. Ibid., 60.
62. Renwick 2006:8.
63. Urban Institute 2006.
64. Stepping stone model is discussed in Marchansky and Theoharis 2006:173–174 and Peck and Theodore 2000:126.
65. Brock, Kwakye et al. 2004: 115, Marchevsky and Theoharis 2006:136.
66. Poppe et al. 2004.
67. Renwick 2006:8.
68. Gooden 2003:275.
69. See Peck and Theodore 2000:126.
70. Hanagan 1988; Tilly 1988; Tait 2005:189.
71. Goldberg 2001:211.
72. Tait 2005:181.
73. Ibid., 180.
74. Rank 2004:103.
75. U.S. Department of Health and Human Services, Office of Family Assistance 2006.
76. Ehrenreich and Hochschild 2002; Romero 1992.
77. Roberts 1997:6.
78. Berrick 2005:142.
79. For a discussion of "other mothers" see Collins 2000.
80. Gooden 2003:274.
81. Naples 1997.
82. U.S. Commission on Civil Rights 2002; also see Gordon:5.
83. Goodin 1988.
84. Soss, Schram, Vartanian, and O'Brien 2001.
85. U.S. Commission on Civil Rights 2002.
86. National Urban League, Institute for Opportunity and Equality:7.
87. Gooden 2003:267.
88. Clarke, Jarmon, and Langley 1999:122 in Gooden 2003:268.
89. Holzer and Stoll 2000:16, 26 in Gooden 2003:268; also in Brown 2003:53.
90. Korteweg 2003:455–456.
91. U.S. Commission on Civil Rights 2002.
92. Ibid.
93. Marchevsky and Theoharis 2006:229.
94. Goode and Maskovsky 2001:3.
95. U.S. Commission on Civil Rights 2002.
96. Cazanave and Neubeck 2001.

97. Technical Assistance for Caseworkers on Civil Rights Laws and Welfare Reform (www.hhs.gov/ocr/taintro.htm). The Grass Roots Innovative Policy Program has placed on its website (www.arc.org/gripp) a document called "Putting Welfare Reform to the Test: A Guide to Uncovering Bias and Unfair Treatment in Local Welfare Programs." That guide provides the information needed to document welfare racist practices." Cazanave and Neubeck 2001.

98. U.S. Commission on Civil Rights 2002.

99. Ibid.

100. Gooden 2003:254.

101. Ibid., 269.

102. Ibid., 254.

103. Ibid., 269.

104. See Tait 2005; Goldberg 2001; Ridzi 2007.

105. Cruikshank 1999:120. See the National Welfare Rights Organization (NWRO) in Gilliom 2001:110; also Burton 1991 and Kingfisher 2001.

106. Fraser 1990 cited in Cruikshank 1999:118.

107. Piven and Cloward 1979:5 in Gilliom 2001:113.

108. Ewick and Silbey 1998:187 cited in Gilliom 2001:164 note 6.

109. Scott 1990.

110. Ibid., 16.

111. Fraser 1990 cited in Cruikshank 1999:118.

112. Burton 1991; Kingfisher 2001.

113. Cruikshank 1999:119.

114. See Ridzi 2007.

115. Cruikshank 1999:113.

116. Ibid., 120.

117. Haney 1996.

118. Peck 2002:353. See also Evans 1995:75 in Peck and Theodore 2000:124. Jamie Peck examines work-first approaches as philosophically "workfarist" because they require activities designed to increase employment prospects as a precondition of aid.

119. Collins 1997:29; Carr 1997.

120. For instance, the assumption that the market is a neutral entity is questioned by McClusky 2003. Also see Rosenbloom 2002; Ridzi and Banerjee 2006.

121. Bourdieu 1998:3.

CHAPTER 8

1. See for instance Orloff 2001:137, 142–143.

2. See for instance Polanyi 1944; and Esping-Andersen 1990:79.

3. Quadagno 1998:13, cited in Neuman 2005.

4. Smith 1987:221.

5. Smith 1987.
6. Schram 1995, cited in Marchevsky and Theoharis 2006:201.
7. Polanyi 1944; Blyth 2002.
8. Polanyi 1944:33, 56, 76.
9. Ibid., 76.
10. Ibid.
11. See for instance Polanyi's 1944:72 discussion of false commodities.
12. Peck 2002b:215.
13. Clarke 2001:10, emphasis in original. Also Morgen and Maskovsky 2003:322; Maskovsky and Kingfisher 2001:105–123, cited in Morgen and Maskovsky 2003:319.
14. Midgley 2007:20.
15. See Polanyi 1944.
16. Holzerand Demetra Nightingale 2007.
17. Osterman 2007.
18. Polanyi 1944:234.
19. See for instance Kaus 1992; Lasch 1995:20.
20. Walzer 1983, cited in Lasch 1995:21.
21. Kaus 1992, cited in Lasch 1995:21.
22. Lasch 1995:22.
23. Ibid., 123.
24. D'Addio 2007:33; D'Addio and Whiteford 2007.
25. D'Addio 2007:38.
26. D'Addio 2007.
27. Bowles and Gintis 2002:49.
28. Holzer and Nightingale 2007.
29. Turner 2007: chap. 4.
30. Lerman 2007: chap. 3.
31. Lerman 2007.
32. Burtless 2007: chap. 9.
33. Burtless 2007.
34. Waldfogel 2007: chap. 10.
35. Waldfogel 2007.
36. Freeman 2007: chap. 1.
37. Midgley 2007:27.
38. Ibid.
39. Ibid., 28.
40. Maskovsky 2001:470–482.
41. Harrington 1996:N15–N18.
42. Morgen and Maskovsky 2003:332.
43. Hays 2003:59.
44. Rank 2004.

45. Tait 2005:179.
46. Shulman 2005:150.
47. Polanyi 1944:256.
48. Neuman 2005:540. See also Hacker 2002:338.
49. Neuman 2005:540. See also Hacker 2002:338.
50. Titmuss 1974; Esping-Andersen 1990.
51. Esping-Andersen 1990:38. See also Ridzi, Loveland, and Glennon 2008.
52. Esping-Andersen 1989:15.
53. Ibid., 15–16, 21.
54. Esping-Andersen 1990:28–29, 109.
55. Esping-Andersen 1989:29.
56. Esping-Andersen 1989:31; Esping-Andersen 1990: 69, 110; see also Verba, Schlozman, and Brady 1995.
57. Esping-Andersen 1990:130.
58. Ibid., 221.
59. Ibid., 207.
60. Ibid., 47; Esping-Andersen 1989:19.
61. Goodin, Headey, Muffels, and Dirven 2000:260; use data spanning the 10-year period from 1984 to 1994.
62. Ibid., 262, italics in original.
63. Esping-Andersen 1990:43–33 argues that social security actually strengthens the commodity status of labor by off-loading cost from employers and leveling the laissez-faire playing field through universality (i.e., not insuring some but not others).

APPENDIX

1. See Smith 1987, 1990, 1999, 2005; DeVault 2006, 2008; Eastwood 2005; Campbell and Manicom 1995; Campbell and Gregor 2004; and Rankin and Campbell 2006, among other institutional ethnography projects.

2. While I did not attend Drug and Alcohol Screening because it was contracted to an outside provider, I did interview staff about the processes involved.

3. DeVault and McCoy 2000:9.

4. Thus any names used to represent applicants in this book are pseudonyms.

Bibliography

Abramovitz, Mimi. 1988. *Regulating the Lives of Women: Social Welfare Policy from Colonial Times to the Present*. Boston: South End Press.

———. 1996. *Regulating the Lives of Women: Social Welfare Policy from Colonial Times to the Present*. Rev. 2d ed. Boston: South End Press.

———. 2002. The Impact of Welfare Reform on Nonprofit Human Service Agencies in New York City. New York: National Association of Social Workers. Retrieved October 11, 2007, from http://www.unitedwaynyc.org/?id=69.

Acker, Joan. 1990. "Hierarchies, Jobs, and Bodies: A Theory of Gendered Organizations." *Gender and Society* 4:139–158.

Adair, Vivyan. 2002. "Branded with Infamy: Inscriptions of Class and Poverty in America." *Signs: Journal of Women in Culture and Society* 27:451–473.

Alan, Pifer, and Forrest Chisman, eds. 1985. "50th Anniversary Edition of The Report of The Committee On Economic Security of 1935 And Other Basic Documents Relating To The Development Of The Social Security Act." Washington, DC: Project on the Federal Social Role, 1985.

Albo, Gregory. 2001. "Neoliberalism from Reagan to Clinton." *Monthly Review* 52:81–89. Retrieved October 11, 2007, from http://www.monthlyreview.org/0401albo.htm.

Alexander, Jeffrey. 1992. "Recent Sociological Theory between Agency and Social Structure." *Revue Suisse de Sociologie* 18(1):7–11.

———. 1993. "More Notes on the Problem of Agency: A Reply." *Revue Suisse de Sociologie* 19:501–506.

Alexander, M. Jacqui, and Chandra Talpade Mohanty. 1997. "Introduction: Genealogies, Legacies, Movements." In M. Jacqui Alexander and Chandra Talpade Mohanty (eds.), *Feminist Genealogies, Colonial Legacies, Democratic Futures* (pp. xiii–xlii). New York: Routledge.

Amenta, Edwin, Chris Bonastia, and Neal Caren. 2001. "U.S. Social Policy in Comparative and Historical Perspective: Concepts, Images, Arguments, and Research Strategies." *Annual Reviews of Sociology* 27:213–234.

American Enterprise Institute for Public Policy Research. 2002. AEI Homepage, Retrieved October 23, 2002, from http://www.aei.org/.

Amott, Teresa, and Julie Matthaei. 1991. *Race, Gender, and Work: A Multicultural Economic History of Women in the United States*. Boston: South End Press.

Anderson, Steven. 2002. "Ensuring the Stability of Welfare-to-Work Exits: The Importance of Recipient Knowledge About Work Incentives." *Social Work* 47:162–170.

Attewell, Paul. 1987. "The Deskilling Controversy." *Work and Occupations* 14:323–346.

Avery, James, and Mark Peffley. 2003. "Race Matters: The Impact of News Coverage of Welfare Reform on Public Opinion." In Sanford Schram, Joe Soss, and Richard Fording (eds.), *Race and the Politics of Welfare Reform* (pp. 131–150). Ann Arbor: University of Michigan Press.

Bachrach, Peter, and Morton Baratz. 1962. "The Two Faces of Power." *American Political Science Review* 57:947–952.

Bandoh, Evelyn. 2003. "Outsourcing the Delivery of Human Services." *Welfare Information Network Issue Notes* 7:12. Retrieved June 22, 2004, from http://www.financeprojectinfo.org/Publications/outsourcinghumanservicesIN.htm.

Barker, Robert. 2003. *The Social Work Dictionary*. 5th ed. Washington, DC: NASW Press.

Barley, Stephen, and Gideon Kunda. 2004. *Gurus, Hired Guns, and Warm Bodies: Itinerant Experts in a Knowledge Economy*. Princeton, NJ: Princeton University Press.

Bartik, Timothy J. 2001. *Jobs for the Poor: Can Labor Demand Policies Help?* New York: Russell Sage Foundation.

BBC News. 2005. "Blair Shuns US Religion Politics." BBC News, March 22, 2005. Retrieved October 11, 2007, from http://news.bbc.co.uk/go/pr/fr/-/1/hi/uk_politics/4369481.stm.

Beckerman, Adela, and Leonard Fontana. 2001. "The Transition from AFDC to PRWORA in Florida; Perceptions of the Role of Case Manager in Welfare Reform." *Journal of Sociology and Social Welfare* 28(3):29–47.

Béland, Daniel, and F. Vergniolle de Chantal. 2004. "Fighting "Big Government": Frames, Federalism, Social Policy Reform in the United States." *Canadian Journal of Sociology* 29: 241–264.

Berger, Peter L., and Thomas Luckmann. 1996. *The Social Construction of Reality: A Treatise in the Sociology of Knowledge*. Garden City, NY: Anchor Books.

Berrick, Jill Duerr. 2005. "Marriage, Motherhood and Welfare Reform." *Social Policy and Society* 4:133–145.

Besharov, Douglas J. 2002. "Professional Profile." American Enterprise Institute for Public Policy Research. Retrieved October 23, 2002, from http://www.aei.org/scholars/besharov.htm.

———. 2003. "The Past and Future of Welfare Reform." *Public Interest* Winter 2003:4–21. Retrieved October 11, 2007, from www.welfareacademy.org/pubs/welfare/pastandfuture.pdf.

Besharov, Douglas J., and Peter Germanis. 2002. "Chapter 1: Introduction" and "Chapter 2: Welfare Reform Update." In Douglas J. Besharov (ed.), *Family Well-Being After Welfare Reform*. Welfare Reform Academy, College Park:

University of Maryland. Retrieved April 21, 2003, from http://www.welfa-reacademy.org/pubs/familywellbeing/.

Beukema, Leni, and Jorge Carrillo. 2004. "Handling Global Developments, Shaping Local Practices. The Interference of the Global and the Local in Work Restructuring." In L. Beukema and J. Carrillo (eds.), *Globalism/Localism at Work*, vol. 13, Research in the Sociology of Work (pp. 3–22). Amsterdam: Elsevier.

Bloom, Leslie. 1999. "'I'm Poor, I'm Single, I'm a Mom and I Deserve Respect': Advocating in Schools as/with Single Mothers in Poverty." *Educational Studies* 32(3):300–316.

Blyth, Mark. 2002. *Great Transformations: Economic Ideas and Institutional Change in the Twentieth Century*. New York: Cambridge University Press.

Bobo, Lawrence, James R. Kluegel, and Ryan A. Smith. 1996. "Laissez-Faire Racism: The Crystallization of a 'Kinder, Gentler' Anti-black Ideology." Russell Sage Foundation (June 1996). Retrieved May 23, 2008, from http://www.russellsage.org/publications/workingpapers/Laissez%20Faire%20Racism/document.

Boleyn-Fitzgerald, Patrick. 1999. "Misfortune, Welfare Reform, and Right-Wing Egalitarianism." *Critical Review* 13(1–2):1–11. Retrieved October 11, 2007, from http://www.ciaonet.org/olj/cr/cr_99bop01.html.

Bourdieu, Pierre. 1988. *Homo Academicus*. Translated by Peter Collier. Stanford: Stanford University Press.

———. 1998. "Utopia of Endless Exploitation." *Le Monde Diplomatique* December 1998. Retrieved October 11, 2007, from http://mondediplo.com/1998/12/08bourdieu.

Boushey, Heather. 2001. "Last Hired, First Fired: Job Losses Plague Former TANF Recipients." EPI Issue Brief # 171. Washington, DC: The Economic Policy Institute.

Bovens, Mark, and Stavros Zouridis. 2002. "From Street-Level to System-Level Bureaucracies: How Information and Communication Technology Is Transforming Administrative Discretion and Constitutional Control." *Public Administration Review* 62(2):174–184.

Bowles Samuel, and Herbert Gintis. 2002. "The Inheritance of Inequality." *Journal of Economic Perspectives* 16(3):3–30.

Brock, Thomas, Claudia Coulton, Andrew London, Denise Polit, Lashawn Richburg-Hayes, Ellen Scott, and Nandita Verma. 2002. *Welfare Reform in Cleveland: Implementation, Effects, and Experiences of Poor Families and Neighborhoods*. New York: Manpower Demonstration Research Corporation.

Brock, Thomas, Isaac Kwakye, Judy C. Polyné, Lashawn Richburg-Hayes, David Seith, Alex Stepick, Carol Dutton Stepick with Tara Cullen and Sarah Rich. 2004. *Welfare Reform in Miami: Implementation, Effects, and Experiences of Poor Families and Neighborhoods*. New York: MDRC. Retrieved May 1, 2008, from http://www.mdrc.org/publications/387/full.pdf.

Brodkin, Evelyn Z. 1997. "Inside the Welfare Contract: Discretion and Account-ability in State Welfare Administration." *The Social Service Review* 71:1–33.

Brookings Institute. 2002. "Child Support Collections and Paternity Establish-ments Are Up." Prepared by The Brookings Welfare Reform & Beyond Initiative. Retrieved December 8, 2007, from http://www.childwelfare.com/pres_200202_full.ppt.

———. 2008. "Blueprint for American Prosperity: Unleashing the Potential of a Metropolitan Nation." Event Summary. Retrieved January 12, 2008, from http://www.brookings.edu/events/2007/1106blueprint.aspx.

Brown, Amy. 1997. *Work First: How to Implement an Employment-Focused Ap-proach to Welfare Reform. A How-to Guide.* New York: Manpower Demonstra-tion Research Corporation.

Brown, Michael. 2003. "Ghettos, Fiscal Federalism, and Welfare Reform." In Sanford Schram, Joe Soss, and Richard Fording (eds.), *Race and the Politics of Welfare Reform* (pp. 47–71). Ann Arbor: University of Michigan Press.

Burstein, Paul. 1991. "Policy Domains: Organization, Culture, and Policy Out-comes." *Annual Reviews of Sociology* 17:327–50.

Burtless, Gary. 2007. "Income Supports for Workers and Their Families: Earnings Supplements and Health Insurance." In Harry J. Holzer and Demetra Smith Nightingale (eds.), *Reshaping the American Workforce in a Changing Economy* (pp. 239–272). Washington, DC: Urban Institute Press.

Burton, Alice. 1991. "Dividing Up the Struggle: The Consequences of "Split" Wel-fare Work for Union Activism." In Michael Burawoy (ed.), *Ethnography Un-bound: Power and Resistance in the Modern Metropolis* (pp. 85–107). Berkeley: University of California Press.

Bush, George W. 2004. "State of the Union Address." The White House. Wash-ington, DC. Retrieved October 11, 2007, from http://www.whitehouse.gov/news/releases/2004/01/200401207.html.

Byrne, David. 1999. *Social Exclusion.* Buckingham, UK: Open University Press.

Campbell, Marie L., and Frances Gregor. 2004. *Mapping Social Relations: A Primer in Doing Institutional Ethnography.* Lanham, MD: Rowman Altamira.

Campbell, Marie L, and Ann Manicom. 1995. *Knowledge, Experience, and Ruling Relations.* Canada: University of Toronto Press.

Carby, Hazel. 1992. "The Multicultural Wars." In Michele Wallace and Gina Dent (eds.), *Black Popular Culture* (pp. 187–199). Seattle: Bay Press.

Carr, Leslie. 1997. *"Color-Blind" Racism.* Thousand Oaks, CA: Sage Publications.

Cazanave, Noel, and Kenneth J. Neubeck. 2001. "Fighting Welfare Racism." *Pov-erty & Race* March/April. Retrieved May 1, 2008, from http://www.prrac.org/topic_type.php?topic_id=2&type_group=10.

Cherlin, Andrew. 2001. *Public and Private Families: An Introduction.* New York: McGraw-Hill.

Cho, Chung-Lae, and Deil S. Wright. 2004. "The Devolution Revolution in Inter-governmental Relations in the 1990s: Changes in Cooperative and Coercive State–National Relations as Perceived by State Administrators." *Journal of Public Administration Research and Theory* 14:447–468.

Clarke, John. 2001. "Globalization and Welfare States: Some Unsettling Thoughts." In Robert Sykes, Bruno Palier, and Pauline M. Prior (eds.), *Globalization and European Welfare States* (pp. 19–37). New York: Palgrave.

Clarke, Leslie, Brenda Jarmon, and Merlin Langley. 1999. "Qualitative Study of Wages: People Who Have Left Wages." In Florida Inter-University Welfare Reform Collaborative, Fall (p. 122).

Clinton, William. 1996. "Presidential News Conference: Clinton Says Welfare Bill Is a 'Real Step Forward.'" *Congressional Quarterly Weekly Report* 54 (August 3):2216–2218.

Close Up Foundation. 1998. "Devolution Revolution." Alexandria, VA. Retrieved May 15, 2003, from http://www.closeup.org/federal.htm.

Cohen, Benjamin. 2002. «Bretton Woods System.» *Routledge Encyclopedia of International Political Economy*, pp. 84–91. Routledge, UK: Routledge. Retrieved May 20, 2008, from http://www.polsci.ucsb.edu/faculty/cohen/recent/pdfs/bretton%20woods%20system.pdf.

Collins, Jane. 2006. "The Specter of Slavery: Workfare and the Economic Citizenship of Poor Women." Paper Prepared for School of American Research Seminar: New Landscapes of Inequality, March 11–16, Santa Fe, NM, pp. 1–37.

Collins, Patricia Hill. 1997. "How Much Difference Is Too Much?: Black Feminist Thought and the Politics of Postmodern Social Theory." *Current Perspectives in Social Theory* 17:3–37.

————. 2000. *Black Feminist Thought: Knowledge, Consciousness, and the Politics of Empowerment.* 2d ed. Boston: Unwin Hyman.

Crouse, Gil. 1999. "State Implementation of Major Changes to Welfare Policies, 1992–1998." Assistant Secretary for Planning and Evaluation, Office of Human Services Policy, U.S. Department of Health and Human Services: Washington, DC. Retrieved December 2, 2007, from http://aspe.hhs.gov/hsp/Waiver-Policies99/W5fam_cap.htm.

Cruikshank, Barbara. 1999. *The Will to Empower: Democratic Citizens and Other Subjects.* Ithaca, NY: Cornell University Press.

D'Addio, Anna Cristina. 2007. "Intergenerational Transmission of Disadvantage: Mobility or Immobility across Generations? A Review of the Evidence for OECD Countries." Working Paper No. 52. Paris: OECD (Organization for Economic Cooperation and Development) Social, Employment, and Migration. Retrieved November 22, 2007, from http://www.oecd.org/dataoecd/27/28/38335410.pdf.

D'Addio, Anna Cristina, and Peter Whiteford. 2007. "Intergenerational Transmission of Disadvantage: Policy Implications." Presented at the Social Policy Division Directorate for Employment, Labour and Social Affairs, Organization for Economic Cooperation and Development (OECD), VU-ICSW (International Council on Social Welfare) Conference, Vilnius, June 2007. Retrieved November 1, 2007, from http://www.icsw.org/doc/Intergenerational_Transmission_of_Disadvantage_Policy_Implications.pdf.

Dehner, Rachael. 2002. "Mandatory Dispute Resolution: New York's Recall on Welfare Recipients' Due Process Rights." *Cardozo Journal of Conflict Resolution* 3(1):2–17. Retrieved November 22, 2007, from http://www.cojcr.org/vol3no1/notes01.html.

DeVault, Marjorie L. 2006. "Introduction: What Is Institutional Ethnography?" *Social Problems* 53(3):294–298.

———, ed. 2008. *People at Work: Life, Power, and Social Inclusion in the New Economy.* New York: NYU Press.

DeVault, Marjorie L., and Liza McCoy. 2002. "Institutional Ethnography: Using Interviews to Investigate Ruling Relations." In Jaber Gubrium and James Holstein (eds.), *Handbook of Interview Research* (pp. 751–776). Thousand Oaks, CA: Sage Publications.

DiMaggio, Paul. 1997. "Culture and Cognition." *Annual Review of Sociology* 23:263–288.

Dominelli, Lena. 2002. Anti-Oppressive Social Work Theory and Practice. New York: Palgrave.

Donovan, Patricia. 1999. "The 'Illegitimacy Bonus' and State Efforts to Reduce Out-of-Wedlock Births." *Family Planning Perspectives* 31: 94–97. Retrieved November 22, 2007, from http://www.guttmacher.org/pubs/journals/3109499.html#3a.

Downs, Anthony. 1998. *Political Theory and Public Choice.* Northampton, MA: Edward Elgar.

Eastwood, Lauren. 2005. *The Social Organization of Policy: An Institutional Ethnography of UN Forest Deliberations.* New York: Routledge.

Edelman, Murray. 1971. *Politics as Symbolic Action: Mass Arousal and Quiescence.* Chicago: Markham Publishing.

Edin, Kathryn. 2000. "How Low-Income Single Mothers Talk About Marriage." *Social Problems* 47(1):112–133.

Edin, Kathryn, and Kathleen M. Harris. 1999. "Getting Off and Staying Off: Racial Differences in the Work Route Off Welfare." In I. Browne (ed.), *Latinas and African American Women at Work* (pp. 270–301). New York: Russell Sage Foundation.

Edin, Kathryn, and Laura Lein. 1997. *Making Ends Meet: How Single Mothers Survive Welfare and Low-Wage Work.* New York: Russell Sage Foundation.

Egan, Daniel. 2003. "'The Undeserving Rich': How the News Media Cover Corporate Welfare." *Humanity and Society* 27:108–124.

Ehrenreich, Barbara, and Arlie Russel Hochschild, eds. 2002. *Global Woman: Nannies, Maids, and Sex Workers in the New Economy*. New York: Owl Books.

Eikenberry, Angela M., and Jodie Drapal Kluver. 2004. "The Marketization of the Nonprofit Sector: Civil Society at Risk?" *Public Administration Review* 64: 132–140.

Ellwood, David. 1988. *Poor Support*. New York: Basic Books.

Esping-Andersen, Gosta. 1989. "The Three Political Economies of   the Welfare State." *Canadian Review of Sociology and Anthropology* 26(1): 10–36.

———. 1990. *The Three Worlds of Welfare Capitalism*. Princeton, NJ: Princeton University Press.

Evans, Patricia M. 1995. "Linking Welfare to Jobs: Workfare Canadian Style." In Adil Sayeed (ed.), *Workfare. Does It Work? Is It Fair?* (pp. 75–104). Montreal: The Institute for Research on Public Policy.

Ewick, Patricia, and Susan Silbey. 1998. The Common Place of Law. Chicago: University of Chicago Press.

Fagan, Patrick F. 2002. "Professional Profile." The Heritage Foundation. Retrieved October 23, 2002, from http://www.heritage.org/About/Staff/PatrickFagan.cfm.

Frankenberg, Ruth. 1993. *White Women, Race Matters: The Social Construction of Whiteness*. Minneapolis: University of Minnesota Press.

Fraser, Nancy. 1989. *Unruly Practices: Power, Discourse, and Gender in Contemporary Social Theory*. Minneapolis: University of Minnesota Press.

———. 1990. "Struggle Over Needs: Outline of a Socialist-Feminist Critical Theory of Late-Capitalist Political Culture." In Linda Gordon (ed.), *Women, the State, and Welfare* (pp. 199–225). Madison: University of Wisconsin Press.

Fraser, Nancy, and Linda Gordon. 1994. "A Genealogy of Dependency: Tracing a Keyword of the U.S. Welfare State." *Signs: Journal of Women in Culture and Society* 19:309–336.

Freeman, Richard B. 2007. "Replacement Demand in a Global Economy." In Harry J. Holzer and Demetra Smith Nightingale (eds.), *Reshaping the American Workforce in a Changing Economy* (pp. 3–24). Washington, DC: Urban Institute Press.

Garfinkel, Irwin. 2002. "Discussant Comments at Public Policy and the Future of the Family Conference." Maxwell School of Citizenship and Public Affairs, Syracuse University, Syracuse, New York, October 25, 2002. Retrieved April 21, 2003, from http://www-cpr.maxwell.syr.edu/moynihan-smeedingconference/conferenceindex.htm.

Gibbs, Nancy. 1994. "The Vicious Cycle." *Time*, June 20, p. 24.

Giddens, Anthony. 1999. *Runaway World: How Globalization Is Reshaping Our Lives*. London: Profile Books.

Gilens, Martin. 2003. "How the Poor Became Black: The Racialization of American Poverty in the Mass Media." In Sanford Schram, Joe Soss, and Richard Fording (eds.), *Race and the Politics of Welfare Reform* (pp. 101–130). Ann Arbor: University of Michigan Press.

Gilliom, John. 2001. *Overseers of the Poor: Surveillance, Resistance, and the Limits of Privacy*. Chicago: University of Chicago Press.

Gingrich, Newt. 1995. *To Renew America*. New York: HarperCollins.

Goffman, Erving. 1952. "On Cooling the Mark Out: Some Aspects of Adaptation to Failure." *Psychiatry* 15: 451–463.

———. 1967. *Interaction Ritual: Essays in Face-to-Face Behavior*. Chicago: Aldine.

Goldberg, Chad Alan. 2001. "Welfare Recipients or Workers? Contesting the Workfare State in New York City." *Sociological Theory* 19:187–218.

Gonzales, Vanna. 2007. "Globalization, Welfare Reform and the Social Economy: Developing An Alternative Approach to Analyzing Social Welfare Systems in the Post-Industrial Era." *Journal of Sociology & Social Welfare* 34(2):187–211.

Goode, Judith, and Jeff Maskovsky. 2001. *The New Poverty Studies: The Ethnography of Power, Politics, and Impoverished People in the United States*. New York: NYU Press.

Gooden, Susan Tinsley. 2003. "Contemporary Approaches to Enduring Challenges: Using Performance Measures to Promote Racial Equality under TANF." In Sanford Schram, Joe Soss, and Richard Fording (eds.), *Race and the Politics of Welfare Reform* (pp. 254–275). Ann Arbor: University of Michigan Press.

Goodin, Robert. 1988. *Reasons for Welfare*. Princeton, NJ: Princeton University Press.

Goodin, Robert, Bruce Headey, Ruud Muffels, and Henk-Jan Dirven. 2000. *The Real Worlds of Welfare Capitalism*. Cambridge: Cambridge University Press.

Gordon, Linda. 1994. *Pitied But Not Entitled: Single Mothers and the History of Welfare, 1890–1935*. New York: Free Press.

Gordon, Rebecca. 2001. *Cruel and Usual: How Welfare "Reform" Punishes Poor People*. Oakland, CA: Applied Research Center.

Gramsci, Antonio. 1971. *Selections from the Prison Notebooks*. New York: International Publishers.

———. 1985. *Selections from Cultural Writings*, David Forgacs and Geoffrey Nowell-Smith (eds.). London: Lawrence and Wishart.

Gray, John. 1998. *False Dawn: The Delusions of Global Capitalism*. London: Granta Books.

Griffith, Alison I., and Dorothy E. Smith. 1990. "'What Did You Do in School Today?': Mothering, Schooling, and Social Class." In *Perspectives on Social Problems*, vol. 2 (pp. 3–24). Oxford: JAI Press.

Guttentag, Marcia, and Paul Secord. 1983. *Too Many Women? The Sex Ratio Question*. Newbury Park, CA: Sage.

Hacker, Jacob. 2002. *The Divided Welfare State*. New York: Cambridge University Press.

Hallums, Melanie R. Esq., Maureen Lewis Esq., Davis, Polk & Wardwell. 2003. "Welfare, Poverty, and Racism: The Impact of Race on Welfare Reform." Washington, DC: Lawyers' Committee for Civil Rights under Law. Retrieved November 23, 2007, from http://www.lawyerscomm.org/features/40thpapers/welfare.pdf.

Hamilton, Gayle, and Susan Scrivener. 1999. *Promoting Participation: How to Increase Involvement in Welfare-to-Work Activities*. New York: Manpower Demonstration Research Corporation (MDRC) Publications.

Hanagan, Michael. 1988. "Solidary Logics: Introduction." *Theory and Society* 17: 309–327.

Handler, Joel. 1973. *The Coercive Social Worker: British Lessons for American Social Services*. Chicago: Rand McNally.

———. 1996. *Down from Bureaucracy: The Ambiguity of Privatization and Empowerment*. Princeton, NJ: Princeton University Press.

Handler, Joel F., and Yeheskel Hasenfeld. 1997. *We the Poor People: Work, Poverty, and Welfare*. New Haven, CT: Yale University Press.

Haney, Lynne. 1996. "Homeboys, Babies, Men in Suits: The State and the Reproduction of Male Dominance." *American Sociological Review* 61: 759–778.

Haney, Lynne, and Miranda March. 2003. "Married Fathers and Caring Daddies: Welfare Reform and the Discursive Politics of Paternity." *Social Problems* 50: 461–481.

Hargadon, Andrew, and Yellowlees Douglas. 2001. "When Innovations Meet Institutions: Edison and the Design of Electric Light." *Administrative Science Quarterly* 46:476–501.

Harrington, Paul. 1996. "Quitting Time." *The Boston Globe*, September 15, 1996, pp. N15–N18.

Harris, Kathleen Mullan. 1996. "Life After Welfare: Women, Work, and Repeat Dependency." *American Sociological Review* 61:407–426.

Harrison, Bennett, and Barry Bluestone. 1988. *The Great U-Turn: Corporate Restructuring and the Polarizing of America*. New York: Basic Books.

Harvey, Robert. 1995. *The Return of the Strong: The Drift to Global Disorder*. New York: Palgrave.

Hasenfeld, Yeheskel. 2000a. "Organizational Forms as Moral Practices: The Cast of Welfare Departments." *Social Service Review* 74:329.

———. 2000b. "Social Services and Welfare-to-Work: Prospects for the Social Work Profession." *Administration in Social Work* 23:185–199.

Hasenfeld, Yeheskel, and Dale Weaver. 1996. "Enforcement, Compliance, and Disputes in Welfare-to-Work Programs." *Social Service Review* 70:235.

Havemann, Judith. 1997. "Making Public Assistance a Private Enterprise: Texas Stews While the White House Ponders a Precedent-Making Decision." *The Washington Post National Weekly Edition*, March 7, p. 30.

Hays, Sharon. 2003. *Flat Broke With Children: Women in the Age of Welfare Reform*. New York: Oxford University Press.

Heinrich, Carolyn J. 2005. "Temporary Employment Experiences of Women on Welfare." *Journal of Labor Research* 26:335–350.

Hercik, Jeanette. 1998. "At the Front Line: Changing the Business of Welfare Reform." WIN Welfare Information Network, Issue Notes 2(7). Retrieved March 21, 2008, from http://www.financeproject.org/Publications/frontline.htm.

Heritage Foundation. 2002. The Heritage Foundation. Retrieved October 23, 2002, from http://www.heritage.org/.

Hochschild, Arlie Russell. 1983. *The Managed Heart: The Commercialization of Human Feeling*. Berkeley: University of California Press.

Holm, Petter. 1995. "The Dynamics of Institutionalization: Transformation Processes in Norwegian Fisheries." *Administrative Science Quarterly* 40:398–422.

Holzer, Harry J. 1996. *What Employers Want: Job Prospects for Less-Educated Workers*. New York: Russell Sage Foundation.

Holzer, Harry J., and Demetra Smith Nightingale, eds. 2007. *Reshaping the American Workforce in a Changing Economy*. Washington, DC: Urban Institute Press.

Holzer, Harry J., and Michael Stoll. 2000. "Employer Demand for Welfare Recipients by Race." Discussion Paper No. 1213-00, Institute for Research on Poverty, University of Wisconsin, Madison.

hooks, bell. 1990. *Yearning: Race, Gender, and Cultural Politics*. Boston: South End Press.

Hudson Institute. 2002. Hudson Institute Website. Retrieved October 23, 2002, from http://www.hudson.org/.

Hwang, Hokyu, and Walter W. Powell. 2005. "Institutions and Entrepreneurship." In Sharon A. Alvarez, Rajshree Agarwal, and Olav Sorenson (eds.), *Handbook of Entrepreneurship Research* (pp. 179–210). New York: Kluwer Publishers.

Hyatt, Susan Brinn. 2001. "From Citizen to Volunteer: Neoliberal Governance and the Erasure of Poverty." In Judith Goode and Jeff Maskovsky (eds.), *The New Poverty Studies: The Ethnography of Power, Politics, and Impoverished People in the United States* (pp. 201–235). New York: NYU Press.

Jencks, Christopher. 1997. "The Hidden Paradox of Welfare Reform." *The American Prospect* May–June 1997:33–40.

Jessop, Bob. 2003. "From Thatcherism to New Labour: Neo-Liberalism, Workfarism, and Labour Market Regulation." Department of Sociology, Lancaster University, Lancaster, UK. Retrieved May 13, 2005, from http://www.comp.lancs.ac.uk/sociology/soc131rj.pdf.

Johnston, David Cay. 2007. "2005 Incomes, on Average, Still Below 2000 Peak." *New York Times*, August 21. Retrieved April 8, 2008, from http://www.nytimes.com/2007/08/21/business/21tax.html?_r=1&scp=1&sq=2005+Incomes%2C+on+Average%2C+Still+Below+2000+Peak&st=nyt&oref=slogin.

Joint Legislative Audit Committee. 2001. An Evaluation: Wisconsin Works (W-2) Program—Department of Workforce Development: 1–221. Retrieved December 8, 2007, from http://www.legis.state.wi.us/lab/Reports/01-7full.pdf.

Jordan, June. 1992. *Technical Difficulties: African American Notes on the State of the Union*. New York: Pantheon Books.

Joseph, Jeffrey. 1995. House Subcommittee on Human Resources of the Committee on Ways and Means. "Statement for the Record on Welfare Reform before the Subcommittee on Human Resources of the House Committee on Ways and Means for the U.S. Chamber of Commerce." Hearing. 104th Cong., 1st sess., pp. 1706–1708.

Katz, Bruce. 2007. "A Blueprint for National Prosperity: What the 2008 Election Should Be About... and How to Make It Happen." Presentation prepared by Bruce Katz, Brookings Council, New York, New York, May 23, 2007. Retrieved January 12, 2008, from http://www.brookings.edu/speeches/2007/0523metropolitanpolicy_katz.aspx.

Katz, Bruce, and Katherine Allen. 1999. "The State of Welfare Caseloads in America's Cities: 1999." *Survey Series* (February 1999): 1–8. Retrieved October 11, 2007, from http://www.brookings.edu/metro/publications/1999caseloads.htm.

Katz, Michael. 1989. *The Underserving Poor: From the War on Poverty to the War on Welfare*. New York: Pantheon Books.

Kaus, Mickey. 1992. *The End of Equality*. New York: Basic Books.

Kettl, Donald F. 1998. "Reinventing Government: A Fifth-Year Report Card." Report from the Brookings Institution's Center for Public Management, Washington, DC.

Kincaid, John. 1990. "From Cooperative to Coercive Federalism." *Annals of the American Academy of Political and Social Science* 509 (May):139–152.

Kingdon, John W. 1984. *Agendas, Alternatives, and Public Policies*. Boston: Little Brown.

Kingfisher, Catherine. 1996. *Women in the American Welfare Trap*. Philadelphia: University of Pennsylvania Press.

———. 2001. "Producing Disunity: The Constraints and Incitements of Welfare Work." In Judith Goode and Jeff Maskovsky (eds.), *The New Poverty Studies* (pp. 273–292). New York: NYU Press.

———. 2002. *Western Welfare Decline: Globalization and Women's Poverty*. Philadelphia: University of Pennsylvania Press.

Korteweg, Anna C. 2003. "Welfare Reform and the Subject of the Working Mother: 'Get a Job, a Better Job, Then a Career.'" *Theory and Society* 32(4):445–480.

Lane, Sandra D., Robert H. Keefe, Robert A. Rubinstein, Brooke A. Levandowski, Michael Freedman, Alan Rosenthal, and Donald A. Cibula. 2004. "The Politics of Marriage Promotion and Missing Men: African American Women in a Demographic Double Bind." *Medical Anthropology Quarterly* 18:405–428.

Lapham, Lewis H. 2004. "Tentacles of Rage: The Republican Propaganda Mill, a Brief History." *Harpers Magazine* 309(185). Retrieved December 8, 2007, from http://www.mindfully.org/Reform/2004/Republican-Propaganda1sep04.htm.

Lasch, Christopher. 1995. *The Revolt of the Elites and the Betrayal of Democracy.* New York: Norton.

Leidner, Robin. 1993. *Fast Food, Fast Talk: Service Work and the Routinization of Everyday Life.* Berkeley: University of California Press.

Lens, Vicki. 2005. "Bureaucratic Disentitlement: Are Fair Hearings the Cure?" *Georgetown Journal on Poverty Law and Policy* 12(2):3–54.

———. 2006. "Work Sanctions Under Welfare Reform: Are They Helping Women Achieve Self-Sufficiency?" *Duke Journal of Gender Law & Policy* 13:255–284.

Lerman, Robert I. 2007. "Career-Focused Education and Training for Youth." In Harry J. Holzer and Demetra Smith Nightingale (eds.), *Reshaping the American Workforce in a Changing Economy* (pp. 41–90). Washington, DC: Urban Institute Press.

Lerman, Robert I., and Caroline Ratcliffe. 2001. "Are Single Mothers Finding Jobs without Displacing Other Workers?" *Monthly Labor Review* 124(7):1–12.

Levy, Paul A. 1992. "The Durability of Supreme Court Welfare Reforms of the 1960s." *Social Service Review* 66(2):215–327.

The Lewin Group, Inc., Mark W. Nowak, Michael E. Fishman, Mary E. Farrell. 2003. Assistant Secretary for Planning and Evaluation Department of Health and Human Services. State Experience and Perspectives on Reducing Out-of-Wedlock Births Final Report. Retrieved December 8, 2007, from http://aspe.hhs.gov/hsp/nonmarital-births03.

Lieberman, Robert. 2003. "Race and the Limits of Solidarity: American Welfare State Development in Comparative Perspective." In Sanford Schram, Joe Soss, and Richard Fording (eds.), *Race and the Politics of Welfare Reform* (pp. 23–46). Ann Arbor: University of Michigan Press.

Lipsky, Michael. 1980. *Street Level Bureaucracy.* New York: Russell Sage Foundation.

Little, Deborah Lynn. 2002. "Denying Motherwork: Welfare-Reliant Women and Welfare State Reconstruction." *Dissertation Abstracts International, A: The Humanities and Social Sciences* 63(2).

London, Rebecca. 2003. "Which TANF Applicants Are Diverted, and What Are Their Outcomes?" *Social Service Review* 77:373–398.

Loprest, Pamela J. 1999a. "How Families that Left Welfare Are Doing: A National Picture." New Federalism Series B, Urban Institute Press, No. B-1.

———. 1999b. "Families Who Left Welfare: Who Are They and How Are They Doing?" Washington, DC: Urban Institute.

———. 2003. *Fewer Welfare Leavers Employed in Weak Economy.* Washington, DC: Urban Institute.

Lower-Basch, Elizabeth. 2003. U.S. Department of Health and Human Services Office of the Assistant Secretary for Planning and Evaluation. "TANF "Leavers," Applicants, and Caseload Studies: Preliminary Analysis of Racial Differences in Caseload Trends and Leaver Outcomes." Retrieved May 21, 2004, from http://aspe.hhs.gov/hsp/leavers99/race.htm#fig1.

Luken, Paul, and Suzanne Vaughan. 2006. "Standardizing Childrearing through Housing." *Social Problems* 53:299–331.

Lukes, Stephen. 1974. *Power: A Radical View*. London: MacMillan.

Luttwak, Edward. 1999. *Turbo Capitalism: Winners and Losers in the Global Economy*. New York: Harper Collins.

Lyon-Callo, Vincent. 2001. "Homelessness, Employment, and Structural Violence: Exploring Constraints on Collective Mobilizations against Systemic Inequality." In Judith Goode and Jeff Maskovsky (eds.), *The New Poverty Studies: The Ethnography of Power, Politics, and Impoverished People in the United States* (pp. 293–320). New York: NYU Press.

Manhattan Institute for Policy Research. 2002. Manhattan Institute for Policy Research Website. Retrieved October 23, 2002, from http://www.manhattan-institute.org/.)

Marchevsky, Alejandra, and Jeanne Theoharis. 2006. *Not Working: Latina Immigrants, Low-wage Jobs, and the Failure of Welfare Reform*. New York: NYU Press.

Marx, Karl, and Friedrich Engels. 1963. *The German Ideology [1845–6]*. New York: International Publishers.

Maskovsky, Jeff. 2001. "Afterword: Beyond the Privatist Consensus." In Judith Goode and Jeff Maskovsky (eds.), *The New Poverty Studies: The Ethnography of Power, Politics, and Impoverished People in the United States* (pp. 470–482). New York: NYU Press.

Maskovsky, Jeff, and Catherine Kingfisher. 2001. "Introduction to Globalization, Neoliberalism and Poverty in Mexico and the United States." *Urban Anthropology and Studies of Cultural Systems and World Economic Development* 30(2–3):105–123.

Matthews, Hannah, and Danielle Ewen. 2005. "Child Care Assistance in 2004: States Have Fewer Funds for Child Care." Center for Law and Social Policy. Retrieved May 23, 2007, from www.clasp.org/publications/childcareassistance2004.pdf.

McClenny, Jackie. 1996. "Hot Topics and Spirited Discussions. National Association of Hearing Officials." Retrieved May 23, 2007, from http://www.naho.org/NL12-96.htm.

McCluskey, Martha T. 2003. "Efficiency and Social Citizenship: Challenging the Neoliberal Attack on the Welfare State." *Indiana Law Journal* 78:783–876.

McConnell, Grant. 1966. *Private Power and American Democracy.* New York: Knopf.

McCormack, Karen. 2004. "Resisting the Welfare Mother: The Power of Welfare Discourse and Tactics of Resistance." *Critical Sociology* 30:355–383.

McCoy, Liza. 1998. "Producing 'What the Deans Know': Textual Practices of Cost Accounting and the Restructuring of Post-Secondary Education." *Human Studies* 21:395–418.

McKenna, Christine. 1998. "Developing Welfare Policy: A Case Study of New York State." *The Maxwell Review* 6(1):1–8.

Mead, Lawrence M. 2005. "Research and Welfare Reform." *Review of Policy Research* 22: 401–21.

Messer-Davidow, Ellen. 1993. "Manufacturing the Attack on Liberalized Higher Education." *Social Text* 36 (Fall):40–80.

———. 2002. *Disciplining Feminism: From Social Activism to Academic Discourse.* Durham, NC: Duke University Press.

Meyers, Marcia K., and Irene Lurie. 2005. "The Decline in Welfare Caseloads: An Organizational Perspective." Paper presented at the Conference on Mixed Methods Research on Economic Conditions, Public Policy, and Family and Child Well-Being. June 26–28, Ann Arbor, Michigan.

Mica, John. 1995. Congressional Record, 24 March, H3766. Cited in "Vicious animal analogies put bite in House debate," *Milwaukee Sentinel*, March 25, 1995. Retrieved May 23, 2008, from http://findarticles.com/p/articles/mi_qn4208/is_19950325/ai_n10190332.

Midgley, James. 2007. "Perspectives on Globalization, Social Justice and Welfare." *Journal of Sociology and Social Welfare* 34(2):17–36.

Mohanty, Chandra. 1989–90. "On Race and Voice: Challenges for Liberal Education in the 1990's." *Cultural Critique* 14 (Winter):179–208.

Monroe, Pamela A., and Vicky V. Tiller. 2001. "Commitment to Work among Welfare-Reliant Women." *Journal of Marriage and Family* 63(3):816–828.

Morgen, Sandra. 2001. "The Agency of Welfare Workers: Negotiating Devolution, Privatization and Self-Sufficiency." *American Anthropologist* 103:747–761.

Morgen, Sandra, and Jeff Maskovsky. 2003. "The Anthropology of Welfare 'Reform': New Perspectives on U.S. Urban Poverty in the Post-Welfare Era." *Annual Review of Anthropology* 32:315–338.

Morgen, Sandra, and Jill Weigt. 2001. "Poor Women, Fair Work, and Welfare-to-Work That Works." In Judith Goode and Jeff Maskovsky (eds.), *The New Poverty Studies* (pp. 152–178). New York: NYU Press.

Moynihan, Daniel P. 1973. *The Politics of a Guaranteed Income: The Nixon Administration and the Family Assistance Plan.* New York: Random House.

Mullings, Leith. 2001. "Households Headed by Women: The Politics of Class, Race, and Gender." In Judith Goode and Jeff Maskovsky (eds.), *The New Poverty Studies* (pp. 37–56). New York: NYU Press.

Murray, Charles. 1997. *What It Means to Be a Libertarian: A Personal Interpretation*. New York: Broadway Books.

———. 2002. "Professional Profile." AEI. Retrieved October 23, 2002, from http://www.aei.org/scholars/murray.htmb.

Naples, Nancy. 1997. "The 'New Consensus' on the Gendered 'Social Contract': The 1987–1988 U.S. Congressional Hearings on Welfare Reform." *Signs* 23:907–945.

———. 1998. *Grassroots Warriors: Activist Mothering, Community Work, and the War on Poverty*. New York: Routledge.

Nathan, Richard P., and Thomas L. Gais. 1999. *Implementing the Personal Responsibility Act of 1996: A First Look*. Albany, NY: The Rockefeller Institute Press.

National Association of Social Workers. 1992. NASW Standards for Social Work Case Management. Washington, DC: National Association of Social Workers, June 1992. Retrieved December 8, 2007, from http://www.socialworkers.org/practice/standards/sw_case_mgmt.asp.

National Urban League, Institute for Opportunity and Equality. 2002. "Differences in TANF Support Service Utilization: Is There Adequate Monitoring to Ensure Program Quality?" June. New York.

Neuberger, Zoë. 2002. "Annual TANF Expenditures Remain $2 Billion above Block Grant." Center on Budget and Policy Priorities. Retrieved December 8, 2007, from http://www.cbpp.org/10-30-02wel.htm.

Neuman, Lawrence. 2005. *Power State and Society*. Boston: McGraw Hill.

New York State Department of Labor. 2000. Welfare-To-Work Division. Welfare-to-Work Policy and Program Framework. New York.

New York State Office of Children & Family Services. 2006. Adolescent Pregnancy Prevention & Services (APPS). Annual Report/Data Book. Retrieved December 8, 2007, from http://www.ocfs.state.ny.us/main/reports/AppsAnnRepDataBook05_06.pdf.

New York State Office of the State Comptroller. 2001. Office of Temporary and Disability Assistance. New York City Human Resource Administration: Fair Hearing Process. Report No. 97-S-42. New York: New York State Office of the State Comptroller Division of Management Audit and State Financial Services. Retrieved December 6, 2007, from http://www.osc.state.ny.us/audits/allaudits/093002/00n6.pdf.

New York Times. 1976. "'Welfare Queen' Becomes Issue in Reagan Campaign." February 15, p. 51.

———. 1976b. "'Welfare Queen' Loses Her Cadillac Limousine." February 29, p. 42.

O'Connell, Lenahan, Michael Betz, and Jon Shepard. 1990. "Social Control and Legitimacy: The Contribution of Accountability Mechanisms." *Perspectives on Social Problems* 2:261–277.

O'Connor, James. 1973. *The Fiscal Crisis of the State*. New York: St. Martin's Press.

Office of Family Assistance. 2007. "Out of Wedlock Birth Reduction Bonus Ranking Data." U.S. Department Of Health and Human Services. Retrieved December 6, 2007, from http://www.acf.hhs.gov/programs/ofa/bonusrank.htm.

Ohmae, Kenichi. 1996. *The End of the Nation State: The Rise of Regional Economies.* New York: HarperCollins.

———. 1999. *The Borderless World: Power and Strategy in the Interlinked Economy.* New York: Harper Business.

Oliker, Stacey J. 2000. "Examining Care at Welfare's End." (In Madonna Harrington Meyer (ed.), *Care Work: Gender, Labor and the Welfare State* (pp. 167–185). New York: Routledge.

Orloff, Ann Shola. 2001. "Ending the Entitlements of Poor Single Mothers: Changing Social Policies, Women's Employment, and Caregiving in the Contemporary United States." In Nancy Hirschmann and Ulrike Liebert (eds.), *Women and Welfare: Theory and Practice in the United States and Europe* (pp. 133–159). New Brunswick, NJ: Rutgers University Press.

Osterman, Paul. 2007. "Chapter 5 Employment and Training Policies: New Directions for Less-Skilled Adults." In Harry J. Holzer and Demetra Smith Nightingale (eds.), *Reshaping the American Workforce in a Changing Economy* (pp. 119–154). Washington, DC: Urban Institute Press.

Papandrea, Karen. 1998. "Memo to Local Commissioners Accompanying WTW Employment Policy Manual." New York State Department of Labor.

Parrott, Sharon, and Nina Wu. 2003. "States Are Cutting TANF and Child Care Programs: Supports for Low-Income Working Families and Welfare-to-Work Programs Are Particularly Hard Hit." Washington, DC: Center on Budget and Policy Priorities.

Pataki, George. 2000. "New York Exceeds All Federal Participation Rates For Third Straight Year." New York State: Office of the Governor Press Release. September 5, 2000. Retrieved August 20, 2006, from http://www.state.ny.us/governor/press/year00/sept3_00.htm.

Payne, Malcolm. 1997. *Modern Social Work Theory: A Critical Introduction.* 2d ed. Chicago: Lyceum Books.

Pear, Robert. 2002. "Study by Governors Calls Bush Welfare Plan Unworkable." *New York Times,* April 4, p. A18.

Peck, Jamie. 2001. *Workfare State.* New York: Guilford Press.

———. 2002a. "Political Economies of Scale: Fast Policy, Interscalar Relations, and Neoliberal Workfare." *Economic Geography* 78:331–360.

———. 2002b. "Labor Zapped/Growth, Restored? Three Moments of Neoliberal Restructuring in the American Labor Market." *Journal of Economic Geography* 2:179–220.

Peck, Jamie, and Nik Theodore. 2000. "Work First: Workfare and the Regulation of Contingent Labor Markets." *Cambridge Journal of Economics* 24:119–138.

Pence, Ellen. 1997. "Safety for Battered Women in a Textually Mediated Legal System." Ontario Institute for Studies in Education of the University of Toronto, Ontario, Canada. Unpublished thesis.

Phillips, Nelson, Thomas Lawrence, and Cynthia Hardy. 2004. "Discourse and Institutions." *Academy of Management Review* 29:635–652.

Piven, Frances Fox. 1997. "The New Reserve Army of Labor." In Steven Fraser and Joshua Freeman (eds.), *Audacious Democracy: Labor, Intellectuals, and the Social Reconstruction of America* (pp. 106–118). New York: Houghton Mifflin.

———. 2001. "Welfare Reform and the Economic and Cultural Reconstruction of Low Wage Labor Markets." In Judith Goode and Jeff Maskovsky (eds.), *The New Poverty Studies* (pp. 135–151). New York: NYU Press.

———. 2002. "Welfare Policy and American Politics." In Frances Fox Piven, Joan Acker, Margaret Hallock, and Sandra Morgen (eds.), *Work, Welfare, and Politics: Confronting Poverty in the Wage of Welfare Reform* (pp. 19–33). Eugene: University of Oregon Press.

———. 2003. "Why Welfare Is Racist." In Sanford Schram, Joe Soss, and Richard Fording (eds.), *Race and the Politics of Welfare Reform* (pp. 323–336). Ann Arbor: University of Michigan Press.

Piven, Frances Fox, and Richard A. Cloward. 1971 [1993]. *Regulating the Poor: The Functions of Public Welfare*. New York: Vintage.

———. 1979. *Poor People's Movements: Why They Succeed, How They Fail*. New York: Vintage Books.

Polack, Robert J. 2004. "Social Justice and the Global Economy: New Challenges for Social Work in the 21st Century." *Social Work* 49:281–290.

Polanyi, Karl. 1944. *Great Transformation*. New York: Rinehart & Company.

Poppe, Nan, Julie Strawn, and Karin Martinson. 2004. "Whose Job Is It?: Creating Opportunities for Advancement." In Robert P. Giloth (ed.), *Workforce Intermediaries for the Twenty-First Century* (pp. 31–73). Philadelphia: Temple University Press.

Powell, Walter W., and Paul J. DiMaggio. 1991. *The New Institutionalism in Organizational Analysis*. Chicago: University of Chicago Press.

Primus, Wendell, Lynette Rawlings, Kathy Larin, and Kathryn Proter. 1999. *Initial Impacts of Welfare Reform on Single-Mother Families*. Center for Budget and Policy Priorities: Washington, D.C. Retrieved October 11, 2007, from http://www.cbpp.org/8-22-99wel.pdf.

Quadagno, Jill. 1998. "Social Security Policy and the Entitlement Debate: The New American Exceptionalism." In Clarence Y. H. Lo and Michael Schwartz (eds.), *Social Policy and the Conservative Agenda* (pp. 72–94). Malden, MA: Blackwell.

Rank, Mark. 2004. *One Nation Underprivileged: Why American Poverty Affects Us All*. New York: Oxford University Press.

Rankin, Janet M., and Marie L. Campbell. 2006. *Managing to Nurse: Inside Canada's Health Care Reform*. Canada: University of Toronto Press.

Raspberry, William. 1995. "Ms. Smith Goes after Washington." *Washington Post*, February 1, A19.

Rector, Robert E. 2002. "The Heritage Foundation Professional Profile." The Heritage Foundation. Retrieved October 23, 2002, from http://www.heritage. org/About/Staff/RobertRector.cfm.

Reese, Ellen. 2005. *Backlash Against Welfare Mothers: Past and Present*. Berkeley and Los Angeles: University of California Press.

Reese, Ellen, Vincent Geidraitis, and Eric Vega. 2005. "Mobilization and Threat: Campaigns against Welfare Privatization in Four Cities." *Sociological Focus* 38(4):287–309.

Reese, Ellen, and Garnett Newcombe. 2003. "Income Rights, Mothers' Rights, Or Workers' Rights?: Collective Action Frames, Organizational Ideologies, and the American Welfare Rights Movement." *Social Problems* 50:294–318.

Reich, Robert. 1988. "Policy Making in a Democracy." In Robert Reich (ed.), *The Power of Public Ideas* (pp. 123–156). Cambridge: Ballinger Publishing.

Relave, Nanette. 2000. "Collaboration between the Welfare and Workforce Development Systems." *WIN Welfare Information Network, Issue Notes* 4(2). Retrieved March 21, 2008, from http://www.financeproject.org/Publications/ workforcecollab.htm.

Renwick, Trudi. 2006. "The Impact of Federal TANF Reauthorization in New York." Fiscal Policy Institute: New York, NY. Retrieved July 20, 2006, from http://www.fiscalpolicy.org/TANFREAUTHORIZATIONREPORT.pdf.

Ridzi, Frank. 2001. "Beyond the Drop in Caseloads: A Look at Welfare-to-Work Hiring and Recycling Across Race and Gender." *Maxwell Review* 9(1):68–78.

———. 2004. "Making TANF Work: Organizational Restructuring, Staff Buy-In, and Performance Monitoring in Local Implementation." *Journal of Sociology & Social Welfare* 31(2):27–48.

———. 2007. "Contingent Government Workers and Labor Solidarity: The Case of Contract Welfare-to-Work Staff and Their Clients." *Qualitative Sociology* 30:383–402.

———. 2008. "Exploring Problematics of the Personal-Responsibility Welfare State: Issues of Family and Caregiving in Welfare-to-Work and Medicaid Consumer-Directed Care Programs." In Marjorie L. DeVault (ed.), *People at Work: Life, Power, and Social Inclusion in the New Economy* (pp. 223–247). New York: NYU Press.

Ridzi, Frank, and Payal Banerjee. 2006. "The Spirit of Outsourcing: Corporate and State Regulation of Labor under the H1-B Visa and TANF Policies in the U.S." *Research in the Sociology of Work* 16:345–373.

Ridzi, Frank, and Andrew S. London. 2006. "'It's Great When People Don't Even Have Their Welfare Cases Opened': TANF Diversion as Process and Lesson." *Review of Policy Research* 23:725–743.

Ridzi, Frank, Matthew T. Loveland, and Fred Glennon. 2008. "Catholics and the Welfare State: How the Preferential Option for the Poor Relates to Preferences for Government Policy." *Journal of Catholic Social Thought* 5(1):45–63.

Roberts, Dorothy. 1997. *Killing the Black Body: Race, Reproduction, and the Meaning of Liberty.* New York: Pantheon Books.

Romero, Mary. 1992. *Maid in the U.S.A.* New York: Routledge.

Rosenbloom, Joshua L. 2002. *Looking for Work, Searching for Workers: American Labor Markets During Industrialization.* New York: Cambridge University Press.

Rosenthal, Alan. 2001. "Racial Disparities in the Local Criminal Justice System: A Report to the NAACP." New York: Center for Community Alternatives.

Ruben, Matthew. 2001. "Suburbanization and Urban Poverty under Neoliberalism." In Judith Goode and Jeff Maskovsky (eds.), *The New Poverty Studies* (pp. 435–469). New York: NYU Press.

Sandfort, Jodi. 1999. "The Structural Impediments to Human Service Collaboration: Examining Welfare Reform at the Front Lines." *Social Service Review* 73:314–339.

———. 2003. "Exploring the Structuration of Technology within Human Service Organizations." *Administration and Society* 34:605–631.

Sarat, Austin. 1990. "'The Law Is All Over': Power, Resistance and the Legal Consciousness of the Welfare Poor." *Yale Journal of Law and the Humanities* 2:343–380.

Savner, Steve. 2000. "Welfare Reform and Racial/Ethnic Minorities: The Questions to Ask." *Poverty & Race* (July/August). Retrieved November 25, 2007, from http://www.prrac.org/topic_type.php?topic_id=2&type_group=10.

Schmidtz, David, and Robert Goodin. 1998. *Social Welfare and Individual Responsibility: For and Against.* New York: Cambridge University Press.

Schram, Sanford F. 1995. *Words of Welfare.* Minnesota: University of Minnesota Press.

———. 2000a. "In the Clinic: The Medicalization of Welfare." *Social Text* 18(1):81–107.

———. 2000b. *After Welfare: The Culture of Postindustrial Social Policy.* New York: NYU Press.

Schram, Sanford F., Joe Soss, and Richard Fording, eds. 2003. *Race and the Politics of Welfare Reform.* Ann Arbor: University of Michigan Press.

Scott, Ellen, and Andrew S. London. 2000. "Looking to the Future: Welfare-Reliant Women Talk About Their Job Aspirations in the Context of Welfare Reform." *Journal of Social Issues* 56:727–746.

Scott, James C. 1990. *Domination and the Arts of Resistance: Hidden Transcripts.* New Haven, CT: Yale University Press.

Seccombe, Karen. 2007. *So You Think I Drive a Cadillac: Welfare Recipients' Perspectives on the System and Its Reform.* Needham Heights, MA: Allyn and Bacon.

Segal, Elizabeth, and Keith Kilty. 2003. "Political Promises for Welfare Reform." *Journal of Poverty* 7(1, 2):51–67.

Sharone, Ofer. 2007. "Constructing Unemployed Job Seekers as Professional Workers: The Depoliticizing Work-Game of Job Searching." *Qualitative Sociology* 30:403–416.

Shulman, Beth. 2005. *The Betrayal of Work: How Low-Wage Jobs Fail 30 Million Americans.* New York: New Press.

Silver, Sheldon, and Herman Farrell Jr. 1998. "Trends in Public Assistance Spending in New York State." Occasional Paper No. 8, Perspectives from the New York State Assembly Committee on Ways and Means.

Simmons, Louise B. 2002. "Unions and Welfare Reform: Labor's Stake in the On-going Struggle over the Welfare State." *Labor Studies Journal* 27(2):65–83.

Smith, Adam. [1776] 1961. *The Wealth of Nations.* Edited by Edwin Cannan. Reprint. London: Methuen.

Smith, Dorothy E. 1987. *The Everyday World as Problematic: A Feminist Sociology.* Boston: Northeastern University Press.

———. 1990. *The Conceptual Practices of Power: A Feminist Sociology of Knowledge.* Boston: Northeastern University Press.

———. 1999. *Writing the Social: Critique, Theory, and Investigations.* Canada: University of Toronto Press.

———. 2005. *Institutional Ethnography: A Sociology for People.* Lanham, MD: Rowman Altamira.

Smith, Victoria. 2002. *Crossing the Great Divide: Worker Risk and Opportunity in the New Economy.* Ithaca, NY: Cornell University/ILR Press.

Solinger, Rickie. 2001. *Beggars and Choosers: How the Politics of Choice Shapes Adoption, Abortion and Welfare in the United States.* New York: Hill and Wang.

Soros, George. 1998. *The Crisis of Global Capitalism: Open Society Endangered.* New York: Public Affairs.

Soss, Joe, Sanford F. Schram, Thomas V. Vartanian, and Erin O'Brien. 2001. "Setting the Terms of Relief: Explaining State Policy Choices in the Devolution Revolution." *American Journal of Political Science* 45:378–395.

Sparks, Holloway. 2003. "Queens, Teens, and Model Mothers: Race, Gender and the Discourse of Welfare Reform." In Sanford Schram, Joe Soss, and Richard Fording (eds.), *Race and the Politics of Welfare Reform* (pp. 171–195). Ann Arbor: University of Michigan Press.

State of New York Office of the State Comptroller Division of Management Audit and State Financial Services. 1998. Office of Temporary and Disability

Assistance: Fair Hearing Process. Report 97-S-42: 1–44. Retrieved December 8, 2007, from http://www.osc.state.ny.us/audits/audits/9899/97s42.pdf.

State Policy Documentation Project. 1999. TANF Applications, Diversion Programs, Emergency Assistance: Pending Application Requirements. Retrieved December 6, 2007, from http://www.spdp.org/tanf/applications/applicpendreq.pdf.

Statistical Abstracts of the United States. 2000. "Table No. 626 Temporary Assistance for Needy Families (TANF)—Recipients by State and Other Area: 1995–1999." *The National Data Book*, 120th edition. http://www.census.gov/prod/www/statistical-abstract-us.html.

Steuerle, C. Eugene, and Gordon Mermin. 1997. "Devolution as Seen from the Budget." *Urban Institute Press New Federalism Series #A-2* (January):1–5.

Stiglitz, Joseph E. 2002. *Globalization and Its Discontents.* New York: Norton.

Street, David, George Martin, and Laura Gordon. 1979. *The Welfare Industry: Functionaries and Recipients in Public Aid.* Beverly Hills: Sage Publications.

Susser, Ida. 1996. "The Construction of Poverty and Homelessness in U.S. Cities." *Annual Review of Anthropology* 25:411–435.

Susser, Ida, and John Kreniske. 1987. "The Welfare Trap." In Leith Mullings (ed.), *Cities in the United States* (pp. 51–68). New York: Columbia University Press.

Swedberg, Richard. 2000. "The Social Science View of Entrepreneurship: Introduction and Practical Implications." In Richard Swedberg (ed.), *Entrepreneurship: The Social Science View* (pp. 7–45). New York: Oxford University Press.

Tait, Vanessa. 2005. *Poor Workers' Unions: Rebuilding Labor From Below.* Cambridge, MA: South End Press.

Tilly, Charles. 1988. "Solidary Logics: Conclusions." *Theory and Society* 17:451–458.

Titmuss, Richard. 1974. *Social Policy.* London: Allen and Unwin.

Touminen, Mary. 2000. "The Conflicts of Caring: Gender, Race, Ethnicity, and Individualism in Family Child-Care Work." In Madonna Harrington Meyer (ed.), *Care Work* (pp. 112–135). New York: Routledge.

Traverso, Susan. 2003. *Welfare Politics in Boston, 1910–1940.* Boston: University of Massachusetts Press.

Turner, Sarah E. 2007. "Higher Education: Policies Generating the 21st Century Workforce." In Harry J. Holzer and Demetra Smith Nightingale (eds.), *Reshaping the American Workforce in a Changing Economy* (pp. 91–116). Washington, DC: Urban Institute Press.

U.S. Census. 2000a. "Households and Families." U.S. Census Bureau. Retrieved December 6, 2007, from http://www.census.gov/prod/2001pubs/c2kbr01-8.pdf and http://www.census.gov/population/socdemo/hh-fam/tabST-F1-2000.pdf.

———. 2000b. "The Black Population: 2000." U.S. Census Bureau. Retrieved December 6, 2007, from http://www.census.gov/prod/2001pubs/c2kbr01-5.pdf.

———. 2000c. "The White Population: 2000." U.S. Census Bureau. Retrieved December 6, 2007, from http://www.census.gov/prod/2001pubs/c2kbr01-4.pdf.

———. 2003. "African-American History Month." U.S. Census Bureau. Retrieved December 6, 2007, from (ttp://www.census.gov/Press-Release/www/2003/cb03ff01.html.

———. 2004. "Poverty Thresholds." U.S. Census Bureau. Retrieved December 6, 2007, from http://www.census.gov/hhes/poverty/threshld/thresh04.html.

U.S. Chamber of Commerce. 2006. "Workforce Development and Welfare Reform Reauthorization." Retrieved December 8, 2007, from http://www.uschamber.com/issues/index/education/workforce.htm.

U.S. Commission on Civil Rights. 2002. "A New Paradigm for Welfare Reform: The Need for Civil Rights Enforcement." A Statement by the U.S. Commission on Civil Rights. Retrieved December 8, 2007, from http://www.usccr.gov/pubs/prwora/welfare.htm.

U.S. Department of Health and Human Services, Office of Family Assistance. 2002. Office of Family Assistance Home Page. Retrieved December 12, 2002, from http://www.acf.hhs.gov/programs/ofa/.

U.S. Department of Health and Human Services. 2003. *Temporary Assistance for Needy Families (TANF)*. 5th Annual Report to Congress. Washington, DC: Administration for Children and Families.

———. 2004. Office of Family Assistance. *Temporary Assistance for Needy Families (TANF)*. 6th Annual Report to Congress. Washington, DC: Administration for Children and Families. Retrieved December 8, 2007, from http://www.acf.hhs.gov/programs/ofa/annualreport6/ar6index.htm.

U.S. General Accounting Office. 2002. *Welfare Reform: Federal Oversight of State and Local Contracting Can Be Strengthened*. Publication No. GAO—02—661. Washington, DC: U.S. General Accounting Office. Retrieved October 6, 2005, from http://www.gao.gov/new.items/d02661.pdf.

———. 2001. *Welfare Reform: Moving Hard-to-Employ Recipients into the Workforce*. GAO-01-368. Washington, DC: U.S. General Accounting Office. Retrieved October 6, 2005, from http://www.gao.gov/new.items/d01368.pdf.

———. 1998. *Welfare Reform: States Are Restructuring Programs to Reduce Welfare Dependence*. GAP/HEHS-98-109. Washington, DC: U.S. General Accounting Office. Retrieved October 6, 2005, from http://www.gao.gov/archive/1998/he98109.pdf p.76.

U.S. Supreme Court. 1970. Goldberg, Commissioner of Social Services of the City of New York V. Kelly Et Al. Appeal from the United States District Court for the Southern District of New York no. 62. Argued October 13, 1969; Decided March 23, 1970. 569 *U.S. Supreme Court Goldberg v. Kelly* 1970.

Urban Institute. 2006. "A Decade of Welfare Reform: Facts and Figures." *Assessing the New Federalism*. The Urban Institute. Retrieved December 6, 2007, from http://www.urban.org/url.cfm?ID=900980.

Valocchi, Steve. 1994. "The Racial Basis of Capitalism and the State, and the Impact of the New Deal on African Americans." *Social Problems* 41(3):347–352.

van Wormer, Katherine. 2005. "Concepts for Contemporary Social Work: Globalization, Oppression, Social Exclusion, Human Rights." *Social Work & Society* 3(1):1–10.

Verba, Sidney, Kay Schlozman, and Henry Brady. 1995. *Voice and Equality: Civic Voluntarism in American Politics*. Cambridge, MA: Harvard University Press.

Vinzant, Janet Coble, and Lane Crothers. 1998. *Street-Level Leadership: Discretion and Legitimacy in Frontline Public Service*. Washington, DC: Georgetown University Press.

Vogel, Lise. 1993. *Mothers on the Job: Maternity Policy in the U.S. Workplace*. New Brunswick, NJ: Rutgers University Press.

Wagner, David. 1990. *The Quest for the Radical Profession: Social Service Careers and Political Ideology*. Lanham, MD: University Press of America.

Waldfogel, Jane. 2007. "Work-Family Policies." In Harry J. Holzer and Demetra Smith Nightingale (eds.), *Reshaping the American Workforce in a Changing Economy* (pp. 273–292). Washington, DC: Urban Institute Press.

Walkowitz, Daniel. 1999. *Working with Class: Social Workers and the Politics of Middle-Class Identity*. Chapel Hill: University of North Carolina Press.

Walzer, Michael. 1983. *Spheres of Justice*. New York: Basic Books.

Weber, Max. 1988. *The Protestant Ethic and the Spirit of Capitalism*. Translated by Talcott Parsons. Gloucester, MA: Peter Smith.

Weigt, Jill. 2006. "Compromises to Carework: The Social Organization of Mothers' Experiences in the Low-Wage Labor Market After Welfare Reform." *Social Problems* 53:332–351.

Wilson, William J. 1987. *The Truly Disadvantaged: The Inner City, the Underclass, and Public Policy*. Chicago: University of Chicago Press.

Woodward, Kerry. 2008. "The Multiple Meanings of Work for Welfare-Reliant Women." *Qualitative Sociology* 31(2):149–168.

Index

About the Author

FRANK RIDZI is founding Director of the Center for Urban and Regional Applied Research and Kauffman Entrepreneurship Professor at Le Moyne College in Syracuse, New York. He is Associate Professor of Sociology.